UNDERSTANDING
CHURCH GROWTH

Third Edition

UNDERSTANDING CHURCH GROWTH

Third Edition

by

DONALD A. McGAVRAN

revised and edited by

C. PETER WAGNER

WILLIAM B. EERDMANS PUBLISHING COMPANY
GRAND RAPIDS, MICHIGAN

Library of Congress Cataloging-in-Publication Data

McGavran, Donald Anderson, 1897–
Understanding church growth / by Donald A. McGavran;
revised and edited by C. Peter Wagner.—3rd ed.
p.   cm.
Includes bibliographical references.
ISBN 0-8028-0463-2
1. Church growth.   2. Sociology, Christian.   I. Wagner, C. Peter.
II. Title.
BV652.25.M293   1990
266—dc20   89-39252
CIP

CONTENTS

81449

PREFACE TO THE THIRD (1990) EDITION

by C. Peter Wagner

One of the greatest privileges of my life has been to associate closely with Donald A. McGavran. After sixteen years as a missionary to Bolivia, I accepted his call in 1971 to join him on the faculty of the Fuller Theological Seminary School of World Mission in Pasadena, California. For ten years, until his retirement in 1981, we worked together teaching church growth, supervising graduate theses and dissertations in the field, training missionaries and pastors, and consulting with churches and mission agencies. I was honored in 1984 to be invited to become the first incumbent of the Donald A. McGavran Chair of Church Growth.

Understanding Church Growth is one of those classics which has become the indispensable foundational text for an academic field. No one can claim to be a serious student of church growth who has not read and absorbed the content of *Understanding Church Growth*. I was one of the first to be introduced to the content of this book, in classroom lectures in the late 1960s while it was yet being written. The first edition was published in 1970, and the revised edition was expanded and updated by McGavran in 1980. In this 1990 edition the language has been modernized, the flow of ideas somewhat streamlined, the content also reduced, mostly by eliminating redundancies, ideas and illustrations updated, and a bit of new material such as the chapter on divine healing introduced. But through it all, Donald McGavran is the one who speaks. This edition is not a Wagnerized version of McGavran. My own contributions are adequately represented in more than thirty books, some of which are listed in the updated reading list at the end of this volume.

Some years ago, Tyndale House Publishers released *Church Growth: State of the Art* (1986), which I had the privilege of editing along with Win Arn and Elmer Towns. The first chapter of that book was a tribute to Donald A. McGavran, the father of the Church Growth Movement. With the permission of the publishers I am concluding this introduction with that tribute. New readers of *Understanding Church Growth* will be well served by taking a few moments to get to know its distinguished author more intimately.

DONALD A. McGAVRAN

"We stand in the sunrise of missions."

This is perhaps the most characteristic phrase proclaimed through the years by Donald A. McGavran, regarded by many as the twentieth century's premier missiologist. At eighty-seven years of age, he still makes that statement with the twinkle in his eye and the determination on his lips that have always been a part of his outgoing and forceful personality.

Donald McGavran was born of missionary parents in India before the turn of the century. His grandparents had also been missionaries to India, sailing around Africa's Cape of Good Hope to get there. He is a graduate of Yale and Columbia. He has climbed the Himalayas. He has produced motion pictures. He was the director of a missionary agency. He managed a leprosarium and supervised a school system. He went one-on-one with a wounded tiger and met a wild boar in combat. He is fluent in Hindi and Chattisqarhee. He stopped a cholera epidemic. He was the founding dean of a prestigious missiological institution. He has written twenty-three books on missions and church growth. His travels have taken him to virtually every nation of the world.

When, one or two generations from now, historians of religion look back to the twentieth century, McGavran will most likely be remembered chiefly as the father of the Church Growth Movement. Seed thoughts for the movement began to germinate in the 1930s when he was executive secretary and treasurer for the United Christian Missionary Society in India. He was in charge of eighty missionaries, five hospitals, many high schools and primary schools, evangelistic work, and a leprosy home. It was a formidable missionary effort. But through decades of hard work the net result of the mission's work had been only twenty or thirty small non-growing churches.

This was the pattern of many missionary groups in India at that time, and still is for some. But Donald McGavran could not live with it. The conventional wisdom among missionaries was that India was a resistant country and that they should not expect many converts. But McGavran did not agree. It occurred to him that obviously there was a way of doing missionary work so as to produce few or no churches. But there must also be other ways of doing missionary work that God would bless with the establishment of many churches. At the time McGavran did not know exactly how the methodologies of the two approaches differed, but he determined to find out. As he declared in the preface to a book he coauthored in the 1930s, he had dedicated himself to "discarding theories of church growth which do not work, and learning and practicing productive patterns which actually disciple the peoples and increase the household of God."

In order to gather the experience necessary to undergird the theories of church growth that were developing, McGavran left his administrative position and spent seventeen years in planting churches. The work bore substantial fruit, and some 1,000 Indians now owe their conversion, humanly speaking, to McGavran's efforts. More significant than the immediate results, however, were the strong convictions about the growth and nongrowth of churches that were forming in McGavran's mind. These convictions led in 1955 to the publication of *The Bridges of God* (rev. ed., Friendship Press, 1981), the landmark volume that launched the Church Growth Movement.

The book was read and discussed by missionaries and mission executives on all six continents. Its ideas were new and controversial. Four principal points of discussion were raised: a theological issue, an ethical issue, a missiological issue, and a procedural issue.

The theological issue suggests that the central purpose of missions was to be seen as God's will that lost men and women be found, reconciled to himself, and brought into responsible membership in Christian churches. Evangelism was seen not just as proclaiming the gospel whether or not something happened, but as making disciples for the Master.

The ethical issue is one of pragmatism. McGavran became alarmed when he saw all too many of God's resources—personnel and finances—being used without asking whether the kingdom of God was being advanced by the programs they were supporting. McGavran demanded more accountability in Christian stewardship. He wanted efforts evaluated by their results. His attitude reflects these words of Bishop Waskom Pickett, McGavran's mentor in the early years in India: "It is disturbing to read book after book about modern missions without finding so much as a hint about either what helped or what hindered church growth. In many books the author seems eager to prove that the missionaries have done everything according to God's leading and that if no church has come into being it means only that God's time for saving souls has not come: 'The disciples' duty is to sow the seed and leave it to God to produce.' How different this is from the command of Jesus, 'Make disciples of the nations!'" (Pickett 1933).

The missiological issue is McGavran's people movement theory. Before the days of the conscious application of cultural anthropology to evangelistic strategy, McGavran intuitively recognized the fact that decision-making processes are frequently quite different from one culture to the next. Whereas most Western missionaries and their converts were preaching an individualistic gospel and expecting people to come to Christ one by one against the social tide, McGavran, with Waskom Pickett's encouragement, concluded that this was not the way multitudes could or would come to Christ. Important decisions, according to their worldview, were community decisions. Therefore, the way to approach many of the world's peoples with the gospel had to be through the encouragement of a multi-individual, mutually interdependent conversion process whereby members of families, extended families, clans, villages, and tribes would become Christian at the same time. This process was labeled a people movement.

A corollary of the people movement theory is the homogeneous unit principle. "People like to become Christians without crossing racial, linguistic, or class barriers," said McGavran. Conversion, he argued, should occur within a minimum of social dislocation. This principle has become the most controversial of all church growth principles because critics have interpreted it as classist or racist. Nothing could be further from McGavran's mind, however. As the prototype of a world Christian, McGavran does not have a racist bone in his body. The homogeneous unit principle is an attempt to respect the dignity of individuals and allow their decisions for Christ to be religious rather than social decisions. It is developed in detail in McGavran's magnum opus, *Understanding Church Growth*.

The procedural issue is the distinction between discipling and perfecting as two discreet stages of Christianization. Discipling brings an unbelieving individual or group to commitment to Christ and to the body of

Christ. Perfecting is the lifelong process of spiritual and ethical development in the lives of believers. McGavran warned that too many mission
activities had been diverted to perfecting when the original mission
charter demanded discipling. He never tires of pointing out that a full 70
percent of the world's population is not yet discipled, and he urges Christian churches worldwide to get on with sending more laborers into those
harvest fields.

Having laid the conceptual groundwork for the Church Growth
Movement in the 1950s, McGavran's crowning achievement was the establishment of the institution which was to become his base of operations.
In 1961 he started an Institute of Church Growth at Northwest Christian
College in Eugene, Oregon. In 1965 he moved the institute to Fuller Seminary and became the founding dean of the Fuller School of World Mission and Institute of Church Growth. Although he stopped teaching at the
age of eighty-three, McGavran continues an active schedule of research,
writing, traveling and speaking, and works in his seminary office daily
when he is in town. His school is the foremost institution of missiological training with a resident faculty of twelve full-time and thirty part-time
members and a student body of over 700.

With over three billion of the world's people yet to believe in Jesus
Christ, Donald McGavran sees the golden years of mission yet ahead. Resources for completing the task have never been greater. Missiological research and knowledge have never been so advanced. Peoples around the
world have never been more open to the gospel. God is on the throne.
Jesus said, "I will build my church," and he continues to do it. No wonder
that Donald McGavran, with a twinkle in his eye and determination on
his lips, says today with more verve than ever, "We stand in the sunrise
of missions."

PREFACE TO THE REVISED (1980) EDITION

by Donald A. McGavran

In the last two decades of the twentieth century the church is hearing anew God's clarion call to bring the peoples of every continent to faith and obedience. Increasingly it is turning its vast resources toward evangelism and church growth. Small denominations, large denominations, Protestants, and Roman Catholics are focusing on the propagation of the gospel at home and abroad. It is becoming crystal clear that there will be no great advance in righteousness, peace, and justice until there are many more practicing Christians and believing churches in every segment of humanity.

Evangelization intends the redemption of individuals and the multiplication of Christ's churches. Concern for evangelism and church growth is an essential part of the Christian faith and an irreplaceable part of the work of the church. The church is the Body of Christ and brings persons and nations to faith and obedience as it proclaims the gospel effectively in every people and incorporates believers from every people into ongoing churches. Believing this, the church girds for action.

However, engaged in many good activities, Christians often take the growth of the church for granted. They neither pray earnestly for it nor work systematically at it. They assume it will take place automatically as Christians study the Bible, do good to others, and worship God. As a result, in the midst of huge numbers of receptive men and women, many churches stop growing and become static enclaves of comfortable middle-class Christians. These feed the hungry, visit the sick, clothe the naked, build attractive houses of worship, train leaders, and influence society for good, but they do not grow. The dynamism of the early church does not dwell in them. Huge populations in the Western world and even larger populations in the Third World remain undiscipled. They do not have the Son. They do not have eternal life. Church growth has been assumed and is, alas, not occurring.

This was the case in Christian missions overseas in the mid-twentieth century. Tremendous resources were spent in mission work, often for very little growth of the church. Where growth was impossible, this outcome was understandable, but sometimes little growth was unnecessary. Christians, pastors, and missionaries were coming out of the ripe fields empty-handed. During recent decades little or no growth has also marked most mainline denominations in the United States. Some biological and transfer growth has occurred but conversion growth has been spotty and slight. Whole denominations have become static or have actually declined. Pastors in America, like their counterparts overseas, often lead congregations that remain at about the same number of members for years, or even lose a few, scores, or hundreds.

Determined efforts to understand church growth, to record where it was and was not happening, and to ascertain the causes for growth and decline began overseas. God granted me unique opportunities to study such matters in many lands. The church growth movement, therefore, between 1955 and 1970 was very largely concerned with growth of churches overseas. How can churches be more faithful to God? Are missions reaping as largely as they can? Are congregations in the Third World multiplying as God desires? How can missionaries engage in more effective evangelism? Which factors accelerate and which factors retard church growth in new denominations? These were the questions asked. On such topics the global *Church Growth Bulletin* published hundreds of articles, authored by Christian leaders in many lands. Career missionaries assembled in church growth seminars, enrolled in the historic Institute of Church Growth in Eugene, Oregon, and later in the School of World Mission of Fuller Theological Seminary to study these matters. Courses on church growth were given, refined to fit aspects of growth that research carried out by career missionaries had discovered. In 1967 the first draft of *Understanding Church Growth* was written. Mimeographed copies of the manuscript served as the basic text in church growth for three years. The book was published in 1970.

In 1971, as church growth writings began to circulate widely in the United States and *Understanding Church Growth* was read and studied by ministers, conviction began to form that growth was fully as much a concern of American churches as it was of missionary societies and Third World churches. Drs. C. Peter Wagner, Ralph D. Winter, Win Arn, and George G. Hunter III played significant parts in the spread of that conviction. The Southern Baptists, Nazarenes, and some other denominations have devoted large resources to church growth. As a result, in America the 1970s have seen a veritable explosion of interest in the growth of the church. Interest is beginning in Scandinavia and England. Books and articles pour from the presses. Hundreds of ministers assemble in church growth seminars. Doctoral programs of church growth are taught in many seminaries. Denominational headquarters make substantial annual allocations to stop the decline and initiate decades of interest.

As American leaders studied the 1970 *Understanding Church Growth* (which they considered the basic book) they found its illustrations came very largely from overseas. Some Americans, therefore, were tempted to think that church growth principles did not apply to the United States. Wiser men realized that they applied fully as much and asked me to revise the 1970 edition so they would be easily seen to do so.

In addition, during the 1970s (a decade rich in insights concerning ways in which the faith is communicated in the tremendously complex mosaic of humankind) leading advocates of church growth had made major contributions to the art. These, I felt, ought to be gathered up in one book. The problem was how to determine which were major contributions and which were needed popularizations and applications. Books on many, many aspects of church growth had been published during the decade. Hundreds of contributions had been made, far too numerous to be covered in one book. In making the revision, therefore, it had to be my steady aim to stick to the *germinal principles*.

Church growth is much wider and deeper than adding names to church rolls. It delves into how persons and peoples become genuinely Christian and revolutionize and bless the cultures and populations in the midst of which God has placed them. Church growth arises in theology and biblical faithfulness. It draws heavily on the social sciences because it always occurs in societies. It continually seeks for instances in which God has granted growth and then asks what are the *real* factors he has blessed to such increase. The Preface to the 1970 edition (which follows immediately) stresses these wide essential emphases of church growth and should be read before beginning the book.

This book is published with the prayer that it may be used of God to aid in the urgent revitalization of his church and the incorporation of sufficient men and women in it so that major social advance may be achieved in all nations. The long-range goal of church growth is the discipling of *panta ta ethne* (all peoples), to the end that rivers of the water of eternal and abundant life flow fast and free, to every tongue and tribe and people in all the earth.

PREFACE TO THE FIRST (1970) EDITION

by Donald A. McGavran

Discipling the nations, reconciling people of all races to God in Christ, bringing all nations to faith and obedience, and preaching the gospel to the whole creation—in short, the missionary enterprise—has arrived at one of the hinges of history.

Vast reinterpretation of what mission essentially is in this rapidly changing world engages voices, pens, and minds. Many see only a small part of the total scene and ardently define what they think mission in that sector should be. Many of the problems of Europe and America—for the simple reason that most Christian writers are provincial Europeans and Americans—occupy the center of the stage. "Mission" becomes what these Western writers think should be done. Furthermore, what the true Christian goals *are* is hotly debated. In this new day what does the triune God demand? And do we understand what he demands on the basis of our reason or his revelation?

The theory and theology of mission is what is in dispute. As God carries out his mission in the world and the church seeks to be found "about his business," what *should* be done? What priorities are correct? Among many good enterprises, which has preeminence? Which should come first and which—if any have to be—should be omitted? How is carrying out the will of God to be measured? What has really been accomplished as the church has spread on new ground? Considerations of anthropology, sociology, theology, and organizational complexity pile up one on the other. Never was a clear mission theory more needed than today—a theory firmly rooted in biblical truth.

Understanding Church Growth has been written in the midst of this welter of opinion. It is speaking to this hinge of history. It has been formed against the confusion of means and ends so typical of today's mission. It is at once a book on mission theology, mission theory, and mission practice. These three do not exist in isolation, but as an integrated whole—theology influencing theory and practice, practice coloring theology and theory, and theory guiding both practice and theology.

This book is not by any means the last word on the subject. Rather, it is an attempt to take the reconciling of women and men to God in the church of Jesus Christ seriously, in view of the empirical churches actually founded. It maintains throughout—and this is one of the stones in its theological foundation—that the establishment of churches (assemblies of baptized believers) is pleasing to God. Furthermore, it maintains throughout—and this is one of the stones in its anthropological foundation—that the size, number, ethnic and cultural composition, and relationship to the undiscipled are matters that, if the Christian is to be a good steward of God's grace, can be measured and *must be known.* I hope many other books about the establishment of churches—units of God's righteousness, peace, and forgiveness—will continue to be written.

Similar books should be made available to the churches of Asia, Africa, and Latin America in the languages of those lands. This book in English will be read by highly educated nationals and missionaries from Europe and America. That is good, but not enough. The younger churches are in grave danger of being misled by the very plethora of good things to do, the intensity of feeling in the older churches about the problems of Europe and America, and the confusion in the theory, theology, and practice of mission. The fact that eight percent and more of the activities of missions today are organized good deeds and social action takes the attention of many younger churches off the propagation of the gospel. They need to center their attention on the basic fact of the gospel, that Jesus Christ died for all and that the "gospel . . . according to the commandment of the everlasting God, [has been] made known to all nations for the obedience of the faith" (Rom. 16:25-26). Until everyone has had a chance to respond to that good news, the mission must go forward.

The great campaigns of evangelism are urgent. They are one way in which the gospel advances. But, as the pages of this book show abundantly, campaigns need to be carried on in such fashion that multitudes of new churches *are* established and multitudes of new converts *do* become reliable members of Christ's body. Furthermore, many other ways to advance the gospel are being and must be used. All of them, including evangelism, must be used in the light of feedback from the ongoing mission enterprise, guided by the degree to which people and *ethne* are being brought to the obedience of the faith, and churches are being multiplied.

PART I

THEOLOGICAL CONSIDERATIONS

1

THE COMPLEX FAITHFULNESS THAT IS CHURCH GROWTH

TREMENDOUS CHURCH GROWTH is going on in the world today. We live in the age of the most rapid forward advance of Christianity that history has ever known. The church is expanding in many towns and cities in North America and overseas in numerous cultures and subcultures, languages and dialects, tribes, classes, kindreds, and people groups.

While such numbers must always be regarded as broad estimates, one study has shown that each day sees some 78,000 new Christians worldwide and each week some 1,000 new churches are established in Asia, Africa, and Latin America (Wagner 1983:20-21). Since those figures were published it became known that in China alone the decade of the 1980s saw up to 20,000 new Christians per day. As the years go by, the proportion of Christians to non-Christians is gradually increasing, especially in the Third World. The percentage is even more dramatic when the growth of evangelicals (as contrasted to all who may vaguely consider themselves Christians) is plotted.

The church is even now expanding in many towns and cities in North America and overseas in numerous cultures and subcultures, languages and dialects, tribes, classes, and kindreds. Whereas in the year 1800 it was confined largely to Europe and the Americas, by the last years of the twentieth century the church had spread to almost every country on earth.

HOW DOES GROWTH HAPPEN?

Frequently a church splits and both sections grow. The divisions of the Presbyterian Church in Korea in the 1950s were widely cited by pessimists as proof of dark days and degeneracy, but during the 1950s the Presbyterian Church in Korea (all branches) more than doubled, erected hundreds of new church buildings, and in 1990 had far more influence in the land than in 1950. Similar phenomena have greatly stimulated the growth of independent churches in Africa, Pentecostal churches in Latin America, and Baptist churches in the United States.

Some Roman Catholic leaders in Chile may bewail the fact that a tenth of their people have become Pentecostal Christians; but wiser heads no doubt praise God for the vitality and growth of the Pentecostal sections of the church. Denominational pride often prevents us from seeing that when our branch of the church loses members to a more vital branch, we are awakened and stimulated to greater effort, and the universal church prospers. Thus when George Fox in Cromwell's time multiplied meetings of Friends across England and these spread around the world, who can doubt that the universal church prospered? Or when reformers left the Syrian Orthodox Church in Kerala, India, about 1890 and established the Mar Thoma Syrian Church (which then grew from a few congregations to a denomination of 400,000 members in 1977), not only did the universal church prosper, but the sleepy Orthodox Syrian Church itself was moved to mission.

Sections of the church, sometimes large, sometimes small, do of course at times face difficulties or new problems and enter a period of malaise. War, famine, pestilence, the spread of some debilitating theology, adjustment to radically new conditions, migration to new lands or cities, and totalitarian oppression are some of the factors that not only check church growth but may enervate the people of God for a time. The hand of Midian sometimes prevails against Israel—until God raises up a Gideon.

This evident truth must not, however, be allowed to obscure the worldwide growth of the church. Just as non-Christian populations are prodigiously growing, so the mere excess of births over deaths in the Christian community vastly increases the number of those who count themselves Christians rather than secularists, Marxists, Hindus, Buddhists, or followers of some other faith; while subsequent personal confession of Christ transforms hundreds of thousands of these every year into convinced Christians.

To these additions from within must be added others from without, through the conversion of unbelievers living on the edge of innumerable existing congregations, intermarrying with their members, and counting themselves as already in some vague way "Christian." Hundreds of thousands of such conversions are constantly going on almost unnoticed. To this new total should be added the dramatic conversions of great numbers of non-Christians.

Between 1936 and 1966, 120,000 Ethiopian pagans became baptized believers in the church founded by the Sudan Interior Mission. During the two decades prior to 1966, 80,000 highlanders became Presbyterian Christians in Taiwan. After India became independent in 1947, the Methodist Church in the Raichur Vikarabad area grew from 100,000 to 200,000. Between 1906 and 1980 the Church of the Nazarene in America has grown enormously. The last half of the twentieth century has seen an explosion of Pentecostal and charismatic church growth. According to David Barrett the Pentecostal/charismatic movements had grown to 96 million in 1975, and then increased to 247 million in 1985 (see Wagner 1988c). The Assemblies of God alone grew from 4.6 million in 1975 to 13.2 million in 1985, a decadal growth rate of 187 percent. By 1987 the Assemblies of God was the largest or second largest denomination in no fewer than 30 nations of the world.

The 1980s also saw the emergence of the metachurch, churches of several tens of thousands. The Yoido Full Gospel Church of Seoul, Korea, under the leadership of Paul Yonggi Cho, led the way by passing the 100,000 mark in 1979 and reaching over 600,000 by decade's end. The Jotabeche Methodist Pentecostal Church in Santiago, Chile, pastored by Javier Vasquez, reported over 300,000 members in 1988. Omar Cabrera's Vision of the Future Church in Argentina numbered 145,000 as of 1987. The Deeper Life Bible Church in Lagos, Nigeria, grew to over 40,000 in 1986 under Pastor W. F. Kumuyi. In the United States several sanctuaries seating 10,000 are either completed or under construction. The Willow Creek Community Church in the Chicago suburb of South Barrington, Illinois, was planted in 1979, grew to an attendance of 9,000 by 1987, and spurted to 12,000 in 1988 under the leadership of Pastor Bill Hybels.

Christians, preoccupied with domestic problems and denominational housekeeping, often fail to see the phenomenon of mighty church growth that God is constantly bringing to pass on all six continents. Some persons, surprised at the extent of this growth, may even doubt its reality. But like Mt. Everest, it is there. It is going on all the time. And understanding it is an urgent task.

CHURCH GROWTH IS FAITHFULNESS TO GOD

Anyone who would comprehend the growth of Christian churches must see it primarily as faithfulness to God. God desires it. Christians, like their Master, are sent to seek and save the lost. Rather than gaining something for oneself, finding the lost is to become "your servant for Christ's sake." Church growth is humane action: the strong bearing the burdens of the weak and introducing to the hungry the bread by which humans live. Nevertheless, God's obedient servants seek church growth not as an exercise in improving humanity, but because the extension of the church is pleasing to God. Church growth is faithfulness.

Only where Christians constrained by love obediently press on, telling others the good news of the Savior, does the church spread and increase. Where there is no faithfulness in proclaiming Christ, there is no growth. There must also be obedience in hearing. Churches do not multiply and spread across a land or through a city unless among the multitudes who hear there are many who obey and—loving Christ more than father or mother—deny themselves, take up their crosses daily, and follow him.

Church growth follows where Christians show faithfulness in finding the lost. It is not enough to search for lost sheep. The Master Shepherd is not pleased with a token search; he wants his sheep found. The purpose is not to search, but to find. The goal is not to send powdered milk or kindly messages to the son in the far country. It is to see him walking in through the front door of his Father's house. For church growth also requires obedience in being found. It never takes place among the indifferent or rebellious, save as they renounce their indifference and rebellion.

Church growth follows where the lost are not merely found but restored to normal life in the fold—though it may be a life they have never consciously known. Faithfulness in folding and feeding—which unfortunately has come to be called by such a dry, superficial term as "follow-up"—is essential to lasting church expansion. When existing Christians, marching obediently under the Lord's command and filled with his compassion, fold in the wanderers and feed the flock, then churches multiply; but when they indolently permit men and women who have made costly decisions for Christ to drift back into the world, then indeed churches do not grow. Faithfulness in proclamation and finding is not enough. There must be faithful aftercare. Among the found, also, there must be fidelity in feeding on the word. Quality goes hand in hand with quantity.

The multiplication of churches nourished on the Bible and full of the

Holy Spirit is a *sine qua non* in carrying out the purposes of God. Conversely, would-be disciples must be joyfully built into his body—they must not wander alone in the wilderness. Because some churches appear to give the empirical church a value and authority beyond that which they accord to Jesus Christ, the Lord, some misguided Christian leaders speak as if the natural goal were a vague kingdom of God toward which we all automatically proceed—as if the multiplying of Christian churches among all peoples were an unworthy aim. Though God's triumphant reign will not come in its fullness until Christ returns in power, it is clear that in this era the more who love Christ and live "in him" as part of his body, the more goodness and truth will prevail in their communities. Righteousness and peace will surely spread as sound churches multiply throughout the more than three billion persons who now feel no allegiance to Jesus Christ.

SOCIOLOGY AND SPIRITUALITY

Church growth is no mere sociological process. To be sure, a secular humanist would see it as merely the outcome of an interplay of anthropological, historical, economic, and political forces. Humanists, believing in no transcendent source of truth, understand reality through empirical reason. But I am not a secular humanist; I am a convinced Christian. I believe in God the Father almighty, maker of heaven and earth, and in Jesus Christ his Son. The truth to which I am bound inheres in the ultimate stuff of the universe: the Word that was in the beginning with God, by whom all things were made, without whom was not anything made that was made—he is truth, and to him I give answer for everything I think and say and do.

I am not free to indulge my prejudices or to slight any of the evidence. I must take into account what comes in through the filter of my small reason and what comes to me through revelation and in every other way. All evidence must be weighed before the bar of truth. Therefore I cannot consider church growth merely a sociological process. It is that, to be sure; but much more than that, it is what happens when there is faithfulness to the God and Father of our Lord Jesus Christ.

Much of the energy of the church growth researchers in the 1960s and 1970s was spent on discerning factors of church growth informed by the behavioral sciences, especially cultural anthropology. As a result, many helpful insights on how to turn around church plateauing and de-

cline, how to avoid growth slowdowns, how to multiply new congregations, and how to diagnose and remedy the various problems of growth
were discovered, taught, and published. While this was all done in the
context of the biblical understanding that Jesus said, "I will build my
church," only passing attention was given to the role of the Holy Spirit in
church growth. The decade of the 1980s has seen an increasingly higher
priority given to the spiritual dynamics of growth by leaders of the Church
Growth Movement. Two of these areas which have become especially
prominent are the role of supernatural signs and wonders in church growth
and the part prayer plays in the extension of God's kingdom.

CHURCH GROWTH AS THEOLOGY

Church growth is basically a theological stance. God requires it. It looks
to the Bible for direction as to what God wants done. It holds that belief
in Jesus Christ, understood according to the Scriptures, is necessary for
salvation. Church growth rises in unshakeable theological conviction.

But since church growth has been born in an interdenominational milieu and taught to missionaries and pastors of many theological persua-
sions, and does not allow denominational differences to hide God's desire
that his lost children be found and his churches be multiplied, therefore
advocates of church growth have avoided voicing their own theological
convictions, which are not—at this time under these circumstances—
either causing or preventing church growth.

Naturally, therefore, to some denominational theologians church
growth looks inadequately theological. They consider it as method, not
theology. Baptismal regenerationists complain that church growth does
not sufficiently stress the sacraments. Some Calvinists complain that
church growth overlooks the sovereignty of God. Those fighting for social justice like to say that church growth teaches cheap grace. Those interested in liturgy find that church growth may say very little about their
concerns.

From the beginning the Church Growth Movement has been rooted
in biblical, evangelical, conversionist theology. But it has refused to take
sides on issues such as whether baptism should be administered to infants
or only to believers, whether churches should be governed by a presbyterian, episcopal, or congregational system, whether tongues proves that
one has been baptized in the Holy Spirit, whether Christians should or
should not drink, whether women should be ordained to the ministry,

whether Christ is truly or symbolically present in holy communion, and on any number of other areas of disagreement among theologians.

Individual church growth leaders have and live by their own personal theological convictions, but they do not seek to superimpose them on the universal church. However, on one thing there is total agreement: men and women without a personal relationship with Jesus Christ are doomed to a Christless eternity. The decisions they make for or against Jesus Christ in this life will make the difference. Therefore, faithfulness to God implies doing our part, empowered by the Holy Spirit, to persuade all men and women to become disciples of Jesus Christ and responsible members of his church.

THIS FAITHFULNESS IS COMPLEX

Very many kinds of church growth are found in the world today, each varying from people to people, from time to time, and from denomination to denomination. Understanding the nature of church growth is impossible unless we apprehend the many different types of growth and their various stages.

The five following illustrations of church growth will reveal something of the tremendously complex process by which the church multiplies congregations among the tongues and cultures of the world, and how God brings about his beneficent reign among all who believe.

In the Central Philippines

When the Japanese occupied the Philippines in 1942, the Rev. Leonardo G. Dia and his wife, refusing to collaborate with them, withdrew from the city of Cebu to the mountainous interior of the island and threw in their lot with three small neglected Presbyterian congregations. These had never had a resident pastor, let alone an able man like Mr. Dia. For the first few months the couple steadily visited the scattered homes of Christians, an arduous task in that mountainous country. They found the second-generation Christians friendly but largely ignorant of the Bible or of why they were evangelicals. At Mr. Dia's urging, three small chapels of bamboo and thatch were built in well-hidden locations. Regular worship and instruction began.

The pastor had R. H. Brown's book on the use of the Bible in personal evangelism in the Philippines, prepared years before by a Presbyterian missionary, which anchored the main Christian truths to about a hundred key passages in the New Testament. Instruction consisted in finding these in the Bible, explaining their meaning, and having the passages memorized. As fast as anyone learned all the passages with their references, and could explain what they meant, his or her name was written on the wall of the chapel. The competition stimulated everyone to learn, and having one's name inscribed on the wall became a status symbol.

As the congregations learned the passages, the believers turned to one another in amazement, saying, "Our religion is true!" Then they rushed out to persuade their loved ones and friends to become believers. In the first six months membership doubled. In the next year it doubled again. Other congregations were established.

The growth of these churches was made possible by seven underlying factors that converged at the same moment. (1) Neglected Christians began to receive highly competent pastoring. (2) They received it from a minister-patriot who refused at the risk of his life to collaborate with the enemy. (3) He gave them not merely good preaching, house-to-house visitation, and Bible teaching but also a clear system that made these neglected Christians masters of an outline of the Christian way. (4) The second-generation evangelicals were living in close contact with their nominally Roman Catholic relatives and friends. Once the evangelicals had the gospel they could readily communicate it. (5) The evangelicals were largely literate, thanks to the American emphasis on schools in the Philippines. (6) The Roman Catholic priests, partly no doubt due to wartime confusion, did not bring instant persecution upon those who attended the Protestant chapels or became evangelicals. (7) Mr. Dia was faithful in proclaiming Christ, finding the lost, feeding them, and building them into growing churches.

This particular kind of church growth would not be seen in all parts of the world. Other kinds of growth will occur in other places and at other times.

In Ongole, South India

In 1840 the American Baptists started a mission at Nellore on the eastern coast of India. For twenty-five years they labored among the upper castes, winning less than a hundred converts.

In 1865 John Clough (rhymes with "how") and his wife came out as new missionaries. As they learned the language and studied the Bible to see what God would have them do, each independently came to the conclusion that, on the basis of 1 Corinthians 1:26-28 ("not many wise according to the flesh, not many mighty, not many noble are called"), the policy followed rigorously by the older missionaries of seeking to win only the upper castes was displeasing to God (Clough 1915:133). The Madigas (untouchables), known to be responsive to the Christian message, had been bypassed lest their baptism make it still more difficult for caste Hindus to become Christians. The Cloughs moved from Nellore, opened the station of Ongole, and began baptizing some remarkably earnest and spiritual Madiga leaders. By 1869 hundreds were being added to the Lord.

In 1877 a great famine swept that part of India. Many of the 3,000 baptized believers died of hunger. To save those he could from starvation, John Clough contracted to build three and a half miles of a canal that the government was putting through as famine relief work. He thus provided labor and food for 1,500 Christian men and women who had found it impossible to get work on sections of the canal where caste Hindus were supervisors. Then, besieged by their starving non-Christian relatives and other Madigas, he also put 1,500 pagan Madigas to work. In the famine camps along the canal, the Christians assembled in the evenings for worship and teaching. Pagan Madigas, too, heard the word with joy and wonder, but were not baptized. Lest they become Christians for the loaves and fishes, Clough had stopped baptizing early in 1877.

As the canal was finished, the famine became more acute. Government and missions started other work projects and even distributed free food. A hundred thousand dollars passed through Clough's hands, and thousands of lives were saved.

After the crisis was over, requests for instruction and baptism poured in from the pagan relatives of the Christians. Clough and his helpers visited and preached in scores of villages. They taught, examined, and helped organize potential churches. Then on July 2, 3, and 4 of 1878, 3,536 believers were buried with their Lord in baptism. On one day alone 2,222 were baptized. Within a few months over 6,000 others had followed them into the church, making the number for that year 9,601, in a total membership of 12,806. Adherents were not counted but formed a much larger number (Clough 1915:284).

This kind of church growth differs enormously from the growth in the Philippines. Its conditioning factors—oppression, untouchability, burning conviction that the oppressed ought not to be denied salvation, a terrible famine, and a canal passing through the district—were utilized by a missionary who was enough of an engineer to take a contract for part of the canal, devout enough to preach the gospel to untouchable laborers, wise enough to defer baptism until they had gone back to their villages, and courageous enough to baptize 9,601 in a single year. These particular factors may never again fall together. Other favorable elements will converge at a single time and place, but not these. Exactly this kind of church growth should not be expected to occur often.

In Rhodesia and Zambia

A distinctive kind of church growth is found in Rhodesia (now Zimbabwe) and Zambia. This part of Africa was occupied by missions in the last third of the nineteenth century. The London Missionary Society began work there in 1859, the South African Dutch Reformed Church in 1872, the Anglicans in 1888, the English Methodists in 1891, and the American Methodists in 1898. Many other missions also have entered these lands.

By 1950 communicants totaled 125,266 and places of worship, 3,883.

The degree of growth these figures indicate might at first glance be considered satisfactory. When it is remembered, however, that (1) a considerable fraction of the 125,266 full members were Europeans (out of a European population of 213,000 at least 35,000 were communicants); and (2) the total African population in 1950 was about 3,500,000, it is readily seen that the African communicants (about 90,000) comprised a mere 2.6 percent of the African population.

Assuming 300 places where worship in English was carried on, the 90,000 vernacular-speaking African communicants were distributed in about 3,500 places of worship. Assuming about two hundred large African congregations with a total of possibly 30,000 communicants in towns, mission stations, and educational centers, this leaves 60,000 African communicants distributed in 3,300 places of worship. The average place of worship would have about 15 communicants.

What kind of church growth was this for the first hundred years of missionary labor in David Livingstone's land?

It was a special variety that I shall call "school-approach church growth." Missions carried on schools as an essential part of their evangelistic work. It was government policy to do all education through the missions. Only missions that promised to maintain schools and dispensaries were permitted to enter these countries, and were assigned territories of their own. Before 1950 almost the only way African children could get an education was to go to a mission school, where, as they were taught the Bible day after day by Christian teachers, they often became Christians. The picture is one of many small congregations, led by teachers and convening in school buildings, while the pagan power structures of the tribe, composed of the mature men, remained intact. At the larger towns and mission stations, with their complexes of institutions and employment, a few score large congregations led by ministers met in church buildings.

In Rhodesia and Zambia the school approach produced this distinctive kind of church growth. It is a common variety in Africa south of the Sahara. For it to occur, a delicate balance of tensions in tribal society must make it possible for children of pagan parents to become Christians without seriously rupturing family relationships. In India, the Middle East, and many other lands, church growth of this sort cannot readily occur. Minors cannot become Christians unless their parents lead the way into baptism.

The unformulated assumptions behind this approach have yet to be dug out of the letters, mission and government policies, allocations of mission budgets, and other sources so that we can see them clearly. Until this is done, one can only hazard a guess that the following considerations bulked large: (1) Tribal life is so pagan, illiterate, and evil as to be beyond redemption. (2) The goal of missions-cum-government is to break up the tribes and bring converts out into a modern, Christian posttribal social order. (3) Polygamy is so entrenched in tribal life that it is impossible for most adults of the tribe to become Christian. (4) The correct way to Christianize, therefore, is through prolonged schooling. The argument was this: Many boys and girls will become Christian before their marriage. Many will remain Christian despite the pull of the tribe. The old generation will die off. Educated Christians will gradually control society. (5) The British government will continue on indefinitely to the great advantage of the Africans. Over the centuries the old pagan order will gradually wither away and a Christian African population take its place. (6) The establishment of mission stations, dispensaries, hospitals, schools, and—in connection with them—churches is therefore the chief task of missions and the only sound way to proceed.

So long as the British framework remained, the school approach had much to commend it. It was not based on New Testament practices; but then African conditions between 1880 and 1950 were so very different from the New Testament world. Since the British framework has collapsed, however, the contemporary situation is quite different. Education is being rapidly taken over by the African states. Secularism, materialism, and Marxism bid for the allegiance of the educated, and no one can count on hundreds of years of peaceful evolution within any given system of government.

In Rhodesia and Zambia this narrow kind of church growth, which during the years 1880-1950 was developed to fit one kind of government and social structure, must speedily be transformed into one that fits the political and social realities of the closing years of the twentieth century in southeast Africa. For example, the tribe must be recognized and welcomed as a significant political and social entity in the new Africa. Even if a hundred years from now tribes should cease to exist (which is highly improbable), they are a powerful part of the contemporary scene. A mode of evangelization must be perfected that spreads rapidly through people groups. The adult power structures of most villages and wards must be made up of Christians. The tribes must come to have as much consciousness of being Christian as the Scottish clans once had. This will require a type of church growth very different from that generated by the school approach.

In Iceland About A.D. 1000

The Saga of Burnt Nyal (Dasent 1960) is a bloody tale of family feuds in one part of Iceland. It would have merely antiquarian interest, except that a few chapters recount how the natives turned from paganism to Christianity. Burnt Nyal is not history. The turning actually took many decades, as first one group of families and then another became Christian. Eric the Red, who settled Greenland about A.D. 1000, died a pagan, while his wife Thjodhild and son Leif, who discovered America, became Christian. Nevertheless, the events recounted are either the actual ones or the kind of happenings that did take place.

Icelanders were the farthest out of the seafaring communities along the shores of Denmark, Norway, the Orkney and Shetland islands, and Iceland. They lived by fishing, raising animals (ponies are frequently mentioned), and raiding villages in more favored lands. They were a hard-bitten, savage, and ruthless lot, who kept slaves and thought little of killing them. Constant feuds between extended families killed off the weaklings. Female infanticide was practiced—probably to keep the community from being burdened with surplus women.

Into the saga comes passing mention of Kolskegg, who went to Denmark and bound himself to Forkbeard, the Danish king. He was there baptized, then fared south to Micklegarth (Constantinople), took service with the Emperor, and married a Christian lady (Dasent 1960:142).

Then the islanders heard that

there had been a change of rulers in Norway . . . and a change of faith. They had cast off the old faith and King Olaf had in addition baptized the western lands, Shetland, the Orkneys, and the Faroe Isles. . . . Many men said it was a strange and wicked thing to throw off the old faith; but Njal said, "It seems to me as though this new faith must be much better and he will be happy who follows this rather than the other, and if those men come hither who preach this faith, then I will back them well." That same harvest a ship came out into the fiords [of Iceland] at Gautawick. The captain Thangbrand was sent by King Olaf to preach the faith. Along with him came that man of Iceland whose name was Gudlief—a great manslayer and one of the strongest of men (Dasent 1960:176).

As these traveled from fiord to fiord, some accepted and some re-fused Christianity. Thorkell, an Icelander, spoke vigorously against the faith and challenged Thangbrand to one-on-one combat. The end of it was that Thangbrand slew Thorkell. A typical sentence of the saga reads, "Then Hildir the Old and all his household took upon them the new faith."

After many families and lineages became Christian, the islandwide Thing, where rough justice was meted out and feuds adjudicated, was convened at the Hill of Laws. Men rode to the Thing that year in battle array, because it seemed likely that pagans would fight Christians to determine which faith would hold Iceland. Both sides went to the Hill of Laws. Christians and heathens declared themselves "out of the other's laws." A great tumult arose. At the critical moment the Christian spokesman turned to the pagan witch doctor, Thorgeir, priest of Lightwater, and "gave him three marks of silver to utter what the law should be."

Thorgeir lay all that day on the ground and spread a cloak over his head, so that no man spoke with him. . . . The day after, men went to the Hill of Laws and Thorgeir spoke thus: "It seems to me as though matters were come to a deadlock, for if there is a sundering of the laws, we shall never be able to live in the land. So I will ask both Christian men and heathen whether they will hold to these laws which I utter." They all said they would. . . . "This is the beginning of our laws," he said, "that all men shall be Christians and believe in one God . . . but leave all idol worship, not expose children to perish, and not eat horseflesh. It shall be outlawry if such things, done openly, are proved against any man; but if these things are done by stealth, then it shall be blameless."

But all heathendom was done away with within a few years' space, so that those things were not allowed to be done either by stealth or openly (Dasent 1960:184).

This unique kind of church growth, so questionable and repugnant to us today, was not unusual in northern Europe a thousand years ago. It may never occur again. The special conditions that produced it have ceased to exist. All must regret the savagery, illiteracy, and isolation that made knowledge of the Bible and the Savior so scarce in the dark ages in Europe that only a low form of Christianity could develop; but we nevertheless rejoice that those rough peoples did decide to "follow the new faith." They took the one essential step by which later advances in Christian living could be made by the Wycliffes, Knoxes, Luthers, Foxes, Wesleys, Careys, and others. Icelandic church growth a thousand years ago was part of the complex faithfulness that pleases God.

In Aracaju, Brazil

In 1964 the evangelical church leaders in Aracaju, Brazil, in conjunction with the missionaries, planned a city-wide, year-long evangelistic campaign. They divided the city into sections and assigned one to each congregation. They organized cells in each to pray for revival and ingathering. Ministers preached on the lostness of unbelievers and the blessedness of those who repent of their sins and accept Jesus Christ as Lord and Savior. Joint open-air services were held. Those to whom God had granted special effectiveness as evangelists were invited in from other cities. The program progressed from congregational assemblies to gatherings of all the evangelicals in each ward. Hundreds of thousands of tracts and Bible portions were distributed. Evangelical processions wound their way through the streets of the city. Christians two by two called on all houses in the urban area, inviting people to meetings and offering to teach them the way of the Lord.

All the evangelical churches, from the Assemblies of God to the United Presbyterian, cooperated in this campaign. A sense of expectation arose in congregation after congregation. Men and women, boys and girls, were won to Christian faith from week to week and joined in winning their neighbors and friends. Sins were confessed. Restitution for wrongs was made. Broken families were reunited. Instruction classes for inquirers and catechumens were opened in every church. When the campaign ended and inquirers had been instructed and baptized, it was found that the membership of the evangelical churches had more than doubled, from 1,200 to 2,400 baptized believers in one year.

This church growth in Aracaju is more akin to North American patterns than some others described. Some Americans feel that this is more real and more spiritual than what occurred in Ongole or Rhodesia. That it is more spiritual may be doubted, but certainly it is different. Growth of this particular variety is possible only in certain circumstances. The general public must already consider itself Christian in some fashion. It must believe the Bible is its own scripture, and read tracts and Bible portions and hear sermons and witness with that in mind. Opposition from leaders of the majority community must be mild or even nonexistent. Numerous existing evangelicals must live in close contact with their unconverted neighbors and relatives. The existing congregations and denominations must be indigenous enough to appear thoroughly national, yet have enough missionary aid to finance a city-wide campaign. The churches must have missionary and national leaders who believe that accepting the Lord Jesus is the most important thing any person can do.

SUMMARY

These five summarized cases of church growth indicate in bare outline the complexity of the process by which God is pleased to multiply his churches. When the church plants congregations in the many cultures of America or any other nation, it multiplies credible witnesses who can readily be understood by the people of those cultures. While it will be done differently depending on time and place, it must be done. Church growth will lead to saving faith in Jesus Christ the "ten thousand times ten thousand and thousands of thousands" whom Christ is redeeming from "every kindred, and tongue, and people, and nation."

The limitless intricacy of church growth may be further understood by locating each church at its proper place on the following five lines of distribution, or axes:

A. DEPENDENCE VERSUS INDEPENDENCE

B. INDIVIDUAL VERSUS GROUP CONVERSION

C. PROPORTION OF TOTAL POPULATION

D. RATE OF GROWTH

E. INDIGENEITY

On Axis A the "most dependent churches" will be placed at the far left and the "most independent churches" at the far right. All others are placed in between according to their degree of independence.

A DEPENDENCE VERSUS INDEPENDENCE

1	2	3	4	5	6

To qualify for position 1, a church would be heavily dependent, spiritually and materially, on its founding mission. To qualify for position 6, it would receive no missionary aid from abroad, carry on all its domestic labors effectively, and propagate Christianity inside and outside its own language area.

Similarly churches can be located, according to their characteristics, on the other four axes whose two ends are defined.

B INDIVIDUAL VERSUS GROUP CONVERSION

1 Church has arisen by pure individual decision.	Church has arisen by pure group decision.	6

C PROPORTION OF TOTAL POPULATION

1 Church forms 1% or less of class or tribe concerned.	Church forms 90% or more of class or tribe concerned.	6

D RATE OF GROWTH

1 Church has grown at less than 10% per decade.	Church has grown at more than 200% per decade.	6

E INDIGENEITY

1 Church has been formed in mold of foreign founder.	Church has been formed in indigenous mold.	6

If on the following axes churches in the Philippines (1942), Ongole (1900), Rhodesia and Zambia (1952), Iceland (1000), and Aracaju (1964) be represented by their initial letters, something like the following distribution will be obtained:

Axis A   DEPENDENCE VS. INDEPENDENCE

O	R	A	P		I

Axis B   INDIVIDUAL VS. GROUP CONVERSION

R	A	P		O	I

Axis C	PROPORTION OF TOTAL POPULATION					
A P	R O					I

Axis D	RATE OF GROWTH					
R			A	O	P	I

AXIS E	INDIGENEITY				
R		O	A	P	I

In the coming millennium, as Christianity spreads throughout the myriad cultures of the world, many factors varying from place to place and time to time will combine to give each church a unique growth pattern and to locate it at a particular place on each axis.

THREE SETS OF FACTORS

As we look at any case of growth or nongrowth, whether it be a local church or an entire denomination, we find that understanding it involves consideration of three important sets of factors. The first set we call contextual factors. These are political, sociological, cultural, and environmental factors over which the church or the mission has no control. They may be local factors or they may extend to regions and entire nations. Church growth is slow in a country like Albania, for example, because of a national contextual factor: religion is outlawed and offenders are severely punished.

The second set is institutional factors. These are factors that the church or denomination can control. Most mainline denominations in the United States suffered severe membership losses in the 1965-1990 period. This was due, at least to a significant degree, to a national institutional factor: in the mid-1960s their national leaders decided to prioritize social ministries over evangelism and church planting.

The third set of factors is spiritual. The Holy Spirit is sovereign, and he is not subject to contextual or institutional factors. He frequently acts in surprising, nontraditional ways, and it is up to those Christian leaders who want to be effective in growth to have an ear to hear what the Spirit is saying to the churches.

2

GOD'S WILL AND CHURCH GROWTH

CHRISTIAN MISSION must be carried on today in the parish and abroad in a kaleidoscopic world, with its divisions, hatreds, and wars—where Russia captures Kabul before hundreds of millions, and visions of world peace both elude and inspire leaders. In this world, men and women long attached to old faiths and loyalties are faced with new scientific truth, world civilization, dreams of abundant life, principles of democracy and Communism, and the revolutionary revelation of God in Christ. Jolted out of old adjustments and social, political, economic, and religious patterns, they are searching for better, truer, and more satisfying ways of life. The population explosion is raising up countless multitudes, alike in new cities and old countrysides, who will be even more exposed to change than were their parents.

In this world, mission must be what God desires. It is not a human activity but *missio Dei,* the mission of God, who himself remains in charge of it. Hence the problems of mission should be viewed in the light of his revealed will. Being the kind of God he has shown himself to be in Christ, what kind of mission does *he* desire? For that is what mission essentially and theologically is.

Mission defined as "God's program for humans" is obviously many-sided. Each aspect of it can be called mission. Has God assigned any priority among these myriad good activities? For example, in his eyes does establishing equality of educational opportunity for all citizens of the United States have a higher priority than beautifying the highways? We believe that God, indeed, has assigned priorities. His will in these matters can be learned from his revelation and is mandatory for Christians.

WHAT DOES GOD DESIRE?

It is not necessary to consider a thousand aspects of God's mission one by one. The live options today come conveniently grouped. Using "what God desires" as a compass to help us pick our way among the baffling good alternatives that confront the church, let us look briefly at two of the easier groups of choices, first considering good works as against reconciling men and women to God in Christ.

As in the light of Christ we look at the world—its exploding knowledge, peoples, revolutions, physical needs, desperate spiritual hunger and nakedness, and enslavement to false gods and demonic ideologies—we realize that Christian mission must certainly engage in many labors. A multitude of excellent enterprises lies around us. So great is the number and so urgent the calls, that Christians can easily lose their way among them, seeing them all equally as mission. But in doing the good, they can fall short of the best. In winning the preliminaries, they can lose the main event. They can be treating a troublesome itch, while the patient dies of cholera. The question of priorities cannot be avoided. In this fast-moving, cruel, and revolutionary era, when many activities are demanded, a right proportioning of effort among them is essential to sound policy. And "rightness"—a true and sound proportion in our labors—must be decided according to biblical principles in the light of God's revealed will.

Among other desires of God-in-Christ, he beyond question wills that lost persons be found—that is, be reconciled to himself. Most cordially admitting that God has other purposes, we should remember that we serve a God *who finds persons.* He has an overriding concern that men and women should be redeemed. However we understand the word, biblical witness is clear that people are "lost." The finding God wants them *found*—that is, brought into a redemptive relationship to Jesus Christ where, baptized in his name, they become part of his household. He is not pleased when many findable sheep remain straggling on the mountain, shivering in the bitter wind. The more found, the better pleased is God.

Among other characteristics of mission, therefore, the chief and irreplaceable one must be this: that mission is a divine finding, vast and continuous. The chief and irreplaceable purpose of mission is church growth. Social service pleases God, but it must never be substituted for finding the lost. Our Lord did not rest content with feeding the hungry and healing the sick. He pressed on to give his life a ransom for many and to send out his followers to disciple all nations. Service must not be so disproportionately emphasized at the expense of evangelism that findable persons are continually lost. In the proportioning of social ministries and church planting, the degree of growth being achieved must always be taken into account. God's servants carry on mission in a fast-moving world and must constantly adjust the proportions of service and evangelism, as the church grows from a few scattered cells to churches forming substantial majorities of the population, so that *maximum finding occurs.*

CHRISTIANIZING THE SOCIAL ORDER

Second, let us consider the Christianizing of the social order as against the multiplication of cells of Christians throughout "every kindred and tongue and people and nation." Today the sinfulness of the social order offends thoughtful Christians everywhere, particularly where they are numerous and powerful. The great inequalities of wealth and poverty among the haves and have-nots and the revolting treatment meted out to oppressed minorities are clearly contrary to the will of the God and Father of our Lord Jesus Christ. Christians of all shades of theological opinion recognize this and, in varying measure, work to rectify it in the areas of their responsibility. They carry on a widespread war against these sub-Christian practices and are remarkably alike in their degree of involvement in them.

But Christian leaders differ dramatically in the relative importance they attach to evangelism and to Christian social ministries. One school of thought assigns weight on the basis of immediate reason—what seems most urgent to them today as they and others of goodwill look at the tragic human scene. The other school, to which I adhere, assigns importance on the basis of biblical principles in the light of the life, death, and resurrection of Jesus Christ. It maintains that Christianizing the social order is a fruit of new life in Christ and of church multiplication and must, therefore, receive a lower priority.

Under some circumstances, to be sure, and for a limited time, Christianizing some aspect of the social order may legitimately be assigned a higher priority and receive greater attention than evangelism. Some Christian leaders under the circumstances prevailing in the 1960s, and for a limited time, did well to turn from winning souls to Christ to winning the civil rights battle. But as a rule, the multiplying of cells of reborn Christians continues to have the higher priority. But for the presence of millions of practicing American Christians of all races, the battle for civil rights could never have been mounted.

George G. Hunter III speaks powerfully to this point. In the March 1977 *Church Growth Bulletin* he says,

> I address those in the Church whose "holy bag" is Christian social action—peace, food, reconciliation, justice. . . . Wherever, anywhere in the world over the last 19 centuries, when the Christian Movement has emphasized disciple-making, two things have happened. . . . We have made some new disciples and planted some churches and have had a social influence out of proportion to our numbers. But, whenever the Christian mission has neglected disciple-making and concentrated on the other facets of Christ's work, we have not made many disciples or planted many churches and have not had much social influence either! *Our social causes will not triumph unless we have great numbers of committed Christians.*

It is comforting to know that the broad consensus among evangelical Christian leaders today affirms the priority of evangelism over social ministries. The 1974 Lausanne Covenant uncompromisingly states that "In the church's mission of sacrificial service, evangelism is primary" (Paragraph 6). Years of debate followed the drafting of the covenant, but this biblical position was reaffirmed both in the Consultation on the Relationship between Evangelism and Social Responsibility held in Grand Rapids, Michigan, in 1982 and in the Lausanne II Congress held in Manila in 1989. The Grand Rapids report stresses that while many human agencies can relieve social needs, only Christians have the message that saves souls. It recognizes that, in the final analysis, eternal salvation is more important than temporal well-being.

SEARCH THEOLOGY AND A THEOLOGY OF HARVEST

To many, mission is widely defined as "God's total program for humans," and we have considered the alternatives arising from that definition. Mission may now be defined much more meaningfully. Since God as revealed in the Bible has assigned the highest priority to bringing men and women into living relationship to Jesus Christ, we may define mission narrowly as *an enterprise devoted to proclaiming the good news of Jesus Christ, and to persuading men and women to become his disciples and responsible members of his church.* Even after establishing the priorities among social service, social action, and evangelism, the church still has many baffling alternatives, and this definition is necessary if we are to discover among them the path desired by the God who finds.

God, who "became flesh and dwelt among us," is primarily concerned that people be saved, and his mission must also be so concerned. Christian outreach in today's responsive world demands a theology of harvest that the New Testament uniquely offers. Yet at this critical time many Christians are firmly committed to a theology of seed sowing, which might also be called a theology of search. It arose in the former, more discouraging era of missions. It maintains that in evangelism the essential thing is not the finding, but going everywhere and preaching the gospel— for which there is some excellent biblical authority.

THE ROOTS OF SEARCH THEOLOGY

Search theology framed its major beliefs under the impact of four chief factors, and it cannot be understood except as we see the part these have played in its genesis.

First, it arose in the face of indifference at home and hostility abroad. At home, the Western churches did not naturally engage in mission. The conversion of non-Christians of other lands seemed to the church expensive, politically inexpedient, meddlesome, dangerous, and not the will of God. Denomination after denomination had to be roused by its prophets before it would engage in foreign missions. Missionary societies had to be organized on the fringe of the churches—among the women, the devout, the specially concerned. Abroad, hostility faced Christian mission—both the hostility of Western traders who feared that missionaries would upset their business and that of cultures which regarded Christianity as the spearhead of an invading imperialism. Christian mission needed a theology that would undergird it during the long years when it was weak at home and hard beset abroad. Search theology did this. It strenuously denied that results had anything to do with mission. Search was God's will.

Second, in recent years, a vast relativism, based on the study of non-

Christian religions, has enveloped the West and in a curious way buttressed search theology. It has aggressively attacked the doctrine that Christ is the full, final, once-for-all revelation of God. It also attacks its corollary, that every Christian should proclaim Christ and persuade men and women to become his disciples and responsible members of his church. This relativism is the more powerful for being the product of a fundamentally sympathetic impulse. In fifty years we have become heirs to a transformed world of communications, transportation, cultural interchange, and the validation of all kinds of formerly unfamiliar peoples, lands, national histories, literatures, and folk art, to name but a few strands in this drawing together of human interest and knowledge.

The new, tender relativism among us, rightly anxious to defer, to heal, not to wound—eager to make up for past crude indifferences to which Westerners were sometimes a party—pauses in appreciation before the richness of non-Christian religions. It then wrongly concludes that there are many ways to God, that people are "saved" by the sincerity with which they follow whatever light they have.

To be sure, most committed and informed Christians themselves have not accepted universalism in any such terms; but its intellectual climate has enveloped them and has heavily influenced what they think most worth doing. Those affected by universalism have also agreed to search theology. It is all right, they argue, to look for needy people and proclaim Christ by word and deed (especially by kindly deed), but it is misguided to work for actual conversions. The aim of mission in friendly, cooperative relationships with other religions is to develop a new humanity, a new just and participatory society.

The third chief factor whose impact resulted in "search" theology has been the enormous gap between the rapidly rising standard of living in the West and that of the masses in the Third World. Compared to the West in the twentieth century, the average of health, literacy, nutrition, comfort, production, cleanliness, enlightenment, and general helpfulness in most of the rest of the world has left much to be desired. Missionaries were beset by requests for schools, hospitals, and agricultural demonstration centers. Their Christian message was looked at askance, but their Western cultural adjuncts were much in demand. They could not produce many converts; but they could produce many hospital treatments and grant many school certificates. Against their will and in the face of their sincere protestations that the real task was discipling the nations, they were pushed into all kinds of philanthropic work. These were defended as "a preparation for the gospel," "a more effective way of preaching the gospel," and on occasion "just as good as the gospel." A harvest of souls was not a high priority.

Fourth, search theology emerged as the church in many fields faced very small growth in membership. It had to find a rationale for existence and continuance that did not depend on numbers of converts. Under such conditions it welcomed a theology of mission that proclaimed that "only search" was God's command. Results *should not* be used to evaluate success or failure.

Goaded by these four pressures, search theology fiercely attacked any emphasis on results. Missionary writers vie with one another in deprecating mere numbers. The shepherds, going out to search for lost sheep, meet at the gate to announce that they do not intend to notice particularly how many are found.

IS GOD PLEASED WITH SEARCH THEOLOGY?

Is search theology true to God as revealed in Jesus Christ? Standing in his presence, let us ask the following three questions. Their concreteness may offend some, but I know of no better way to narrow the issue down to the essential question: Is *God* concerned that countable persons be won to Christ?

1. Theologically speaking should the number of people found bear any relation to the direction and intensity of the search?

2. Speaking with the utmost sincerity before God, do we feel that the number of sinners *obeying* the call to repentance and discipleship should or should not influence where and how that call is issued?

3. Is it more pleasing to God to proclaim Christ where people are ready to be reconciled to God than where they are not?

Christians with a theology of search answer each of these three questions with a ringing "No!" They hold mission to be the proclamation of Christ by word and deed, whether people hear or not, whether they obey or not. God commanded Ezekiel, saying, "Go to your people and say to them, 'Thus says the Lord,' whether they hear or refuse to hear." Many hold that the mission of the church is similarly to proclaim Christ. The church is to pay no attention to the response; its duty is complete in proclamation. This position is neutral toward results. To have an eye on results would be immodest toward God and coercive toward fellow human beings.

Some fear numbers because they see one soul as of infinite value.

Christ died for each one, hence every soul is worth the entire effort of all mission from the day of Pentecost on. They argue that a church or a mission that over a period of fifty years leads fifty souls to the feet of Christ is as pleasing to God as one that in the same period wins fifty thousand and plants the church firmly in an entire countryside. Persons evangelizing indifferent or resistant populations usually espouse a theology of search on this score.

Faced with the question, "Theologically speaking should the numbers of those who can be effectively *found* have anything to do with the direction and intensity of the search?" Christians such as I have described would answer, "No! The gospel is to be proclaimed everywhere, and God will gather into his church whom he will."

At base, the trouble is that mere search, detached witness—without the deep wish to convert, without wholehearted persuasion, and with what amounts to a fear of the numerical increase of Christians—is not biblically justified. *Mere search is not what God wants. God wants his lost children found.* Let us examine the evidence.

GOD'S PASSION TO FIND

Four kinds of biblical evidence nourish the conviction that God has a passion to find the lost.

1. Explicit statements of our Lord and his apostles are against the search position. Matthew records that our Lord instructed his disciples to pray that God would send laborers into *his* harvest (see Matt. 9:37). Seeing the responsiveness of a particular population, our Lord recognized the need for reapers. The whitened fields were God's. Simply walking through them proclaiming Christ's lordship was not enough. God wanted the grain cut, bound into sheaves, and carried back into his barns. In Matthew 10:14 Jesus says, "And whoever will not receive you nor hear your words, when you depart from that house or city, shake off the dust from your feet." Our Lord carefully instructed his disciples not to tarry with those who rejected the gospel, but to hurry on to those who welcomed it. Acts 13:51 indicates that Barnabas and Saul knew of this instruction and followed it. It is a fair inference that this was the common practice of the New Testament church. Evangelists did not badger and bother people who resisted the good news, but hurried on to those who were ready to become believers.

These words of the Lord Jesus and this practice of the early church cannot be directly applied in all times and to all populations. There are many instances of decades of work among the unresponsive being followed by rapid growth of the church. Yet this New Testament principle should be the rule, and applied whenever a specific church or mission faces a New Testament situation, that is, where part of its hearers are responsive and part have set their faces like flint against the gospel. There Christians must win the winnable while they are winnable.

2. Our Lord's parables often emphasize an actual finding. The woman does not merely search, but searches *until she finds* the lost coin. The shepherd does not make a token hunt and return empty-handed. He goes "after the one which is lost, *until he finds it.*"

At the great banquet, the master did not commend the servant who brought news that the invited could not come. He did not say, "Continue inviting these indifferent persons until they accept." He said to his servant, "Bring in the poor and the maimed and the lame and the blind." When there was yet room, he said again, "Go out to the highways and hedges, and compel them to come in." Issuing the invitation was not the end: partaking of God's feast was. If one group would not accept the summons, then the servant was to find others who would.

The legitimacy of persuasion does not depend at all on the new course of conduct arising solely in the mind of the persuaded. Its rightness depends entirely on (a) whether the action proposed is good for the persuaded, and (b) whether he or she freely accepts it. A sleeping woman in a burning building is a case in point. Is it legitimate to shake her, wake her, and persuade her to leave? Certainly—even, in fact, if the arouser risks his or her own life merely for the plaudits of others or because payment is made for services. Motives have nothing to do with the legitimacy of persuasion.

3. Behind the specific passages and parables mentioned, however, lies still more weighty evidence. The revelation of God culminating in Christ tells us that God himself is a searching, saving God. He found Israel in Egypt and bound her to himself in the covenant at Sinai. He remained faithful to the covenant when Israel again and again was faithless. God wants people—multitudes of people—reconciled to himself. He was in Christ reconciling *the world* to himself.

Jesus Christ, our Lord, came to seek and save the lost. The lost are always persons. They always have countable bodies. As Scripture says, "We have this treasure in earthen vessels"—vessels that can be numbered. Again, "that the life of Christ may be manifested in our mortal flesh"— flesh that is distributed among persons numerous as the sands of the sea.

Our Lord would have rejected the thought that the number of those found has no bearing on the direction of the search. On the contrary, his very mention of the joy in heaven over a single saved soul is but added testimony to the urgent importance of the many. To God, as he has thus revealed himself, proclamation is not the main thing. The proclamation of the gospel is a means. It must not be confused with the end, which is that men and women—multitudes of them—be reconciled to God in Christ.

4. Finally we note that the New Testament church went where people responded, believing this to be God's will.

For possibly fifteen years, witness was confined almost entirely to the Jews. "They spake the word to none but Jews." During the years when Jews responded by becoming disciples of Christ, the church multiplied itself among the Jews. This is often regarded as a grievous fault in the early church, but in the circumstances then prevailing it was, on the contrary, one of its great virtues. The church won the winnable—while they could be won. If Peter on the day of Pentecost, in an effort to win the Gentiles, had required all would-be converts to practice inclusiveness in eating, marrying, worshiping, and proclaiming, and the apostles had immediately given as much attention to Gentiles living in Jerusalem and Judea as they did to Jews, very few Jews would have become Christian.

This may be why our Lord commanded the gospel to be preached to all peoples "beginning with Jerusalem"—where many would respond, be baptized, and form churches.

After A.D. 48 the church broke out from among the racial Jews—Hebrews born of Hebrews—and spread rapidly in the synagogue communities with their large numbers of Gentile God-fearers. Indeed, had the church not multiplied enormously among the synagogues of the Roman world, their Gentile fringes would never have become Christian.

BEYOND SEARCH TO HARVEST

In view of all this and much more evidence, must we not consider mission in intention *a vast and purposeful finding*? Is it possible biblically to maintain that only "search" is the thing, motives are what matter, and the finding of multitudes of persons is something rather shabbily mechanical and "success ridden"? Can we believe it theologically tenable to be uninterested in the numbers of the redeemed?

Does not the biblical evidence rather indicate that in the sight of a God who finds, numbers of the redeemed are important? God himself desires that multitudes be reconciled to himself in the church of Christ. Indeed, God commands an ardent searching for the lost *in order to find them.*

In the revolutionary churning up of the world in which we live, fantastic increase of churches is obviously the will of God. He it is who shakes the foundations. Since he is the Father almighty and not some blind force or cosmic urge, inherent in his action must be some good purpose. What purpose is more in line with his intent to save men and women than to marshal, discipline, strengthen, and multiply his churches until all people on earth have had the chance to hear the gospel from their own kindred, who speak their own language and whose word is unobstructed by cultural barriers? In many regions, missionaries must start the process; but it is clear that the gospel cannot be proclaimed to every creature, belief cannot become a real option to every person, until churches exist in all groupings of humanity, whether in city or country, of high or low caste, educated or illiterate, throughout the earth. Thus speaks a theology of harvest.

Is then a theology of search false? By no means; but it is partial. It is true for some populations. It is false only insofar as it claims to be the sole theology of evangelism and applicable to all.

As we confront the indifferent or the hostile, we must remember that God yearns for the salvation of all his children. He searches even when he does not find. Our Lord stands at the door and knocks, but enters only if the door is opened. Yes, God is a searcher and commands searching.

As we look at those who respond and are found, however—and their name is legion—we must remember that God finds. It should be easy for us who have been found to remember this: he not only searched, but he also found. God searches until he finds. He searches where he finds. He reconciles people to himself. He has appointed us shepherds. He commands us to find and save the lost.

3

TODAY'S TASK, OPPORTUNITY, AND IMPERATIVE

THE TASK

IT IS DIFFICULT to speak about today's task in the singular when hundreds of tasks lie before the church and God calls his people to every one of them. Internal tasks abound—raising church budgets, helping Christians grow in grace, serving youth, erecting new buildings, training lay leaders, teaching the Bible, and many more. External tasks abound— building community in the midst of racial strife, giving underprivileged youth a chance, working for peace and justice, reaching unevangelized men and women with the gospel, establishing new churches in suitable locations, and scores of others. The calls from across the seas were never more numerous. Great numbers of persons die each year of hunger and malnutrition. Yet there are still refugees to house, illiterates to teach, the sick to heal—and *three billion who have never heard the name of Christ* to flood with knowledge of their Savior.

In spite of all, the thesis of this chapter is that—for the welfare of the world, for the good of humanity—according to the Bible, one task is paramount. Today's supreme task is the effective multiplication of churches in the receptive societies of earth.

Discerning the Urgent

The other good and urgent things to do, far from contradicting this thesis, reinforce it. The many tasks that lie at hand should be done—there can be no two opinions about that. Preaching good sermons, teaching illiterates to read, working at planned parenthood or the world's food supply, administering churches skillfully, applying Christianity to all of life, using mass media, and hundreds of other activities are not sinful. They are good. Some are urgent.

But are they all of equal importance? Even if the mission of the church is broadly defined as everything God wants his people to do, are all these activities of equal value? Does mission consist of a large number of parallel thrusts between which Christians may not discriminate? Does it make no difference which comes first, or which is omitted?

Christians accept the authority of the Bible in its total impact and, believing that God's revelation in Christ and the Bible establishes guidelines for all, they find sure guidance concerning the relative importance of various courses of conduct. They are not left to human wisdom, with some maintaining that humans are responsible beings and some that they are automatons. They do not have to wonder whether the highest good is ethical achievement or being in Christ. Their path is illumined by God's revelation. They can and should draw the distinction between root and fruit, and base their policies in mission and evangelism upon it.

We must not oversimplify the situation, as if Christians could do one task and leave all others undone. They can and should do many tasks together. When Nehemiah built the wall, some carried stone, some brought water, some mixed mortar, and some laid the stones in place. All were controlled, however, by the overriding purpose—all were building the wall. The supreme aim guided the entire enterprise. Stones and mortar arrived at the wall in the right proportions at the right time to guarantee maximum wall-building.

In mission today many tasks must be carried on together; yet the multiplicity of good activities must contribute to, and not crowd out, maximum reconciliation of men and women to God in the church of Jesus Christ. God desires that people be saved, and he therefore commands those of his household to go and "make disciples of all nations." Fulfilling this command is the supreme purpose that should guide the entire mission, establish its priorities, and coordinate all its activities.

Clarifying the Issue

The church today faces deep cleavage among her members at just this point. Some are so deeply impressed by physical needs—and who can deny their urgency?—that meeting these needs becomes for them the highest present purpose of God and the church.

In 1977 my *Conciliar Evangelical Debate: The Crucial Documents 1964-76* presented the writings of fifteen representatives of the conciliar and fifteen of the evangelical wing of the church. Sharply differing opinions as to ends and means mark the volume. In the rough-and-tumble of vigorous disagreement, the writers speak of the basic questions of evangelism and mission. The convictions of major thinkers are weighed in the balance of reason and revelation; when found adequate, they are embraced, but when found wanting, rejected.

In 1979 Harvey Hoekstra, then president of the Reformed Church in America, published his well-researched book *The World Council of Churches and the Demise of Evangelism,* showing how the leaders of the conciliar churches and mission boards, following the theory and theology of "new mission," had all but abandoned evangelism as they sought to minister to physical needs and to rectify the basic injustices of the global social order.

Deeply as I sympathize with the problem and long as I myself have ministered to desperate physical needs (for years I superintended a leprosy home), I cannot ally myself on this point with those who put social action first. On the contrary, my conviction is that the salvation granted to those who believe on Jesus Christ is still the supreme need of human beings, and all other human good flows from that prior reconciliation to God.

Quality and Quantity

Some earnest Christians reject multiplication of churches as today's chief task because they pin their hopes on quality rather than quantity. What use, they ask, to make more Christians unless they are *better* Christians? Throughout much of the world they affirm that education of believers is more important than evangelism. In America they assert that church unity is more important than church extension.

We must inspect closely this attractive plea for quality. As soon as we separate quality from the deepest passion of our Lord—to seek and save the lost—it ceases to be Christian quality. No amount of sophistication can change this very simple fact. To fight for brotherhood is good;

but to proclaim that brotherhood is more important than salvation is misguided. If in the homelands or out there on the mission field we rear Christians who shine with a high polish, speak beautiful English, have an advanced education, but care nothing whatever about their unconverted relatives being reconciled to God, then their vaunted quality as Christians is ashes. Even if we produce Christians who live as equals with those of other races but do not burn with desire that those others may have eternal life, their "quality" is certainly in doubt.

Anyone who seriously pleads for this kind of quality is in danger of advocating works of righteousness and substituting ethical achievement, the fruit of the Spirit, for the gospel. Christians, when true to the Scriptures and to Christ, reject such legalism and insist that ethical achievement *grows out of life in Christ* and must not be made a prerequisite for faith in him.

On a practical plane, church leaders have continually to choose between pressing tasks, all good. They would do well to listen to Ralph D. Winter, who writes,

> I used to be an expert in the gadgets and the gimmicks—the various means and types of ministries common to most missions. Recently it has become steadily clearer to me that the most important activity of all is the implanting of churches. The care, feeding and reproduction of congregations is the central activity to which all the gimmicks and means must be bent (Winter 1966:128).

The Chief Task: Often Left Undone

Christian mission should take serious account of the many churches marked by slight growth. Specialists in carrying water abound, but there are few masons. Tons of mortar arrive, but few stones. The wall does not go up. Slight church growth characterizes many whole denominations, both liberal and conservative. Worse, the lack of growth is taken as natural and unavoidable.

In the state of Sinaloa in the west of Mexico, the Congregational Church, now the United Church of Christ, has been at work for over half a century. During all these years its dedicated missionaries have labored earnestly; yet by 1962 it had only 300 members in 9 small static churches (see McGavran, Huegel, and Taylor 1963:45).

Scores of denominations both large and small in North America have plateaued or declined. For example, three large denominations—the United Presbyterians (now Presbyterian Church [U.S.A.]), the United

Church of Christ, and the United Methodists—lost 10 to 12 percent of their membership between 1965 and 1975, and the decline continued through the 1980s. The Oregon Yearly Meeting of Friends is a typical small denomination. In 1961 the average figure for church membership, Sunday school membership, and Sunday morning attendance in its sixty-one congregations was 5,300. In 1968 the average figure was 5,400 (Willcuts 1979:27).

In Taiwan, the Presbyterian Church has registered great growth, trebling in twelve years from 57,407 in 1952 to 176,255 in 1964 (Taiwan Presbyterians, Synodical Office 1966:76, 80), while the Baptists who came over from the mainland in 1948 with a few hundred numbered 21,783 in 1967 (Coxill and Grubb 1968:181), the Methodists in 1967—despite the fact that Methodist Chiang Kai-shek and Madame Chiang were ardent Christians—numbered only 4,553. The Methodist Church in Taiwan demonstrates that it is quite possible to miss church growth in receptive populations.

In Chile, where Pentecostal denominations in the past forty years have grown from nothing to over 20 percent of the population, one North American mission with thirty missionaries, at work for about thirty years, counts fewer than 300 Chilean Christians in its congregations. It believes that Chile has "an almost Islamic population."

The secretary of a large conservative missionary society said recently, "We have spent $3,000,000 in Japan over the last thirty years; and our churches there now have less than 500 full members."

My interest in church growth was first roused when Waskom Pickett's survey showed that 134 mission stations in mid-India (where I was a missionary) had experienced an average church growth of only 12 percent per decade, or about 1 percent per year (Pickett 1956:ix). The ten stations of my own mission, the India Mission of the Disciples of Christ, were not significantly different from the other 124. They had a staff of over 75 missionaries and a "great work"—but had been notably unsuccessful in planting churches. In the town of Harda where my wife and I with six other missionaries worked from 1924 to 1930, not one baptism from outside the church occurred between 1918 and 1954, a period of thirty-six years.

These cases of little growth have been taken from lands where the church *can* grow, as proved by the fact that some branches are growing. They are significant because in populations where the church *can* grow, some missions and missionaries, churches and pastors, engaged in witness for Christ and "many good works," nevertheless seem content with little or no growth. Faced with a general population in which some segments are accepting Christ, they try to propagate the gospel either among gospel rejectors or by methods that obviously are not blessed of God to the increase of the church.

Finding the Remedy

Illustrations of lack of growth in receptive populations could be multiplied indefinitely. Most missionary societies, both conservative and liberal, if they would chart accurately the growth of the churches they assist, would find many cases of small growth. For example, leaders of the Church of the Foursquare Gospel—a vigorous church of the Pentecostal family—recently had occasion to study the development of ten of its younger churches. They found one greatly growing church of 25,000, three moderately growing churches of around 10,000, and six static churches of less than 2,000 each.

In a few cases, nongrowth or slight growth is irremediable. It can be truly ascribed to the hard, rebellious hearts of those to whom the gospel is proclaimed. Negative contextual factors are insurmountable. Resistance is too high, hostility too great, for unbelievers to obey or even "hear" the gospel. There are counties and cities in almost every nation in which Christians can preach, teach, and heal for decades with practically no one accepting Christ. Such resistant populations exist. Procedures in these cases will be discussed later. Remembering our Lord's command that the gospel must be preached to every creature, we should not bypass these resistant populations.

In most cases, however, the situation is remediable. Arrested growth can be ascribed to faulty procedures. Institutional factors can be adjusted positively. Sometimes, when shepherds return empty-handed, it is because the sheep refuse to be found and flee at their approach. Sometimes, however, empty-handedness becomes a habit and is caused by peering into ravines where there are no sheep, resolutely neglecting those who long to be found in favor of those who refuse to be. Sometimes it is a question of sticking for decades to methods that have proved ineffective. Suffice it to say that lack of church growth is an unnecessary trait, or experience, of many branches of the church and many missionary societies. It can, and should, be remedied.

TODAY'S OPPORTUNITY: RECEPTIVE POPULATIONS

The urgency of church growth is heightened by the fact that the church now faces a most responsive world. Alongside many nongrowing churches are some that are growing moderately, and some with great vigor. Alongside lack of growth in far too many instances goes an amazing amount of real, sometimes spectacular growth. When we realize that much of the standstill is unnecessary and can be replaced by a steady, healthy increase among those who have become new creatures in Christ, the extent of today's opportunity can be better assessed.

North America is believed by some to be a difficult field. Indifference to Christ marks its secular pluralistic populations. Contextual factors are blamed for empty pews. Denominations decline. Church growth is most unlikely. Why strive for it? Thus it appears to the leaders of static churches. Yet in this very land, the General Conference Baptists grew from 40,000 in 1940 to 125,000 in 1978. The Assemblies of God grew from 627,000 in 1970 to 2,037,000 in 1986 a DGR (decadal growth rate) of 108 percent. Independent charismatics show a 1979-1984 DGR of 557 percent. The fact is that ripe harvests abound in North America—but harvesters with scythes are needed. Conviction that the Lord of the harvest has sent them in to work is essential if the fields are to be reaped.

Overseas, comparison with conditions a hundred years ago heightens appreciation of today's responsiveness. Then a chief goal of most missions was to get into closed lands and manage to stay there. Dread diseases killed off many Westerners. Non-Christian rulers and governments with the power of life and death considered missionaries the advance agents of Western imperialism and often prohibited entry as long as they could. When the missionaries finally got in, they encountered incredible difficulties.

Today in countless areas all this has changed. Danger to health has been dramatically reduced. Missionaries come and go, harassed by nothing more than delays and paper work. It is true that some countries present hindrances to mission—China, India, Egypt, Russia—but by contrast with earlier days the world is full of mission opportunities and eager populations, with relatively little risk to life and limb. Six-month journeys on foot are rare. Missionaries arrive by jet to find large and flourishing churches glad to receive them. If they know where to look and want to evangelize the people whom God has prepared, they can generally find hundreds or thousands who, like the common people in the day of our Lord, will hear the gospel gladly and obey it.

Responsiveness, to be sure, must not be overstated. Well over half the world is still indifferent or even hostile to the good news. Millions have set their faces like flint against Christ. Christian missionaries have been thrown out of Russia, China, Cuba, and other Communist lands. A few million souls in Afghanistan and Saudi Arabia are still closed to evangelization. All this and more must be taken into account. Nevertheless, many lands *are* responsive, many populations *are* receptive. Compared to a time when almost everyone was hostile, now only some are.

Outside the Middle East it is a rare land where there is not some receptive segment of the population. Segments of the upper and middle classes in Chile may be as scornful of evangelical Christianity as they were in 1900, but the Chilean masses, as the rise of large Pentecostal denominations testifies, are abundantly able to hear the good news and obey it. Most touchable castes in India have yet to ripen, but since 1947, in two Indian Methodist conferences alone, that church has grown from 100,000 to 200,000 (Seamands 1968:121). When the British left, many denominations in India—including the great United Churches of North India and South India—decided to lie low and not court persecution by active evangelization. These two sections of the Methodist Church, however—enduring persecution joyfully—doubled from among the lower castes. In short, the Methodist Church, rejecting the counsels of the fainthearted that the church cannot grow in independent India, established a multitude of congregations in receptive segments of the population.

In Ethiopia (before the Communist takeover), missions that had evangelized the responsive groups saw great church growth. The Sudan Interior Mission was in 1967 assisting a church of 100,000 baptized believers (Coxill and Grubb 1968:67) despite the fact that most of its missionaries still worked in resistant sections of the country. Had the mission concentrated its efforts on those who were responsive, it would have seen a still greater increase. Despite Marxist persecution the Mekane Yesus Church in Ethiopia has emerged as the fastest-growing Lutheran church in the world with an increase from 140,000 in 1970 to 750,000 in 1986, a DGR of 186 percent.

In the first decades of this century, southern Brazil was flooded by hundreds of thousands of Italian immigrants. Most were cool toward the Church of Rome. They came from the laboring section of the Italian population that later became Communist. The first generation or two spoke Italian. They were highly responsive to the evangelical message. The Methodists, Presbyterians, Lutherans, and Baptists, however, were busy among Portuguese-speaking Brazilians. The leaders of their churches knew nothing but Portuguese and did not even glimpse the Italian opportunity.

An Italian convert from Chicago, however, totally without financial resources, moved from North America to Brazil and preached Christ. The church he founded, which until 1936 conducted its services in Italian, by 1965 had grown to 400,000 baptized believers. Its mother church in São Paulo is a beautiful structure seating 4,000. In general it may be said that responsive segments exist in many lands, but they are not always found by missionaries or national church leaders (Read 1965:20-44).

More winnable people live in the world today than ever before. There are far more winnable men and women in Illinois or British Columbia than there were a hundred years ago. The general population in many states and regions is more favorable to Christ and more open to conversion. India has far more now than in the days of Carey or Clough. Africa has myriads who can be won. Latin America teems with opportunity. For the gospel, never before has such a day of opportunity dawned.

These populations have not become receptive by accident. In their responsiveness to the gospel, those who have eyes to see can discern God at work. His sunshine and rain, his providence and Holy Spirit, have turned population after population responsive. One hears a great deal today about the Lord of history and his action in human affairs.

One thing can delay a vast discipling of the peoples of earth. If, in the day of harvest—the most receptive day God has yet granted his church—his servants fail him, then the ripened grain will not be harvested. If slight church growth persists, then the winnable will not be won. If missions and churches continue content with little growth, God's preparations for the feast may be wasted.

TODAY'S IMPERATIVE

Today's task and opportunity reinforce the biblical imperative. This is the day par excellence to reconcile men and women to God in the church of Jesus Christ. We must not be limited by the small expectations of our forebears, nor measure tomorrow's advances by yesterday's defeats. Modes of mission that suited a hostile population should not be continued when that population turns receptive. Concepts of what God desires our church to do, formed during the frozen decades when our predecessor did well merely to hang on, must not deter us from planning to double the churches when, for at least some segments of the population, the climate moderates.

Verse 5 of the first chapter of the Epistle to the Romans gives direction here. One can call this the great commission as given to Paul. In the light of the last verses of Matthew and the redemptive purposes of God as portrayed in the entire Bible, it also speaks to the whole church. The commission is found in three places in Romans, but I quote it from 16:25-26 as it appears in the New English Bible. "The Gospel I brought you . . . [is] now disclosed, and . . . by eternal God's command made known to all nations, to bring them to faith and obedience." For exact rendering of the Greek words *panta ta ethne,* "all nations" should read "all peoples." The apostle did not have in mind modern nation-states such as India or Mexico. He had in mind cultural groupings—tongues, tribes, castes, and lineages. That is exactly what *ta ethne* means both here and in Matthew 28:19.

In a day when few nations as wholes are turning responsive, but many segments of them are, an exact rendition is vital to understanding. When peoples are turning responsive as social classes, as peasants moving into cities, as minorities, tribes, castes, tongues, occupational groups, and numerous other *ethne,* the biblical mandate to bring the *ethne* to faith and obedience falls on our ears with particular force. Not only is there the command, but God has provided the opportunity.

Christians might be excused for neglecting the divine directive in ages when most peoples were hostile to the gospel; but when many segments of society at home and abroad are ready for change, can hear the gospel, and can be won, what answer shall we give to God if we neglect the work of reconciling them to him? What answer shall we make to our fellow human beings if, while providing them with all the lesser furnishings of the banquet of life, we withhold from them the bread and meat we know is true nourishment?

Thus today's paramount task, opportunity, and imperative is to multiply churches in the increasing numbers of receptive peoples of all six continents.

PART II

DISCERNING THE OUTLINES

4

THE MARVELOUS MOSAIC

A S WE PONDER God's desire that all peoples (note the plural) everywhere hear the gospel, have a real opportunity to set their faith intelligently on Jesus Christ, and become members of his body, the church, a shocking fact confronts us. Of the vast population of the world (five billion in 1988) *over three billion have yet to believe the gospel.* Most of these have yet to hear it in a way that enables them to become Christ's disciples and responsible members of his church. This three billion is now almost four, and by A.D. 2,000 may be approaching *five billion.*

This shocking fact has been concealed by an understandable euphoria that during 1920-1980 accompanied the transfer of authority from the missionary societies to the recently founded churches of the non-Western world.

THE EUPHORIA

During these years the missionary societies were broadcasting the following cheerful message:

> The heroic labors of our missionaries have borne good fruit. God has blessed them to the establishment of strong churches in many lands. Wonderful Christians have been reared. We thank God for their ded-

ication and ability. In their now self-governing nations, these nationals, not our missionaries, should be in control. Good missionaries work themselves out of a job. They prepare their successors and come home. Rejoice in the successful completion of the task. From now on mission means not world evangelization but a moderate amount of fraternal aid to our sister churches and the restructuring of our own society so as to bring in a just, peaceful and righteous world.

National church leaders rejoiced so greatly in their new responsibilities and took so seriously the kind words the missionary societies spoke of them, that they seldom called the attention of the world church or their founders to the colossal *undone* task lying all around them. Some of them, indeed, wanting more power and more money from the West, cried, "Missionary go home" and demanded a moratorium on missions. They never pointed out that in most cases it was impossible for them alone to evangelize and church a tenth (or even a twentieth) of the enormous non-Christian population round about them—the 100 million non-Christians living in Bangladesh, 900 million in the Muslim world, 700 million in India, and 950 million in China. National church leaders seldom beseeched the older churches to "send multitudes of missionaries on beyond us to the unreached peoples of this land."

To be fair, neither did most Western missionary societies and most missionaries. The promotional euphoria of "transferring authority to our sister churches" led most mission thinkers to believe that missions in the future would be the rapid evangelization of the remaining unevangelized by the great younger churches. "We must not flood them with money, or push them around. They—not we—are now in charge of missions in the third world," said many Western leaders.

THE COMFORTABLE DOGMA

The World Council of Churches' Commission on World Mission and Evangelism meeting in Mexico in 1963 declared that from now on mission was each church in its own place proclaiming the gospel and carrying on mission.

This comfortable dogma—which so cheerfully disregarded the fact that in most places the church in the Third World was only a tiny part of the total population and confined to one or two sections of it—gave most Western Christians a comfortable feeling that the main task of world evangelization was now *finished.* "The great new fact of our time" was that the church was in every land of earth. From now on, it would grow naturally as devoted Christians of each nation evangelized their neighbors. They would be so much more effective than foreign missionaries. Such was the wisdom of the times.

THE BOMBSHELL

In 1974, into this relaxed scene Ralph D. Winter threw a bombshell. To understand that bombshell, it will be necessary to see the background. Ralph Winter had been a Presbyterian missionary to Guatemala. In 1965 searching for faculty for the School of World Mission at Fuller, I asked him to write an article for the *Church Growth Bulletin.* His "Gimmick-itis" article was published in the January 1966 issue—and is still well worth reading. In it he stresses that the central task of missions must always be the multiplication of churches.

I immediately saw that Winter belonged on the faculty of a School of World Mission that intended above everything else to look at the *facts* of world mission in the light of Christ's mandate to disciple *panta ta ethne*—all the classes, tribes, castes, ethnic units, and economic groupings of the world—and to devise strategies for churching them as rapidly as possible. I invited him to become a member of our faculty.

At Fuller he became the professor responsible for the accurate portrayal of the facts of church growth for all theses and dissertations. His academic background was civil engineering combined with theology and anthropology. He began to see and measure the church growth situation in hundreds of regions from which career missionaries and leading nationals came to study with us. He soon discerned that the comfortable dogma was a vast illusion.

The promotional voice of missions—which was uncritically accepted by most missionaries and Third World leaders—spoke as if the population of any nation was homogeneous—made up of one kind of people, having one language and one culture, and enjoying instant communication with all other citizens. In Nigeria lived Nigerians, in China Chinese, and in Indonesia Indonesians. Promotional writing also assumed that since all the citizens were one kind of people, the church there was of the same kind and could therefore spread the gospel to everyone. That was the illusion. The reality was something very different.

The reality is that most nations are mosaics. In the United States, for example, as C. Peter Wagner points out in his 1979 landmark book *Our Kind of People,* ninety million Americans arranged in eight major groups (and hundreds of minor groupings) make up the unassimilated part of the American mosaic. When educational and economic distinctions are added to ethnic divisions, it is seen that even in America (where "everybody speaks English and all are Americans") the reality is hundreds of what Wagner calls "ethclasses"—pieces of the mosaic. A church strong in one piece does not spread easily to another. For example, a congregation of native-born whites in Georgia would find it very difficult to evangelize a tight-knit Cuban or Gypsy community recently arrived in Atlanta.

To cite other examples, in Mexico eighty Indian languages have survived four hundred years of Spanish domination and are spoken by eighty communities of considerable size. In India, the population is divided into more than 3,000 castes and tribes, each of which is endogamous and ostracizes any of its members who marries outside it. India has thirteen major languages and hundreds of dialects. The Lutheran Church in Andhra State has arisen very largely from depressed classes converts. Ninety-eight percent of all Lutherans there are of Mala or Madiga origin. It is ludicrous to suppose that *that* church—despite the great degree of liberation granted it by the Christian faith—can successfully evangelize the middle and upper castes. One could hardly imagine that renewal in England will come as Jamaican Christians in east London persuade the secular and Anglican populations of wealthy west London to become members of Jamaican congregations!

As I said in 1974 at the International Congress on World Evangelization:

> The Christian faith flows well within each piece of the mosaic, but tends to stop at linguistic and ethnic barriers. Most congregations are shut up to one language, one ethnic unit and frequently to one social or economic class (Douglas 1975:100).

As Chapter 13 of this book insists, "People like to become Christians without crossing racial, linguistic, or class barriers."

In short, enormous numbers of men and women belong to pieces of the mosaic from which very few have become Christians. They will not be evangelized by their neighbors. They will not be evangelized by any except cross-cultural missionaries, whether those missionaries be sent out by Western or Third World churches. American Christian John Doe, who speaks English, earns $40,000 a year, lives in a middle-class home, and attends a typical congregation of about three hundred members, will not win to Christ and bring into that congregation many Lebanese, Portuguese, Polish, French Canadian, Chinese, or Indian immigrants to the United States. Even if they were to believe on Jesus Christ and be welcomed in that congregation, converts from these and other ethnic units would rarely feel at home. Those who come for one service ordinarily do not return next Sunday. If they join the church, they more often than not drop out after a few months.

The bombshell to which I refer was the address given by Ralph D. Winter to the plenary session of the International Congress on World Evangelization held in Lausanne, Switzerland, in 1974. The title of his paper was carefully chosen: "The Highest Priority: Cross-Cultural Evangelism." Recall that the wisdom of the day was suggesting that because there was a national church located in virtually every country of the world, the age of foreign missions could be considered a thing of the past. Winter almost single-handedly put a stop to such missiological nonsense. Through a careful analysis of the world population of 1974 he showed that of the world's approximately 2.7 billion non-Christians, a full 87 percent (or 2.4 billion) would not be evangelized other than through cross-cultural missionaries. The agents for cross-cultural evangelism would not necessarily have to be from the traditional Western sending churches, of course. South Indians could send missionaries to tribes in North India. Kenyans could send missionaries across tribal boundaries within their own country. Brazilian churches could undertake the evangelization of Portugal. But having said this, the urgent missiological priority of someone moving from their culture to another, learning a new language, eating strange food, and loving those who formerly appeared unlovable was convincingly established by Ralph Winter in that prestigious international forum.

RALPH WINTER'S FINDINGS

With characteristic clarity of thinking, Winter devised both a new terminology and an enlightening diagrammatic representation of the true world situation.

First, the terminology. The evangelistic typology that distinguishes between E-0, E-1, E-2, and E-3 evangelism has since become widely accepted missiological and church growth vocabulary. Pointing these out was his way of taking the mosaic seriously, and became one of Winter's brilliant contributions to missiology. E-0 evangelism aims to bring existing church members to a personal commitment to Christ. E-1 is near-neighbor evangelism of non-Christians whose language and customs are those of the Christian who is witnessing. E-2 is evangelism across a small ethnic, cultural, or linguistic gap. E-3 is evangelism across a large linguistic, cultural, or ethnic chasm. Note the important fact that the distinguishing feature on the spectrum from E-1 to E-3 evangelism is culture, not geography. An E-2/E-3 challenge can exist even in the same immediate neighborhood, as I pointed out above.

Secondly, the diagram. The figure below is a somewhat simplified version of the diagram Winter presented in Lausanne (for the original diagram see Douglas 1975:229). Keep in mind that the numbers are 1974 figures. A current diagram would differ in some details. The world population, for example, is much larger. The percentage of non-Christians who need cross-cultural evangelism would be reduced from 87 percent in 1974 to about 72 percent in 1990 due to the unprecedented growth of the Christian movement in China beginning around 1976. But my purpose in including the diagram here is to show the process through which missiological thinking changed, particularly among evangelicals, to see the true picture of the world's marvelous mosaic.

As you can see, about 30 percent of the world's population was Christian in 1974. This means that if a world religious census were taken, about 30 percent would check the box that said "Christian." But most of them are nominal; Christian in name only. An estimated 200 million could be considered committed, obedient Christians. They constitute God's force for evangelism. Their primary ministry to the block of nominal Christians is E-0 evangelism or Christian renewal, depending on the situation.

The 70 percent of the world population that does not profess to be Christian in any sense (numbering 2.7 billion in 1974) can helpfully be divided into two segments. The upper rectangle contains 336 million non-Christians of the same ethnic, linguistic, and cultural groupings as the committed Christians. They can be reached by E-1 evangelism. The lower rectangle contains 2.4 billion souls of quite different languages, cultures, and ethnic make-ups. These myriads can be reached only by E-2 and E-3 evangelism—across barriers of language, economic and educational achievement, and culture. Such evangelism can be carried out only by missionaries, of course. Cross-cultural evangelists (missionaries) should be prepared and sent out by all sections of the church in all nations. The numbers assigned to each block in the diagram are careful estimates. Readers should not waste time debating whether they are exactly right or not. Whatever the precise figures, something like this exists.

In subsequent writings, Ralph Winter shows the degree to which traditional mission agencies have been neglecting the 2.4 billion, which have come to be known as unreached peoples (see Winter 1977a and 1977b). He points out that, while the most urgent task for world evangelization was the 2.4 billion who required the E-2/E-3 evangelism, the evangelistic efforts of existing committed Christians were almost entirely focused on E-1 ministry among nominal Christians. He found, for example, that in India some 98 percent of current evangelistic efforts, whether carried out by nationals or missionaries, were attempts by committed Christians to reach out to nominal Christians and bring them back into the fold (Winter 1977a:125). It goes without saying that this is a poor way to strategize intelligently the completion of God's great commission.

THE WORLD

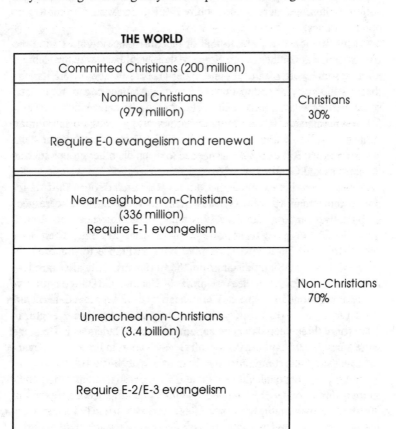

Committed Christians (200 million)

Nominal Christians
(979 million)

Require E-0 evangelism and renewal

Christians
30%

Near-neighbor non-Christians
(336 million)
Require E-1 evangelism

Unreached non-Christians
(3.4 billion)

Require E-2/E-3 evangelism

Non-Christians
70%

E-1 OR E-2?

In the marvelous mosaic, the "cultural distance" between the multi-tudinous pieces varies considerably. In the neighborhood where I live are found some of my relatives, some colleagues, both black and white, some university professors, teachers in the public schools, business leaders who are Christians, Jews, and secular materialists, some Hispanic-Americans, some wealthy black Americans, some Armenians, and others. They all speak excellent English and live within a mile of my house; but the cultural distance between me and each of these groups varies greatly. So does the kind of evangelism that will reach each. I could evangelize some of these by E-1 and expect them to join my church, Lake Avenue Congregational Church. Others would require E-2/E-3 and would prefer to join other churches.

My situation is parallel to that of the Christians in Palestine in the first fifteen years of the church. Some of their neighbors were the Hebrew masses, some were Sadducees and upper-class Jews, some were Italians there as the army of occupation, some were Arabian pagan merchants, some were Greeks, some Cretans. The church was enormously successful in winning the Hebrew masses, but not very successful in winning scribes, Pharisees, and Roman soldiers. E-1 evangelism reached the Jewish masses. But E-2/E-3 was needed to reach the other groups such as Samaritans and Gentiles.

To take another example, the May 1974 *Church Growth Bulletin* reported more than 100,000 Gypsies living in France. These were geographically near to millions of Christians, both Protestant and Roman Catholic. The Gypsies all spoke French—but not at home. There they spoke Romany. The Gypsies, despite living in France for hundreds of years, were culturally far distant from the Christians. Only after missionary Clement le Cossec of the Assemblies of God in 1958 started multiplying congregations of Gypsies, which heard the Bible, prayed, and worshiped in Romany, did the Gypsy people movement gather strength. In 1961 (only three years later) he appointed Gypsy leaders as pastors and colleagues. In 1974 about a third of all Gypsy leaders in France were evangelicals. The total community numbered thirty to forty thousand. From France the Gypsy people movement to Christ spread to many other lands. In the summer of 1979 I attended a service of a Gypsy congregation of 300 that met for worship about ten miles from my home in Pasadena. Until missionaries bridged the chasm, Gypsies never thought of becoming Christians in the churches that they passed every day as they earned their living in France, the United States, and many other lands. Clearly these Gypsies would not have been reached by E-1 evangelism. Someone had to cross the cultural barrier through E-2 evangelism.

Similarly, churches made up of Spanish-speaking Mestizos in Peru or Ecuador are not effective in winning Quechua-speaking Indians. Missions in Bangladesh creating congregations from scheduled caste Namashudras do not consider the sixty million Muslims in that fertile land their business at all. In a very real sense, such missions do not see the Muslims. In Kenya, hundreds of Kamba congregations seem to have little concern for the 300,000 Turkana two hundred miles to the north. They are not Kamba: they are not us. It is easy to overlook them.

THE HIDDEN PEOPLES OF THE MOSAIC

Seeing the myriad peoples of the world as a vast mosaic, most pieces of which are hidden from the sight of both missionary societies and churches, has vastly expanded our understanding of the task of missions. The new vision has been emphasized in various ways. Ralph Winter and his U.S. Center for World Mission focus Christian attention on the *hidden peoples*. Others such as C. Peter Wagner and Edward R. Dayton refer to them as *unreached peoples*. All are speaking of very large numbers of homogeneous units— ethnically, geographically, culturally, and economically separate segments of mankind. Depending on how such segments are defined, there are thousands or tens of thousands of them—the hidden peoples.

The important and very numerous hidden or unreached peoples of the world can be grouped in two sections. First, they are the hundreds of millions in the Chinese and Islamic worlds, to which Marxist and Muslim governments deny Christian missionaries access. Second, they are the peoples who live in great cities and in extensive countrysides geographically intertwined with Christians of other linguistic, ethnic, and cultural backgrounds. For instance, scores of Brahmin castes in India are well aware of Christians. They know of church buildings and sometimes walk past them every day. But between Brahmins and Christians is an enormous social and racial gulf. Consequently to Christians, the fifty or more Brahmin castes and subcastes are truly unreached or hidden peoples. There are thousands of Chinese in Peru. Protestant denominations and missions in Peru are made up almost exclusively of Spanish-speaking Mestizos and Aymara or Quechua-speaking Indians. Consequently, to most Protestants in Peru the thousands of Chinese are a hidden people.

WHEN ARE THEY REACHED?

Wagner and Dayton pioneered a series of *Unreached Peoples Annuals* that identified and described over 5,000 unreached people groups from 1979 to 1986. Hopefully, as the years pass, some peoples will be taken off the list. They will have been reached. But now a nice question arises. What does it mean to reach a segment of humanity, a piece of the mosaic? When the first missionary gets there, has that segment been reached? Or shall we count it as reached only after a substantial minority in that segment has become Christian and has been incorporated in viable congregations?

In my judgment, a people has been reached only when many of its members have become disciples of Christ and responsible members of his body. Until the church is well rooted in that society, it has not been reached. With that definition, it is clearly seen that the remaining task is immense. Christ commanded his followers to disciple all the ethnic units of the earth. After nearly two hundred years of modern missions only a few out of the myriad peoples of the world have been incorporated in the church, that is, been discipled.

In September 1979, Lal Rema, field secretary of the General Conference Baptists in India, was telling me that of the 600,000 Boro Kacharis in Assam, about 20,000 have become Christian. We rejoice in that beginning people movement, while noting that one can scarcely say that the Boro Kacharis have been reached. Though more than 300 congregations are scattered through them and three mission-assisted Indian churches carry on work among them, nearly 97 percent of them have yet to believe. They are still unreached.

With the Mizos and Nagas the case is otherwise. Both of these people groups are now more than seventy-five percent Christian. They are no longer unreached. It would waste valuable time to haggle over the exact proportion of the total population of a given people that must be incorporated into ongoing congregations before it may properly be called reached or discipled. Furthermore, any such discussion would miss the main point. Whatever measure is used, it is clear that thousands and thousands of whole peoples, whole segments of society, whole classes and neighborhoods have yet to be evangelized effectively, that is, have yet to be reached.

SUMMARY

If God's plan for the salvation of the world is to be carried out, a mighty multiplication of living congregations must occur in most pieces of the mosaic in most countries. Through it multitudes of men and women will find peace, joy, and power in the forgiveness of their sins and assurance of salvation. And because of the large numbers of citizens who will then be living and voting, serving and ruling as dedicated followers of the Lord Jesus, tremendous increase in individual and corporate righteousness will become possible. Churches are the most potent instruments of social advance known. They must be multiplied in every piece of the marvelous mosaic. That is the challenge of church growth.

5

A UNIVERSAL FOG

MORE THAN 350,000 congregations dot the counties and cities of the United States. Each of them was planted and grew to its present size. Literally millions of men and women have become members of these churches. A tremendous amount of church growth has been going on. Yet until quite recently not much was known or written about it. How churches grow and how they die remained largely a mystery. Did great evangelistic campaigns really increase the church? Did all Sunday schools make churches grow or only some? Could churches survive in the inner city? How much has this congregation grown in the past decade, and what parts of it are growing most? These questions seldom received satisfactory answers. Fog enveloped the church.

Sixty-seven thousand North American Protestant missionaries were reported in 1985, the largest number ever active in the world. Churches numbering many millions of members dot Asia, Africa, and Latin America. Many segments of society in those lands have become responsive. Hundreds of missionary societies write into their constitutions that carrying out the Great Commission is their foremost aim. Why, then, is so very little known about church growth?

Why is it so seldom even seen? Why has it not been understood long ago? We have discovered so much about how plants and animals and human beings grow—why do we know so little about how churches grow? When we devote enormous sums to teaching agriculture and to research in that field, why do we spend so little in learning about or teaching church culture—the planting and care of self-propagating churches?

Many partial answers are given to these questions. Lack of holy living militates against the spread of faith. Worldliness in all its forms is a potent enemy of the infectious Christian life. Yet these answers apply more to Christians indifferent to evangelism than to missionaries and ministers actively engaged in it, and my questions concern the latter. Why is so little known and done about church growth in Asia, Africa, and Latin America? And in Europe and America as well?

WHO SEES THE GROWTH?

An initial obstacle that, like the cork in a bottle, must be removed first, is that church growth is seldom seen. Every church and mission has its committees for education, medicine, finance, and the like; but one seldom finds one whose principal purpose is the planting of churches. Possibly leaders intend all these other activities to bring men and women to Christ and propagate the gospel. But if this is so, one wonders why they do not check up on their intention now and then to see if it is being achieved. The evidence inclines one to believe that, instead, these activities become ends in themselves and shut out awareness of propagating Christianity. Few leaders of church or mission are acutely conscious of church growth.

Missionary training schools have many good and necessary courses on the Bible, cultural anthropology, non-Christian religions, tropical medicine, languages, and so on; little is taught of the many ways in which the church has arisen in the lands to which missionaries go. Missionary candidates are not drilled as to the factors in those particular circumstances that have stimulated or suppressed church growth. Conferences of every sort are commonly held; but until very recently few have dealt with the multiplication of churches.

Should anyone object that evangelism itself is essentially concerned with church growth and has formed a substantial part of most Christian activity, it must be answered that much evangelism neither results in church growth nor is expected to. When evangelism is presented, it may be assumed that proclamation or seed-sowing evangelism will usually be meant. Searching or embarrassing questions as to how churches arise and how much they have increased will be avoided. In the mainline literature on the theology of evangelism the increase of Christians and churches is seldom mentioned. One can read literally volumes without suspecting that it is pleasing to God to have churches multiply. If theologians assume that evangelism will result in church growth, they are proceeding on a very shaky assumption. In all these manifestations of outreach, church growth remains hidden. It is seldom seen, or even focused upon.

A VARIETY OF CAUSES

A strange combination of factors keeps us from perceiving church growth and keeps church leaders from measuring what has occurred and planning for more. These factors render the phenomenon as invisible as if blotted out by a physical fog. Pastors and missionaries, surrounded by this opaqueness, carry on programs, preach sermons, do assigned work, raise budgets, administer departments, baptize converts, teach schoolchildren, and recruit new workers. But only occasionally—when the cloud lifts— do they glimpse briefly the state of church growth. It is taken for granted that everyone knows about it and assumes its importance.

That churches and missions should tolerate this obscurity is the more remarkable in view of the fact that to see, study, and understand church growth is crucially important to all pastors, missionaries, executives of mission boards, and leaders of churches. Until the ways of growth form part of the common knowledge of all those who are engaged in the work of the church, the reconciling of people to God-in-Christ will limp when it should run. The time has now come to eliminate the sources of the fog and focus attention directly on the problem.

Until 1970 amazingly few books had been written on church growth. Poring over the card catalog in any seminary library one would find little on growth of the church—which is at least a major and irreplaceable pur- pose of every denomination and every Christian mission. Books on the churches of the various countries—their structure, membership, rates of growth, prospects, geographical locations, aids to growth, obstacles to growth, and causes of growth—would even in 1990 be very few.

The Southern Baptists in the United States grew from about two mil- lion in 1900 to about thirteen million in 1980. Yet I know of no book care- fully analyzing this healthy increase and telling us exactly what theolog- ical convictions fueled it, what organizational structures nurtured it, in which states the denomination prospered and in which it languished, and what were the methods that God most signally blessed.

In *Cross and Crisis in Japan* (Iglehart 1957), Chapter I is entitled "Some Japanese Churches." One might hope for light on at least the United Church of Christ in that land, but in vain. The chapter was written after World War II to say to American supporters that Japanese churches are just like theirs. One may applaud the friendliness that prompted these pages while observing that, where less than one person in a hundred is a Christian and the typical congregation has less than forty worshipers on Sunday morning, saying "they are just like yours" does not help anyone to understand the churches of Japan.

As we contemplate the consistency with which church and mission writings omit any reliable and meaningful picture of church growth, we must not imagine there has been a conspiracy of silence. Simple fog is not only a kindlier but a more correct explanation. Omission of this vital information is both curious and disastrous, but it is strictly unintentional.

Since 1965 the Church Growth Movement has stimulated books that describe accurately the growth of some congregations and denominations in America and abroad. But in thousands of regions in the Third World and in over 300,000 congregations in America, visibility is still very poor. All one can say is, the fog has begun to lift.

An informational fog over an entire subject can only be dispelled by dealing with it at its sources. It becomes important therefore to recognize the factors that produce it. Each by itself hinders the discipling of the nations. Together they could be fatal to mission. This overwhelming obscurity in a crucial area demands the immediate attention of the churches and their missionary enterprise.

Statistical Causes

Exact understanding of the increase of the church is prevented partly by haphazard or inaccurate membership accounting. Approximations blur the picture, omissions distort it, and changed definitions mislead the unwary. As an example of the last, observe that when a certain denomination defined members as "those who contribute to the church," the membership stood at 4,800. When it ruled that "all baptized believers in good standing" are to be counted members, without adding a single soul membership jumped to 6,000.

Accurate accounting, easy within one denomination, becomes very difficult when extended across the whole spectrum of Protestant churches. To Baptists, members mean "baptized believers in good standing"; to Episcopalians, they mean "all the baptized, infants and adults." Community is defined so variously by different branches of the church that figures of community are meaningless. Some report that their community is exactly the same in number as their communicants; others that it is ten times as large.

In America, the reputable *Yearbook of American and Canadian Churches* solemnly publishes church memberships, some of which are baptized believers only and some the total community including baptized infants. Thus the Episcopal Church with three million members appears larger than the Churches of Christ with just under three million baptized believers, but is actually considerably smaller.

Overseas, many denominations are made up of hundreds of scattered rural congregations worshiping in thatch and wattle churches. Termites eat the church records. The membership register (a cheap notebook) is used on urgent occasions as a source of writing paper, and the sheets torn out sometimes have entries on them. Village pastors have little education and have no idea of the importance of accuracy. They continue the names of members who move to the city, expecting them to send money to their home church while they are away and to come back soon.

City pastors and missionaries who send in reports to headquarters seldom visit the villages and almost never the homes of individual Christians, so the initial inaccuracy is built into the final total. Day school figures will be exact, for a government inspector visits the schools and checks reports; but no one checks the rolls of the congregations.

All this creates a serious fog when it comes to real numbers. Church administrators pay little attention to church statistics, partly because they question their accuracy.

Administrational Sources of Fog

Mission and denominational administration, at local, national, and board levels, frequently proceeds as if church growth did not matter. Budgets are distributed equally to all whether churches multiply or not. An increase of $10,000 sent out by the board is prorated to all stations. When on occasion a reduced amount is sent out, the cut is distributed proportionately to all. By its adherence to this egalitarian procedure, administration unintentionally but effectively proclaims that what matters is faithful work; the outcome in the spread of the gospel is immaterial.

It is easy to describe this universal phenomenon in church and mission administration but difficult to avoid it. To see the need for priorities is one thing; to put them into effect quite another.

The gospel must be preached to every creature. "Can we leave these hundred thousand Hindus, to whom three generations of missionaries have given their lives, without any witness to Christ, simply because they will not hear?" exclaimed one missionary. To determine a true course, as between "preaching to every creature" and "bringing the nations to faith and obedience," is not easy.

Even administrators who conclude that in fidelity to the Lord gospel acceptors have a higher priority than gospel rejectors, and that the church, mission, or mission board is going to plant churches that march under the Great Commission, face difficult decisions. They must allow time for germination and growth before they expect harvest. It is hard to judge when seed is germinating and when it has rotted, and even harder to withdraw support from a weak, static congregation, for it is "our church" and all we have in that district, county, or suburb.

But acknowledging all these difficulties, mission administrators must not—dare not—act as if church growth did not matter. This is to betray the gospel. Mere continuation of an uncritical egalitarianism is not the answer. Yet it characterizes much Christian work. Itself a result of the fog that hides church growth, it generates much obscurity of its own and leads many missions and denominations to do what they earnestly do not want to do.

Cultural Overhang Causes Fog

A veil that hides church growth effectively is the ethnocentricity of missionaries, or, more simply, their cultural overhang. Individuals naturally tend to see everything in their own cultural frame of reference.

Mission leaders know something of how churches grew in their own homelands. That knowledge, they think, is sufficient. "Christians preach the gospel, bear witness to Christ, pray for God's blessing, and work hard. God gives the increase. Our denomination in this state has grown from 79 to 134 congregations in twenty-five years. That is the way the church grows."

In any increase of the church, the activities mentioned and God's sovereign pleasure are of immense importance. Yet if any one thing is certain, it is that churches in the varying cultures of the world do *not* grow in the same way as in the wealthy, educated, individualistic Protestant populations of the U.S.A. The gospel is surely one, and the church is one; but the visible churches that God creates in every corner of the world differ enormously one from the other. Some speak Mandarin and others Tagalog. Some exist as tiny minorities oppressed by the powerful, others as the power structure itself. Some are literate, healthy, and fat; others illiterate, sick, and hungry. Some are led by highly educated professional ministers; others untrained, unpaid laypersons. The processes of growth that cause these differences are themselves extremely different.

Strong denominationalism (which, to the surprise of some, God has blessed to great and good growth of churches) also frequently keeps Western missionaries from understanding the length and breadth of church growth in the Third World. They think of the younger churches as Episcopal, Free Methodist, Disciples, or Friends. They forget that churches which have arisen through any given mode of growth are much more like each other than like their founding denominations at home. A Lutheran church in India, which arises by gathering in famine orphans and occasional converts, will resemble a Baptist church there that arose in the same way much more than it will the Lutheran church of Germany or Minnesota.

The Semantic Cause

Vague words of many meanings are common in this field and contribute to the fog. The word church is an example. We read that a mission is "working with a hundred churches" in such and such a country. Does this mean a hundred churches that have an average membership of 200, permanent buildings, and trained ministers paid entirely by the churches? Or are we to understand a hundred worshiping groups of 10 to 30 illiterate members each, meeting in homes and village courtyards?

A mission reports that it is giving *evangelism* a place of first importance. This may mean it is putting most of its energies into distributing tracts to an indifferent population, touring a thousand villages annually, preaching the gospel but expecting no converts, or planting a dozen new churches a year. The vague word assures us that good work is going on, but tells little about what it is. Obscure approximations rather than exact understanding are precisely one trait of the fog.

In recent years the foggy word *work* has become popular. This least common denominator includes all kinds of activities. Preaching, teaching, healing, theological training, broadcasting, building, and chicken raising—all are work. Ardent church planters like the Southern Baptists, addicted to the idiom, even when they begin a church in some town in Mexico are likely to say, "We have opened a work there." Wherever used, the word hides what is being done. It says in effect: "Mission is many good works; you can never tell quite what." Where this notion of mission prevails, there church growth—if it occurs—is hidden by fog.

Witness also adds to the obscurity: "We extended our witness this year to seven new barrios," writes a missionary. Does he mean, "We have planted seven new churches"? Or "As we toured this year, we reached seven barrios that we never expect to see again and preached the gospel at the crossroads"? Usually his supporters have not the faintest notion. When a United Church missionary wrote, "We established a witness in that province," it meant a witness to the desirability of church union, not a witness to Christ—but readers did not know it.

Similarly the words *friendly interest, response, outreach, encounter,* and the like are so vague and cover so many activities that they tell little about the increase of congregations. The more such terms are used, the less possible it is to see exact outcomes in terms of the physical increase of sound churches. Fog swirls along in the wake of these words. The semantic cause is a considerable one in America and other lands.

Psychological Causes

Fog also arises from psychological sources. Of these, rationalization is the chief. Church leaders getting little church growth defensively declare they are not interested in it and do not want it. We are not afflicted by "numberitis," they retort. We would not be so carnal or hungry for quick and easy results as to seek or count conversions! We are aiming at something much higher and nobler—like building Christian character. Manufacture of high-sounding phrases that do not involve church growth is a specialty in some quarters. One of the best came out of China some years ago. "We are engaged," it ran, "in building Christ into the foundations of China." Under that broad and impressive umbrella a missionary doing almost anything could raise ample funds.

Western expectations of church growth comprise another psychological source of fog. In well-churched lands it is normal for a congregation of 400, let us say, to remain year after year at about that figure. Over a decade, should it increase to 500, that would be thought exceptional. The growth of the congregation is, alas, not often thought to be its main business. Increases in Christian devotion, social action, missionary sendings, and participation in denominational activities are considered more important. Unfortunately, these meager expectations of growth and these patterns of relative values are often carried abroad and applied unthinkingly in lands where not one in a hundred is a Christian and the chief business of congregations is precisely to grow. Such standards lead us to judge slight growth excellent where great growth could be obtained, and thus again shroud churching the unchurched in fog.

In North America and around the world the excuse "I am interested in quality not quantity" must be listed chiefly as a defense mechanism, used by those not getting growth. In *Crucial Issues in Missions Tomorrow,* Ralph D. Winter has an effective chapter dealing with this common excuse. He writes:

> Every task has dimensions of both quality and quantity. . . . All quantitative measures are measurements of certain qualities. . . . Highly important qualities have measurable dimensions. The proper way to look at quantitative measurements is to regard them—properly handled—as reliable indications of qualities (McGavran, ed. 1972:178).

Anyone troubled by this psychological cause of the fog should read Winter's whole essay. It legitimizes the use of statistics and graphs in a striking way.

Promotional Causes

No more potent producer of confusion abroad exists than the promotional activities needed to carry on the missionary enterprise. The 1.4 billion dollars spent annually by foreign missionary societies in North America do not come rolling in of themselves. They must be raised. The worldwide North American Protestant missionary force of 67,000 must be constantly renewed from young people who hear about missions chiefly in the promotional speeches of missionaries on furlough. Promotion is absolutely essential to missions. It is an important part of what, in one way or another, most missionaries and all mission executives do.

Yet promotional writings and addresses, whose steady aims are to give satisfaction to donors past, present, and future and to present missions in a favorable light, cannot give the accurate picture of outcomes—in terms of churches planted and people reconciled to God in the church of Jesus Christ—that mission must have. It is in the very nature of promotional speaking and writing to present an optimistic picture, packed with human interest. It inevitably creates a deluding cloudiness that prevents the multiplication of churches from being seen accurately, or even sometimes from being seen at all.

Even when conversions and church growth are reported, a striking conversion or successful church planting made into a vivid illustration and used again and again gives the impression that it is typical—even when the speaker assures the audience that it is exceptional. For example, John Clough's 2,222 baptisms on a single day at Ongole formed a regular part of his speeches and have since been used by thousands of others. Thus the true situation is obscured by the single telling instance.

Hopes and purposes are sometimes stated as if they had been realized. "Thus," reads a communication from Japan, "through Christian bookshops and literature distribution, Japan is being led to the feet of Christ." This is hope, not accomplishment. The hope blots out the reality.

Missionaries and denominational executives are both promoters and diagnosticians. They occupy two chairs. Sitting in one, they are raising support for a glorious work commanded by the Lord, in which lies the surest hope for the ultimate welfare of humanity. Since they are given thirty minutes in which to present their message to supporters, they must tell the story in dramatic pictures. They must fire imaginations with what they confidently expect to come about. Sitting in the other chair, however, they are stewards rendering an exact account and should present precise figures concerning what now exists by way of church and distinguish carefully between aims, hopes, and outcomes. They must describe what now prevents normal increase and what remedial actions should be taken, and set forth a defensible projection of what growth may be expected during the years to come.

Were missionaries or denominational executives to spend adequate time in each chair and never be in doubt which one they occupy when they speak, much of today's fog would evaporate.

Theological Causes

Today's tremendous theological shifts cause uncertainty about the aim of missions, with consequent vagueness as to outcomes and goals. The reinterpretation of mission that is going on and the attempted capture of the wealthy missionary establishment by certain schools of thought deserves a volume of its own. Here only two brief illustrations can be given of the more common new departures.

Many Protestant leaders appear to be saying that the church is purely instrumental: that is, it has no value in itself, but is only a means to bring in a better world. According to this viewpoint, God loves the world (John 3:16), not the church. He is not primarily concerned with the spread of the church. He spreads his kingdom of justice, peace, and righteousness among all people, whether they call themselves Christians or not. To the extent that churches aflame with social passion are established, and bring about changes in the direction of a more humane society, their existence is in line with God's purposes; but it is selfish to establish churches of those who merely believe in Jesus Christ and accept the Bible as their rule of faith and practice.

Where any such theology and philosophy prevails, interest in church growth declines. The main task is something else. Publications and pronouncements dominated by this viewpoint add to the obscurity.

A second theological shift concerns the complex question of what attitudes Christians should take toward non-Christian religions. Some, heavily influenced by a pluralistic society and freeing themselves from the authority of the Bible, opt for the view that God has revealed much in other religions and consequently the best attitude Christians can take toward them is to learn from them. Joint search for truth through dialogue with adherents of other faiths is, they proclaim, the contemporary mode of "mission." That the Bible as a whole is opposed to this view does not seem to trouble these leaders. This school of thought considers church planting outmoded. Its words and actions, describing mission in entirely other terms, naturally settle on the mission scene as a dense, damp miasma.

RESULTS OF THE FOG

Churches and missions that operate regularly in this complex obscurity as to church growth, and take no steps to dissipate it, find it forcing them to the decision that winning souls to Christ is less important than proclaiming the gospel. This subtle but far-reaching distinction constitutes in reality another theological decision. The question should be decided on biblical grounds; but once fog has taken over and church growth has been obliterated, what remains is proclaiming the gospel whether unbelievers hear or not, whether they accept it or not.

A second result is that parallelism is seen as the right policy in mission. This is the doctrine, conscious or unconscious, that all the many activities carried on by missions are of equal value. They are parallel thrusts. No one of them has basic priority. Recently parallelism is being camouflaged under the new attractive term "holism." "It would be narrow and partisan," say some influential leaders, "to hold that evangelism had the highest priority. Rather Christians should hold that all works of the church are of equal value. This is holism." I disagree. Certainly many things should be done. The task *is* extremely complex; but this complexity must never be made to mean an aimless parallelism. World evangelization is a chief and irreplaceable work of the church.

The fog keeps the sending churches in the dark. They are "supporting missions" but are kept from having any idea as to the growth of the church. One missionary society uses great church growth in a few of its stations to make all the rest look promotionally desirable. It fears to tell its supporters where growth is not going on lest they withdraw support from the less productive stations. Could it be that many societies fear to give the facts of church growth to the supporting churches, lest money gravitate to where churches are multiplying?

Fog also prevents intelligent action toward discipling the nations. If churches and missions deny themselves exact, current, and meaningful accounts of the degree of church multiplication that has—and has not—taken place, how can they take remedial action? The owners of a chain of supermarkets or any other business would think it folly not to know promptly which units are making and which are losing money. How otherwise can they rectify conditions?

In the Chingrai province of the Church of Christ in Thailand, congregations had been multiplying. Communicants had doubled in the previous decade, and I was searching for reasons for the growth. A missionary administrator believed that the great growth (at that time the most notable in Thailand) was due to the establishment in the province of an agricultural center, to which $50,000 worth of tractors had been given and which was asking for a further $50,000 to shift from wheeled tractors to caterpillars. The Thai moderator of the church in that province, however, giving many illustrations assured me that the basic reason for the growth of the churches was that Christians in those rural congregations were experiencing the supernatural power of the Holy Spirit over demons, breaking their ancestral bondage to the evil spirits. This one factor, he declared, brought person after person and family after family out of animistic Buddhism to Christian faith.

I do not know whether the local moderator or the missionary was right; but might it not have paid the mission to find out? It would have allowed the mission to direct efforts along the most productive channels. It might also, possibly, have saved it $50,000.

SUMMARY

Those who believe that the chief and irreplaceable purpose of Christian mission is to proclaim Christ and to persuade men and women to become his disciples and responsible members of his church should systematically dissipate the fog that envelops the growth of the church. It might cost two percent of their annual budget to accomplish this task. It is easily possible for any branch of the church, month by month, to see clearly the degree of church growth that has been achieved and to feed this knowledge back into the administration of the enterprise. It is entirely practical to understand very much more about the complex processes that God blesses to the increase of his churches; but to do so, Christians must recognize the fog that swirls around their heads and take steps to dispel it.

6

THE FACTS NEEDED

THE NUMERICAL APPROACH is essential to understanding church growth. The church is made up of countable people and there is nothing particularly spiritual in not counting them.

The numerical approach is used in all worthwhile human endeavor. Industry, commerce, finance, research, government, invention, and a thousand other lines of enterprise derive great profit and much of their stability in development from continual measurement. Without it they would feel helpless and blindfolded. The vast programs of education, to which advances in every country owe so much, employ numerical procedures at every turn. The counting of pupils by sex and grade, place of residence and intellectual ability, and degree of learning and rates of progress is never questioned. Without it, effective administration and accurate forecasts would be impossible.

It is common to scorn church statistics—but this is part of the fog. Advocates of this, casting about for biblical support, sometimes find that God was displeased with King David for taking a census of the people (2 Sam. 24:1-10), conveniently overlooking many chapters of Numbers in which God himself commands a meticulous numbering of all Israel and every part of every tribe. "Take ye the sum of all the congregation of the children of Israel, after their families, by the house of their fathers, with the number of their names, every male by their polls; from twenty years

old and upward, all that are able to go forth to war in Israel: thou and
Aaron shall number them by their armies" (Num. 1:2-3). Also frequently
overlooked is Luke's great emphasis on numbers in the book of Acts and
his careful record of the numerical increase of the church. As Alan R. Tippett points out, the motive for numbering has much to do with God's approval or disapproval (1965:28). On biblical grounds one has to affirm
that devout use of the numerical approach is in accord with God's wishes.
On practical grounds, it is as necessary in congregations and denominations as honest financial dealing.

To be sure, no one was ever saved by statistics; but then, no patient
was ever cured by the thermometer to which the physician pays such close
attention. X-ray pictures never knit a single broken bone, yet they are of
considerable value to physicians in telling them how to put the two ends
of a fractured bone together. Similarly, the facts of growth will not in
themselves lead anyone to Christ. But they can be of marked value to any
church that desires to know where, when, and how to carry on its work so
that maximum increase of soundly Christian churches will result.

WHAT ARE THE FACTS WE NEED?

First come *field totals* across the years. We should know the number of
Christians in all congregations for our denomination in a given field. The
field may be a whole nation, a state, a province, a district, or a part of a
district. The number of full members for each field is almost always recorded by the denomination or missionary society. From its headquarters
the annual records are easily available. As the number for each year from
the beginning to the present is ascertained, part of the pattern according
to which the church has grown becomes clear. Periods of great growth,
little growth, plateau, and decline will be evident. A brief inspection of
the figures will tell the church leader as much about the church as an elec-
trocardiogram tells the physician about the patient.

Figures, having been gathered, should be refined. In the course of
years, various geographical districts are added to or taken away from
ecclesiastical administrative units. For example, a congregation at Lexington, Kentucky, gives birth to several daughter congregations. At first
these are counted as part of the mother church and their memberships
swell hers. Then they separate. The mother church experiences a sharp
drop in membership; but the field total at Lexington should show a steady
rise.

Church membership at the Bolenge station of the Disciples of Christ in Zaire grew year after year until it reached 12,000. Then in a given year Bolenge reported only 9,000. This looked like a loss of 3,000 but was not. The Bosobele cluster of congregations, fifty miles away across the great river, which until that year had been considered part of the Bolenge Church, had been constituted a church unit and reported separately. Field totals should be refined until such meaningless ups and downs are fully understood.

Grimley and Robinson (1966:135) show a graph portraying a drop from 800 to 200 in the membership of the Lutheran Church in the Languda tribe in Nigeria. But there really was no loss! In 1953 the Languda Church ruled that only those who paid a membership fee would get a membership card and be counted full members. Out of 800 baptized believers only 200 paid the fee that first year; though in other respects, Grimley and Robinson say, "they were convinced Christians and were living a life in accordance with the precepts of the church. At any rate, in 1961 there were 603 card-bearing Christians, at least 1,000 other baptized believers, and 8,108 attending church each Sunday. . . ." Grimley and Robinson would have done better to refine their figures before graphing them. Their graph, built on the raw figures, shows a dramatic decline, whereas the number of baptized believers was steadily increasing. Changing definitions of membership should not be allowed to confuse the picture. Refining the figures is essential to understanding.

Field totals, however, are a thin measure. They reveal little. In fact, they often conceal more than they reveal. By themselves, they can deceive the observer. They must be used with discretion, knowing the pitfalls that lie before the unwary. As the researcher seeks to discern church growth outlines, field totals are a good beginning, but they must be amplified by other kinds of information before safe deductions can be drawn from them.

Homogeneous Unit Totals

The second fact needed is each *homogeneous unit total* across the years. The *homogeneous unit* is simply a section of society in which all the members have some characteristic in common. The homogeneous unit is frequently a segment of society whose common characteristic is a culture or a language, as in the case of Puerto Ricans in New York or Chinese in Thailand. In the island of Taiwan, for example, one sees four main homogeneous units: the Taiwanese-speaking 11,000,000; the Mandarin-speaking 4,000,000 who came over from the mainland in

1948; the Hakka-speaking 2,000,000; and the 300,000 aboriginal tribespeople, the Highlanders.

The homogeneous unit might be a people or caste, as in the case of Jews in the United States, Brahmins in India, or Uhunduni in the highlands of Irian Jaya. The Taiwan aboriginals mentioned above have six main tribes that together compose one homogeneous unit as regards the total population of the island; but if one were considering the Highlanders alone, each tribe would be such a unit. One might ask, How many Christians are there in each of the tribes? The answer would be given in six homogeneous unit totals.

Within a tribe subunits usually appear. These may be clans or lineages, language or dialect groups, or political or geographical units. For example we read, "As the Lord commanded Moses, so he numbered them in the wilderness of Sinai. And the children of Reuben, . . . by their generations, after their families, by the house of their fathers . . ." (Num. 1:19-20). Moses, by his numbering, obtained a homogeneous unit total for each clan and lineage. Similarly, within a modern city subunits appear—usually castes, tribes, or vocational or language groups.

For instance, Zairians from many different tribes have flooded into Kinshasa, each speaking a different tongue. It would be profitable for the Protestant churches to know the total Protestants from each tribe. These homogeneous unit totals would indicate to the churches the size of their shepherding task in following up Protestants who have moved to Kinshasa. When Norman Riddle and I did this in 1977 we found that 600,000 claimed to be Protestants, of whom less than 100,000 were on the rolls of all Protestant churches taken together (McGavran and Riddle 1979:145).

As these illustrations indicate, the homogeneous unit is an elastic concept, its meaning depending on the context in which it is used. However, it is a most useful tool for understanding church growth. The field total includes figures both from areas where the church is growing and from those where it is declining. Victories and defeats are added together to make the total figure that hides all details. But when the field total is broken down into homogeneous unit subtotals, one sees exactly where the church is advancing and where it is not. For example, in Latin America between 1916 and 1926 the number of Protestants doubled. This appears encouraging, but for Latin America as a whole it is falsely so, since most of the growth took place in the Baptist, Methodist, and Presbyterian Churches in one small section of Brazil. For most missionary societies in Latin America, that decade was one of slow growth; for some, of no growth at all. The general outlook was far from encouraging.

To cite a second example from Brazil: since 1946 there has been enormous growth of evangelicals. Most of this has occurred in Pentecostal denominations, some in Baptist and Presbyterian, and very little in the conservative missions that entered Brazil after World War II. An exact and meaningful assessment of the church growth situation would be concealed by any field total for all evangelicals in Brazil. It comes to light only in the securing of homogeneous unit totals for all churches at work there. William Read, in his remarkable book *New Patterns of Church Growth in Brazil,* has provided the first adequate understanding of the memberships of the larger evangelical churches in that big country. He shows clearly the homogeneous units that comprise the Protestant church in Brazil (Read 1965).

A *homogeneous unit church* may be defined as that cluster of congregations of one denomination which is growing in a given homogeneous unit. Thus in Central Provinces (Madhya Pradesh), India, the General Conference Mennonites assist three homogeneous unit churches. The largest is growing in the Gara caste in the southern third of the field, where the unit is a caste. The next largest is the northern church, made up of individual converts, famine orphans, and their descendants. In this case the unit is a geographical area. The smallest church is a cluster of congregations just starting in the Uraon caste, in the northeast corner of the field (Waltner 1962).

Three Kinds of Church Growth

Three kinds of church growth should be distinguished: biological, transfer, and conversion. Biological growth derives from those born into Christian families. The world is littered with tiny static denominations that obtain chiefly or solely this kind of growth. In times past a small Christian community has come into existence through occasional converts, famine orphans, and refugees. When the flame of evangelism burns low this community increases, if at all, by the excess of births over deaths. Biological growth is exceedingly slow. It often does not equal the normal population increase for the nation, for while some children become ardent Christians, some are lost to the world, or through marriage are sucked back into the other community.

Biological growth is good growth. God commanded us to "be fruitful, and multiply, and replenish the earth." Christians should, truly, bring up their children in the fear and admonition of the Lord. Yet this type of growth will never bring the nations to faith and obedience. At best it becomes a holding action.

What a providential occurrence it was that the 120 Christians before the day of Pentecost did not rely on biological growth! One wonders whether they might not have done so, but for the intervention, entirely beyond anything they had imagined, of the Holy Spirit.

By transfer growth is meant the increase of certain congregations at the expense of others. Nazarenes or Anglicans move from the country to the city, or from overpopulated areas to new lands the government is opening up. City or new land congregations flourish; those from which they have come diminish. Transfer growth is important. Every church should follow up its members and conserve as many of them as possible. But transfer growth will never extend the church, for unavoidably many are lost along the way.

The third kind is conversion growth, in which those outside the church come to rest their faith intelligently on Jesus Christ and are baptized and added to the Lord in his church. This is the only kind of growth by which the good news of salvation can spread to all the segments of American society and to earth's remotest bounds. The goal of mission is to have a truly indigenous congregation in every community of every culture. When that occurs, and only when that occurs, we may be sure that the gospel has been preached to every creature. Patently, this goal requires enormous conversion growth.

Internal, Expansion, Extension, and Bridging Growth

Another concept, helpful in understanding church growth, sees it occurring in four ways. (1) *Internal growth:* increase in subgroups within existing churches and the continually perfecting Christians, men and women who know the Bible and practice the Christian faith. E-0 evangelism, or bringing nominal Christians to active commitment to Christ, is included here. Some refer to internal growth as "quality growth." (2) *Expansion growth:* each congregation expands as it converts non-Christians and takes more of them, as well as transfer members, into itself. (3) *Extension growth:* each congregation plants daughter churches among its own kind of people in its neighborhood or region. (4) *Bridging growth:* congregations and denominations find bridges to other segments of the population and, crossing the bridges of God, multiply companies of the committed on the other side.

Ralph D. Winter and C. Peter Wagner share the credit for discovering and popularizing this creative classification, which has greatly enriched the entire church. All four ways should be familiar to and used by healthy congregations in all six continents.

Even in lands where virtually the whole population has become Christian and almost every name is on a church roll, the number of nominal Christians, backsliders, doubting Thomases, and confessed pagans who take their infants to the church to be baptized is very large. For example, in Sweden perhaps 90 percent of the population falls in this category. Also, among the Mongo tribes in the Equatorial Province of Zaire, where whole villages are Christian and most people, as boys and girls, went for years to Christian schools and were baptized after much instruction and after confessing Christ before the whole congregation, more than half the baptized seldom attend public worship. In that region in the late 1970s, belief in witchcraft was reasserting itself with great power. In both Sweden and the Equatorial Province, congregations of the dominant church ought to engage in much internal growth.

When one comes to those parts of the world where Christians are still a tiny part of the total population, major emphasis should be laid on expansion and extension growth. Where the church is a tiny part of the population, internal growth is seldom neglected.

In all churches, young and old, bridging growth or cross-cultural evangelism needs to be emphasized. Homogeneous unit churches that are only evangelizing their homogeneous unit are not pleasing to God. Disciples must be made of *panta ta ethne,* all the peoples.

Baptismal Figures

If baptisms from all sources—believers and infants, the Christian community and the world—are added together and recorded as a single figure, they are not extremely helpful. But if baptisms from the church and from the world are recorded separately, and a distinction made between the baptism of believers and that of infants, baptismal figures are well worth study. They can add a new dimension to understanding church growth.

For example, a large Asian church reports about 4,000 baptisms of believers a year. This is striking at first glance, but when we realize that this church of 200,000 members, if it conserves all its own children, should baptize more than 4,000 a year as they come to the age of discretion, then the number is far from impressive. This church, we observe, is static. It is baptizing most of its children and at best a few converts here and there.

If the record of baptisms from the world is obtained year after year and superimposed on a graph of growth, it will be seen that growth takes place only when there are sizable numbers of baptisms from the world. Nothing produces real church growth except baptisms from the world. No baptisms: no growth! Aftercare is, of course, crucially important; but the refinement does not vitiate the statement: No baptisms: no growth. The church through baptisms must obtain new Christians before it can care for them properly.

Family Analysis

A family analysis furnishes useful facts in understanding the patterns of church growth. In Thailand, for example, an analysis revealed that in a small congregation of 49 members, 44 were women, most of whom were married to Buddhist men. In another congregation in Thailand—this one of Chinese Christians—it became clear that if the mother alone was a Christian, all the children were likely to be Christians, whereas if the father alone was a Christian, none of the children was likely to be.

A family analysis of the congregation reveals the number of full families (where husband and wife are both Christians), half families (where only one partner is Christian), and singles. Obviously a congregation of 34 composed of 4 full families, 17 half families, and 9 singles is much different from a congregation of 34 made up of 12 full families and 10 of their believing children. Theoretically, the first congregation has much greater contact with the outside, but in practice this contact may leave it much more open to erosion. How half families come about is also important and should be ascertained. Sometimes they arise as out of non-Christian families only one partner becomes a believer. In other cases they arise as Christians marry non-Christians. In some cases half families bring loss to the church and in others the believing partner wins the unbelieving. Much depends on the fervency of the believers and much on other factors.

In Jamaica, in 1958, a family analysis revealed that most members of congregations of the masses were over forty years of age and consisted of elderly married couples and elderly single ladies. Youth and young adults of the masses, because they were living in a series of temporary unions, could not become members of the church—though in a vague way they counted themselves Christians and brought their infants to the church to be baptized or dedicated. Congregations of the upper classes, however, consisted of a normal spread of youth, young adults, and elderly people.

Family analysis reveals the intricate network of blood and marriage relationships that tie communities together and have so much to do with the inner life of any congregation. These webs of relationship also indicate the probable modes of future growth. They are important to know as one estimates the real possibilities of church increase.

Community or Communicants

In thinking about church expansion, nothing is more confusing than the various categories, usually undefined, according to which members are recorded. For example, in 1966 Episcopalians in the United States reported 3,410,657 members and the Churches of Christ 2,350,000 (Jacquet 1967:209, 201, 196). However, since Episcopalians were reporting all their baptized, including infants, and Churches of Christ were reporting only baptized believers, the figures are noncomparable, and they must be interpreted in that light.

If Episcopalians were to report communicants in good standing, their three million would shrink to less than the Churches of Christ figure. Responsible reporting should never give community and communicant figures under the same heading. Fortunately researcher David Barrett is compensating for such differences in his valuable worldwide research.

When Queen Elizabeth visited Uganda in 1954 to open the Jinja Dam, the Anglican bishop in Ruanda, who drove up to attend the ceremony and meet the royal party, told her that the Anglican Church in Ruanda numbered "a hundred thousand souls." At the time its communicant membership stood at about 16,000. "Souls" in that parlance meant all the baptized (infants and adults) plus all catechumens and their children.

Some conservative Latin American missions report numbers of *believers,* counting into their field total *baptized believers, unbaptized believers,* and *unbaptizable believers.* This last class of persons is fairly common in Latin America and consists of sincere men and women who as young people were married in the Roman Catholic Church, whose marriages have broken up, and who at the time they came to believe the gospel were living with someone not their original marriage partner. Divorce is difficult. Since each of the partners to the original marriage has settled down with some other person and has children by him or her, it is unthinkable for the original couple to be reunited. However, until the marriage is "regularized," some missions will not baptize these believers. They are therefore encouraged to come to church, give, pray, read the Bible, lead a Christian life, and bring others to Christ. They are "unbaptizable believers"—second-class Christians. Evidence indicates that some evangelical churches have grown greatly when, free from strict supervision by evangelical clergy, they have taken in numbers of unbaptizable believers and accorded them full status in the congregations.

Two other categories are commonly used: *adherents* and *sympathizers*. Horace Underwood wrote from Chung Do in Korea in 1888, before there were any Christians there at all, saying that several were asking for baptism and seventy were adherents. He meant that seventy were deeply interested in Christianity. In other cases, adherents is used in the sense of unbaptized, born again members of a declared Christian community in which many are baptized believers. Sympathizers is a common term in Latin America, where it denotes several different kinds of people: (1) those who attend evangelical teaching and worship but do not join the church, (2) those who are strongly anticlerical and who are friendly to the Protestants, and (3) those who are related to evangelicals and help them out when they are persecuted.

Community, communicants, full members, members, believers, baptized believers, adherents, sympathizers—accurate measurement of the growth of the church becomes impossible unless in this welter of different sociological entities, one can be found that means the same thing in all denominations and countries. Fortunately, there is such an entity—the *baptized responsible membership*. This hard core of the church is called "members" by some and "communicants," "full members," "resident members," "active members," or "baptized believers" by others.

To be sure, variation exists even in this category. In a few denominations, "full members" are not admitted to communion; that is reserved for an inner elite who can relate a saving experience, recognized as such by the church. Some denominations record not only communicants but "active communicants." Some, such as Quakers and the Salvation Army, do not practice water baptism. However, by and large, full members or communicants, defined as those who have a right to commune if they appear in church, is a category that is comparable across the length and breadth of Protestant churches.

Membership of Individual Congregations

A most useful fact in discerning the mode of growth of any denomination is the membership of its congregations across the years. Nothing grows but individual congregations. Until one knows how they are growing or not growing, reality is elusive. In Puerto Rico in 1955, I did a survey for the United Christian Missionary Society of Indianapolis. Its denomination in Puerto Rico had grown vigorously for twenty years, and I was sent down to understand and describe it. The reality escaped me until, almost by accident, I discovered the record of growth of every congregation. Then it became clear that the denomination consisted of four kinds of congregations—big urban churches, little urban churches, small-town churches, and little rural churches. During the years from 1948 to 1955, *all* the growth had been secured by the six large city churches. Industrialization of the island was proceeding apace. Rural Christians, flocking to the big cities, were making good money, and the six large city churches under able leadership were getting both transfer and conversion growth. Several small beginning congregations in these same cities, on the contrary, had made little progress. The small-town congregations were (with one exception) static, with memberships around forty, and all eighteen little rural churches were static or dying (McGavran 1956:16-20).

The Record of Each Worker

Even more difficult to obtain and even more illuminating in understanding the spread of the gospel is the record of each Christian worker. Workers are often the most influential single factor in the multiplying of churches. In one field two missionaries alternated or succeeded one another in various posts for twenty years. Whenever one came in, churches multiplied. When the other did, growth stopped. The one man was long on engine, the other on brakes. It takes courage and faith to baptize. Timid persons hesitate to create new churches. We marvel at the courage of the apostles, when on a single day they baptized three thousand believers! New members bring problems that plague one during the day and dance on the pillow at night. With no baptisms, one has fewer problems.

The missionary who carries the gospel often makes a difference, as can be clearly seen in the coming of John Clough to Ongole in 1865. His new policy of baptizing the untouchables, to which he was sure God had led him, ushered in a new era for the Baptist Mission in South India. I was puzzling over a sudden rise in membership in a church in Mexico and discovered that it was due to a worker who had been employed by the mission for a few years. He was a pearl of great price—a man through whom God was establishing new congregations in rancho after rancho—and yet twenty-five years later no one knew why he had left or where he was. From the time he left, the denomination had continued its dull way on a plateau of about 800 members.

KEEPING FOCUSED ON CHURCH GROWTH

It cannot be said too emphatically that the facts needed are not general facts concerning church activity. Some past studies of the church fail at just this point. They describe what has come into being from the total church program. They relate all kinds of interesting data about numerous facets of church life. They record the number of Sunday schools, women's societies, and youth organizations. They duly note the number, training, and salary schedules of pastors, evangelists, catechists, and workers. They set forth the number of men and women missionaries and their relation to the national leaders of the church. They list and value church buildings, cemeteries, pastors' residences, and other property. They attempt to photograph the entire ecclesiastical enterprise, without asking whether the details presented have anything to do with the spread of the faith or not.

In sharp contrast with this process, students of church growth are highly selective. They gather only those facts that are needed to understand the thrusts of growth and recession. Instead of presenting a profusion of data, most of it irrelevant as concerns increase of Christians, they present only data having something to do with the theme. To be sure, all life is such a closely woven web that every aspect and activity of the church has at least a distant connection with its reproductive powers. Nevertheless, since many aspects and activities have very little to do with reproduction, students of church growth concentrate on those most directly responsible for propagating the Christian religion. The facts they select are relevant to bringing the nations to faith and obedience. The structures they portray will reveal growth.

Hence they avoid relating the facts of one year only. These, like a single frame from a moving picture, do not tell what is happening. The sequence across many years is of prime importance. Progress from year to year and history of growth are meat and drink to one seeking to understand how churches grow.

RESEARCH IN CHURCH GROWTH

As pastors or missionaries set about gathering up the facts needed, they are likely to conclude that a survey of the growth of the congregation, conference, or diocese must be undertaken. Not ever having done such a survey, they look around for previous models, questionnaires, or forms that they can use. During the fifteen years 1964-79, it was a rare month when

I did not receive an appeal from some church leader, "Tell me how to do a survey of church growth. Send me the forms I ought to use."

Unfortunately, the varieties of churches are so numerous, the size of the baptized membership so varied, and the reasons for growth and stagnation so different that no one set of forms can be used. Each investigator has to construct his or her own instruments of research. They must fit the particular situation. Denominational preferences and terminologies must be taken into account. Are infants counted as members, or only baptized believers? Is tithing required or not? Is record-keeping left up to the local congregation or required by the bishop?

Bearing these difficulties in mind, the Church Growth Movement has attempted to standardize to the extent possible the least common denominators of research and reporting. The pioneering effort resulted in a small pamphlet of mine published by the Fuller School of World Mission called "How to Do a Survey of Church Growth." Thousands of them were distributed around the world. Following that, Southern Baptist missionary Ebbie Smith wrote *A Manual for Church Growth Surveys* (Smith 1976) which contributed many new and helpful insights and which should be used by serious students.

At the present time the standard research tool is *The Church Growth Survey Handbook,* written by Bob Waymire and C. Peter Wagner and available from Overseas Crusades, 25 Corning Avenue, Milpitas, CA 95035. It is a step-by-step, fill-in-the-blank presentation that includes blank graph paper and helpful diagrams. The authors have chosen to make it a public tool, they receive no royalties, and reproduction rights for parts or the whole are open to all who wish to study church growth. Over 1,600 case studies of local congregations and denominations are on file in the Fuller School of World Mission research library, all done using this standard format.

Knowing, for example, that the line graphs invariably represent membership or attendance figures over the diagnostic period and that the bar graphs indicate annual growth rates greatly simplifies comprehension of each individual study and allows for ready comparison of one study to another.

Investigators are well advised to remember that church growth research *accomplished* (even on a small scale) is to be preferred to research *deferred* until it can be done on a more scholarly scale. Battles must be fought on what information is available. Corrections and adjustments can be made later.

HOW TO DO A SURVEY OF CHURCH GROWTH

Christian leaders in increasing numbers are realizing that the growth of the churches, older as well as younger, must be taken with renewed seriousness. It is not sufficient to do excellent church and mission work in the hope that it will, somehow, lead to the multiplication of churches. The sheer physical expansion of sound Christian churches is a central and continuing duty of the church. There is a rising interest in it. We must push on through promotional commendations, encouraging generalities, and the scaffolding of church and mission work to the churches actually being planted and must see them clearly. How to do this careful investigation is described in the four steps following:

Step One: Defining the Study

1. State carefully the purpose and scope of your study. For example:

- To diagnose the reasons for growth or nongrowth in congregation A.
- To discover why, in a certain area, churches of denomination B are growing more rapidly than those of denomination C.
- To investigate the relationship between leadership selection and training and the growth of X cluster of churches.
- To identify the major factors of church growth in a given geographical region or in a given homogeneous unit at a given point in time.

2. Determine the ecclesiastical bodies to be studied. It will give you more light to study several congregations working in one general kind of population than to confine yourself to your own. While you may study your own more thoroughly than you do others, comparisons with others are valuable for understanding.

3. Determine the kind of population or populations involved. Are you going to study church growth among:

- Small town or large city congregations?
- Indians or Mestizos?
- Farmers or city workers?
- The intelligentsia or the illiterate?
- One caste or tribe or many?
- Lowlanders or Highlanders?

4. Once the target population is identified, gather pertinent demographic information on it, answering such questions as how many there are, what their socioeconomic position is, what changes they are going through, and how receptive they are to the gospel. A helpful model for this step is the *Unreached Peoples* annual series edited by C. Peter Wagner, Edward R. Dayton, and Samuel Wilson from 1979 to 1984.

Step Two: Finding the Membership Facts

1. Determine the *field totals* for each denomination at three- or five-year intervals from the beginning of the church until the present. This is not easy. But by writing to your friends, consulting church histories, and reading old yearbooks you can dig up the facts. Secure as much information as you can. Sometimes there will be gaps of several years. You may get the full picture only for your own church or mission, while information for the others will be sketchy—when they began, what their membership is now, and a few points in between.

2. Determine membership totals for each homogeneous unit in the denomination. A homogeneous unit is simply a section of society in which all the members have some characteristic in common. If Baptists in Boston number 20,000, discover how many are New Englanders and how many immigrants from the South. If the Congregationalists in Polynesia number 67,000, how many live in the Society Islands, the Cook Islands, and the Austral Islands? If the Lutherans in Taiwan number 5,000, how many speak Mandarin and how many Minnan?

3. Determine individual church totals over as many years as possible. Nothing grows but local churches. Which congregations are growing, standing still, or diminishing? You will find these figures most revealing, but sometimes difficult to get.

Step Three: Draw the Graphs of Growth

As you draw graphs of growth new insights about the growth or non-growth of your church or churches will come into focus. Draw graphs of your field totals for the history of the church. Also draw separate graphs for each homogeneous unit. When you have done this, begin work on the diagnostic period, which consists of the past ten years. Experience has shown that if you concentrate on the past ten years and analyze the situation well, intelligent decisions can then be made as you project future growth.

Church growth research has settled on the norm of a line graph to indicate the year-by-year changes in membership, attendance, number of congregations, or whatever you are graphing. Here is the format suggested by the *Church Growth Survey Handbook:*

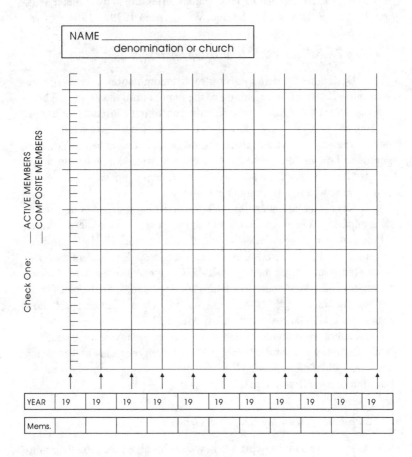

Alongside the line graph of the growth history, a bar graph is used to depict the annual growth rates of the church or group of churches. With a zero horizontal line across the middle of the graph, positive annual rates appear as bars above the line and negative annual rates appear as bars below the line. Here is an example taken from the *Church Growth Survey Handbook:*

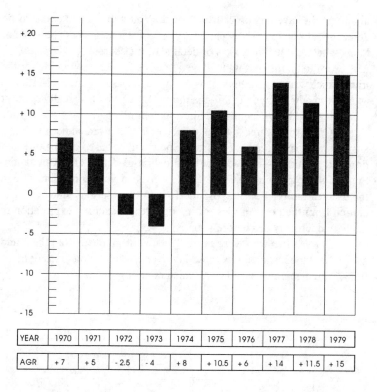

YEAR	1970	1971	1972	1973	1974	1975	1976	1977	1978	1979
AGR	+ 7	+ 5	- 2.5	- 4	+ 8	+ 10.5	+ 6	+ 14	+ 11.5	+ 15

How the information depicted on graphs of growth can be analyzed and utilized for planning evangelization will be dealt with in the next chapter.

Step Four: Ascertaining Causes of Growth and Nongrowth

1. Referring constantly to the graphs, ask what caused sudden rises, long plateaus, and gradual declines.

Look for causes—striking conversions, beliefs and traditions of the converts, changing neighborhoods, oppressions, the work of certain leaders, or their death or retirement. Consider what policies the church or mission has followed in times of membership increase or decrease. Did new programs adopted in hope deliver church growth? Was evangelism stressed?

Until you complete the graphs, you cannot tell what bearing a given action might have had on church growth. You will read an enthusiastic defense of the action—how necessary and wise it was—but you will not know whether it led to growth or decline of the church.

Learn to be ruthless with alleged reasons. You are searching for the truth. Much writing and thinking is really a defense of whatever is. It shies away from admitting defeat. It champions little growth as really the best thing that could have happened. Shun such thinking.

2. Consult the three sources named below, but remember that most answers will be inaccurate or partial. Some will be based on misinformation and prejudice—the accumulated debris of defeat and resignation. Some will be genuine insights. Some will lead you to insight, though themselves faulty. You may be the first to do a serious study of your church from the point of view of its growth. An exciting exploration in uncharted territory lies before you.

a. *The leaders who were there.* Place your graphs before them and ask particular questions. Ask those involved the following kinds of questions, which could be asked about this graph of growth.

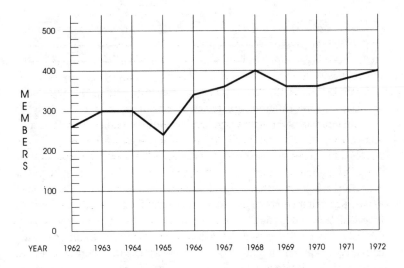

What caused the surge of growth in 1965 after a year of sharp decline?

What stopped growth in 1968 after three promising years?

What were we doing during this long period when our neighbor church grew three times the rate?

Expect to dig. Not every interview will yield information. Church leaders and missionaries, for example, who during their active lives were not interested in the growth of the church will in retirement remember little about it.

Beware of facile explanations. (i) "This was a very difficult field. The church simply could not grow there." If no denomination in the country was growing, that explanation may be accurate; but frequently it is tendered when next-door Presbyterians, Adventists, or Roman Catholics are seeing increase. (ii) Or someone says, "After each surge of growth there must be time for consolidation. This is a natural rhythm of the gospel." Is it? Or is consolidation an excuse for little growth? (iii) "My friend, you have no idea of the cold indifference here." Is the real trouble lack of zeal and warmth—or a ministry so highly trained (and paid) that new churches cannot start?

Consult people in their language. Talk about church growth to older members, recent converts, ministers, missionaries, and retired persons. Make the growth of the church a frequent topic of conversation.

b. *Denominational yearbooks, church records, baptismal registers, magazine articles, mission histories, and old reports.* In these is much chaff and little information about the physical increase of the churches. But if you will patiently winnow the chaff, you will find the wheat. Learn to scan inspirational or promotional articles, written to commend the work to supporters. Look for the sentence or phrase that tells something as to the size, shape, or nature of the church at a given time.

c. *Government statistics, censuses, anthropological studies, sociological expositions, handbooks for social workers, and surveys of the church.* Here again you will have to pan tons of gravel to get an ounce of gold. Do not get wrapped up in panning gravel! A book on theological education may be interested chiefly in lifting the standard of theological education and care nothing for the discipling of the nation. It may be concerned entirely with perfecting rather than discipling. Even so, it may throw both positive and negative light on church growth.

Similarly, anthropological treatises should be perused, not for intellectual interest, but to discover how the church has grown—or has not—and how it can grow in accordance with God's will in given populations.

3. Read all you can on how churches multiply. Since over three billion have yet to believe, millions of new churches will be needed. Thousands of books will be written, describing how particular pieces of the

mosaic have been or are being discipled. You cannot possibly read all of these. First, choose the few that deal with general principles, written by authors who know the whole field. Value highly those written by authors whose primary concern is carrying out Christ's Great Commission. Second, choose books that describe the multiplication of churches in the kind of population to which God has sent you. If you are called to multiply churches among the hundreds of thousands of nominal members of the Greek Orthodox Church, now in America becoming materialists and hedonists, it will not do you much good to read about church growth among the animistic tribes of Irian Jaya. If God has called you to disciple the respectable castes of India, studying how churches multiply in the nominally Protestant black population of Jamaica will not be highly informative; but accounts of how the tribes and castes of India have become Christian will prove a gold mine of information.

RESEARCH IN GROWING CHURCHES

Research aimed to help evangelism become more effective, churches multiply, and missions become more obedient to the Great Commission should concentrate on *growing* churches.

Numerous churches are growing healthily. Many denominations are increasing at 50 or 100 percent a decade. Some are doubling every eight years. The General Conference Baptists of the United States grew from 40,000 to 124,000 between 1940 and 1978. The Southern Baptists grew from about two million to over thirteen million between 1900 and 1978. Even in declining denominations, some congregations show vigorous increase.

Similarly in missions at home and abroad, while some labor for decades and establish only a dozen congregations, many others in a similar time span and population break through to mighty reproduction of the Christian faith. During the 1960s and 1970s in the Philippines, for example, while the largest and most prestigious Protestant denomination (The United Church of Christ) was growing only slightly, several other denominations were setting challenging church growth goals, and achieving them. For example, the Christian and Missionary Alliance increased from four hundred to over a thousand congregations.

Research is carried on in order to find ways God is currently blessing to the liberation of captives, the recovery of sight to the blind, and the acceptance of the good news by the poor. Consequently, research should be *concentrated on growing churches and growing denominations to find out why they are growing.*

The point is important. Much research painstakingly finds out all the facts about a given congregation or denomination. This wastes much time. Most facts, accurate as they may be, have little to do with the growth of the church. The skillful researcher therefore avoids gathering information that has little bearing on growth. An able church leader once came to study with me, bringing five cartons full of data that he had amassed on his own large denomination. After studying church growth for six months, he brought in the cartons one day and said wryly, "All this sheds little light on the real reasons our church is declining. I wasted a year. What shall I do with it?" "Throw it away," I replied, "and determine never to gather any but pertinent information." I have seen large amounts of data pour out of modern computers. Its accuracy is impeccable but its usefulness in discovering facts about a church is minimal at best.

Concentrate on growing churches, because something they are doing is causing them to grow. Research should discover which among the hundreds of activities carried on, convictions held, attitudes demonstrated, and persons engaged in the work are the actual causes of church growth. As these are described and the part they played analyzed, each person reading the study will see which of them are relevant to their situation.

Stagnant congregations and denominations may, occasionally, be studied with profit, but since they have *not* been growing, lessons learned from them are likely to be somewhat discouraging. It is better to commend with joy causes of accomplished growth than to point with dismay toward causes of nongrowth.

Furthermore, since part of stagnancy is a sense of defeat, one of the better ways of motivating Christians to effective evangelism is to persuade them that growth is possible and to show them how the Holy Spirit has caused it. Nothing is more potent in leading defeated pastors or missionaries to attempt church growth than to assemble illustrations of substantial growth from their denominations, kinds of Christians, and institutional machinery.

PART III

CAUSES OF CHURCH GROWTH

7

DISCOVERING THE WHY OF IT

WHEN STUDENTS of church growth carry out the procedures described in the preceding chapter, they will obtain for a given church its homogeneous units, its congregations, accurate pictures of their size, and growth histories from the beginning to the present. They will also obtain sociological analyses of the membership showing where it came from, how it is composed, and what the relationships of its various parts are. The structure of the church will become visible.

Since promotional speaking and writing properly form such a large part of Christian work, those who would understand church growth must be particularly careful that they distinguish between what church leaders hoped would happen, what happened in an instance or two, what ought to happen, and what in fact did happen. The picture built up by patiently assembling accurate statistics concerning the church and its many constituent parts is the foundation of all further knowledge of church growth.

KNOWING WHY IS ESSENTIAL

Statistical knowledge is not enough. To know the structure is interesting but is important only as it leads on to understanding why the church and its homogeneous units have grown, plateaued, and occasionally diminished. The goal of church growth studies is not merely to assemble correct facts as to the quantity of growth. It is not sufficient to see the structure clearly—though that must be done. The goal is through evaluation of the facts to understand the dynamics of church growth. Only as, on the basis of assured growth facts, we see the reasons for increase, the factors that God used to multiply his churches, and the conditions under which the church has spread or remained stationary, do we understand church growth.

Understanding the times and conditions is vitally important. How multitudinous kindreds, tongues, tribes, and nations have accepted the abundant and eternal life that comes through faith in Jesus Christ and membership in his church is the story of "opportune times," the biblical *kairos*.

The answer to the question "Why did church growth occur?" is complex. One reason for lack of growth in the midst of widespread receptivity is that many church leaders, not sufficiently recognizing the intricacies of propagating the gospel, work at it along one simplistic line. The point is so important that two examples will be given here, the first from the world of radio.

As the gospel is broadcast in North America, the message falls on the ears of a potential audience of at least 150,000,000 persons, to whom because they are active or nominal Christians it is more or less familiar. Contained in this multitude are literally millions of nominal Christians—the unconverted or backslidden. As these hear the unchanging, powerful gospel, many believe, repent, and accept Christ. They find a nearby church and join it. If they are already members, they come to new life in it.

Christian broadcasting in the Third World, however, falls on the ears of Marxists, Hindus, Buddhists, animists, and Muslims. At least half of these are illiterate. The Christian message is not familiar. On the contrary, it is totally strange. Under these conditions it is simplistic to suppose that even the unchanging gospel, beamed over the radio waves to this audience *in substantially the same way it is in North America,* will bring non-Christians of many different cultures to Christ—especially where there are no churches with which believers can unite. Recognizing the complexity of church growth, radio should convey the message of salvation to each community in ways that make it possible for obedience to the gospel to become a real option to its members. Fortunately, positive changes in these directions are being made in many broadcasting circles.

Second, those who prepare and distribute Christian literature should know what factors have brought people to a saving knowledge of Jesus

Christ and active membership in his church in the specific populations where they are distributing literature. For example, in Japan because of universal literacy and advanced education, evangelism through literature should be effective in church multiplication, provided tracts and gospel messages fit the Japanese population. Of course, they must be thoroughly biblical. They must set forth Jesus Christ, the sole Savior and Lord, by whom alone men and women come to the Father. Yet even if the literature is biblical and sets forth Jesus Christ faithfully, if it does so in an American manner, it will be read—if at all—with dull eyes. To put it positively, the more the writers of that literature are steeped in the lore of Japan, its culture, worldview, and dreams, the more eagerly will they be read. Literature that tells how typical Japanese have become disciples of Christ will be more effective than that which tells how Americans have. Writers should know thoroughly how churches have multiplied in Japan, how the patterns of growth have varied from class to class and decade to decade, and what factors in the affluent secular Japan of today are most potent in producing self-propagating congregations. The writer of literature should learn about church growth as the surgeon learns anatomy— with complete thoroughness, not by reading a book or two, but by years of study and firsthand research.

ANTHROPOLOGY HELPS UNDERSTANDING

Cultural anthropology, one of the behavioral sciences, describes how people act, how they innovate, how they govern themselves, what restraints they set up for their societies, and a thousand other matters of note. Cultural anthropology has influenced the mind of America more than most pastors realize.

Many secular anthropologists rigorously avoid judging whether actions and customs are good or bad. Some anthropologists, pursuing objectivity, believe that all cultures are equally good and each religion is simply a way of understanding reality that a given society finds agreeable or convincing. In consequence they object to changing a society in any way and particularly to Christianization. Other anthropologists, however, freely use their science to effect all kinds of change that they, their government, or their employers consider desirable.

Christian missionaries who believe that in Jesus Christ God has revealed a way of life rewarding for all, also use anthropology for directed change. They, too, are aware that it is impossible for various cultures to remain in their present state of development. Like other practitioners of applied anthropology, they are opposed to sacrificing the long-range welfare of any people in order to keep it as a museum piece. They are opposed to leaving directed change in the hands of the exploiter, materialist, Communist, blind chance, or selfish racism. They believe that God is calling the church to play its part in bringing about a social order more in harmony with his will—more just, brotherly, and peaceful.

The Christian then turns to anthropology with a good conscience to discover why certain churches have grown and others have not, and to devise customs, institutions, and other configurations that will fill the voids created by rapid social change, in a manner acceptable to the society in question and consonant with the authority of the Bible.

Alan R. Tippett's *Solomon Islands Christianity* is a mine of information concerning the ways in which cultural anthropology can be used in the service of the gospel. In relating how the various denominations in the Solomon Islands grew and stopped growing, flourished and atrophied, became really or nominally Christian, and communicated the Christian faith to others or failed to communicate it even to their own relatives, Tippett uses anthropology to cast a flood of light on the growth, in quality as well as quantity, of the various branches of the church. For example, after describing a dramatic scene in which a taboo banyan tree was cut down by new converts and the whole population thereupon declared for Christ and put themselves under instruction, Tippett devotes two pages to an anthropological understanding of the situation. He concludes:

> [The Western missionary] is working in a Melanesian world, facing a Melanesian philosophy, and will have to learn to understand Melanesian thought forms, and fight for Christianity on Melanesian levels. [The banyan tree incident] is a relevant encounter and a real victory, with many scriptural precedents. Western missions might do well to face up to the statistical evidence that animists are being won today by a Bible of power encounter, not a demythologized edition (Tippett 1967:101).

Anthropologist Charles H. Kraft points out that when the Christian faith moves from one culture to another, the churches in the second culture would not be expected to look exactly like the churches from the missionaries' culture. Missionaries who do not understand this and who feel that their mode of church government, their requirements for ordination, their sense of punctuality, their liturgical tastes, their musical idioms, their rules for baptism, their ethical taboos, and what have you need to be cloned in the churches in the new culture raise artificial barriers to church growth. In his landmark book *Christianity in Culture,* Kraft says, "It is crucial that each new generation and culture experience the process of producing in its own cultural forms an appropriate church vehicle for the transmission of God's meanings." He recommends what he calls "dynamic-equivalence churches" (1979:315).

THE WONDERFUL GRAPH OF GROWTH

Columns of figures giving the membership of any church and its homogeneous units contain locked-up knowledge. By careful study the figures can be forced to reveal their secrets, but the process is tedious. When, however, each set of figures is transformed into a graph of growth, the secrets leap out at the reader. Those who would understand church growth should construct line graphs showing at a glance what has transpired. They can then ask why it happened.

The process of constructing a graph was explained in the last chapter. Now let's think of how to analyze the picture. See the following hypothetical graph of growth. It shows that after twenty years of extremely slow growth, a period of seven years ensued when churches multiplied healthily. Then for eighteen years growth stopped, but started up again in the late forties and, after a brief decline, rose to new heights by 1970.

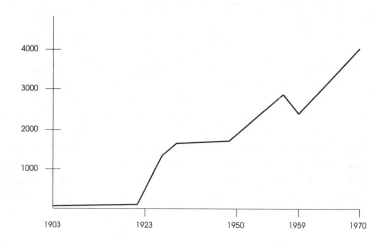

The present lack of information about the growth of the churches may be gauged by the fact that most church leaders have never seen a graph of growth for their own denomination or for the congregation to which they are giving their lives. They no doubt have a vague idea that their own congregation is growing or standing still, but they have no exact knowledge of their church. They work surrounded by fog.

The hypothetical graph of growth above should intrigue all. During the eighteen years from 1930 on, was an insurmountable obstacle encountered? Or did some errant policy, theology, or personality dominate the enterprise? What caused the sharp upturn in 1923? And the recovery of growth in 1948 and 1960? Could the twenty years of no growth at the beginning have been shortened? Most leaders neither know the answers to these questions nor, as a rule, are able to ask them. Most are not familiar enough with their own church history to know what to ask, or where in the story significant changes have taken place.

Many American writers have told us why they thought their churches have grown—frontier conditions, notable leaders, revivals, denominational excellencies, God's blessing, the work of "our great home missionary society," and on and on. Of course, part of this is the exact truth. Yet until the particularity of church growth is seen, and until the many parts of the total picture are described one by one against graphs of the actual increases, there is great danger that the picture presented will be simplistic. Most of the reasons for church growth will not even be seen. A few will be overly emphasized.

Many writers on missions have set forth reasons for the growth of the church. One who roams through the volumes on the history of missions, biographies of missionaries, and records of proceedings of churches and missions will again and again run across statements concerning why and how the church has grown. When these are made about growth in one homogeneous unit during a given period of time, they are usually accurate. They have been formed in view of the actual record. When, however, they are made about large units, such as field totals or "our church in such and such a country," the complex growth history being only vaguely seen, they are apt to be faulty. It is particularly necessary for historians to see the growth history of homogeneous units when they set forth hypotheses as to growth. Otherwise they describe causes for growth that never took place, or relate as true for the whole what was true for only one of several parts.

The Graph Shows Each Plateau, Decline, or Increase

The graph of growth shows trends extending over various periods of time. If causes for church growth are to be understood, these trends must be seen. Consider the instructive graph of growth of the church founded by the English Presbyterians in Taiwan (formerly Formosa) between 1865 and 1900. If one were asked, "How did the Presbyterian Church in Taiwan grow to three thousand communicant members in thirty-five years?" without the graph they would probably reply that missionaries proclaimed the gospel, women and men were healed and taught, and God gave the increase. This vague reply contains elements of the truth, but is far from adequate. It actually conceals the five different kinds of church growth that occurred during these years.

THE PRESBYTERIAN CHURCH IN TAIWAN

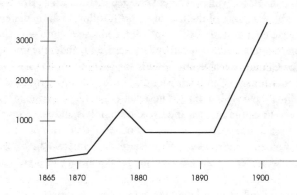

On the graph one can immediately distinguish five periods of growth. The first, of about eight years, was an exploratory phase. Missionaries were learning Chinese and local geography, getting acquainted with the people, buying property, and winning the first few converts from among the Chinese population. During the second, a small movement brought in about 1,500 Pepohwans (see the upward swing of the line of growth). These were the aboriginal inhabitants of Formosa who were being pushed back by the Chinese settlers who had come over from the mainland after A.D. 1600. Pepohwan converts were instructed and shepherded, not in their own language, but in Chinese. Most of them, failing their baptismal ex-

amination, were not baptized. Compared with the congregations of
Chinese Christians, the peasant Pepohwans did not appear promising.
They were improvident and often in debt. They frequently drank to excess.
The rural congregations at some distance from the main mission station
were difficult to look after. The more powerful among the missionaries
came out strongly for Chinese work as opposed to Pepohwan. Considerable Pepohwan reversions set in, which the mission ascribed to instabil-
ity in the people. They may have had something to do with them; but a
more potent cause lay in the shepherding mistakes recounted above. The
reversions account for the third period—that of decline—shown on the
graph.

In the fourth period—the long, low plateau—the remaining Pepohwan congregations and the station congregations made up largely of
Chinese converts were cared for and evangelistic, educational, and medical work was carried on. Chinese were becoming Christians in the smallest numbers and the Pepohwan movement had been arrested. The fifth period (note the upward surge of the line of growth) followed immediately
after the Japanese conquest of Taiwan in 1895. Chinese culture was dis-
credited, Chinese rulers were replaced by Japanese, and, under the impact
of defeat, many Chinese became able to hear the gospel. At just this time
a remarkable missionary, Campbell Moody, toured the western part of
Taiwan preaching the gospel to the Chinese with fire and persuasiveness.
Hundreds turned to Christ in ones and twos, by families and kin groups.
The baptism of each new person or family opened the door to others of
that clan. Many small congregations were established. In 1894 the majority of Christians were Pepohwans. In 1899 the great majority of them were
Chinese.

The graph by itself does not give the details that enable us to understand what really happened in the first thirty-five years of Presbyterian
mission in Taiwan. It cannot reveal the causes of growth and decline.
Those must be dug out of histories and biographies, reports and articles.
But it does clearly indicate when changes in rate and amount of growth
took place and how long each phase lasted. It thus breaks the meaningless whole into its meaningful parts, enabling the student of church growth
to search for causes at the right times.

Further, the graph gives substance and reality to the story. We know
not merely that "some Pepohwans and Chinese were converted in the early
days,"; but that about 1,500 of them were. We can see not merely that
"large numbers of Pepohwans reverted,"; but that the numbers were not
so large and that after the reversions there remained a church of nearly

1,000 members. It becomes clear that not only was there "some growth in the nineties," but that the church more than tripled in five years. In short the outlines of what happened stand out sharply.

The Extent of Gradual Slowdowns

It often happens that after a period of rapid growth, a church in a responsive area will slow down and become introverted, or turn its attention to cultural advance. This frequently happens in the United States. It enters a static stage of its existence. Sometimes growth stops because the kind of converts who constituted the first source of growth are no longer available, and the church does not seek a second source. Often, however, the same kind of converts are available but the emphasis has changed—new pastors or missionaries have come who are busy perfecting the existing Christians and the absence of growth continues year after year or decade after decade. No one is conscious of the stoppage. Good church and mission works proceed onward.

The long plateau graphically portrays stoppage and projects the question whether it was preventable. The plateau, seen in context of previous growth, encourages church leaders to believe that growth is possible and leads to a search for causes that initiated the era of slow growth and bound it on the church.

Consider, for example, the Methodist Church in Gold Coast— Ghana. Between 1907 and 1925 the cocoa boom, the Harris movement in Apolonia, and the Ashanti ingathering under the Prophet Opong lifted the communicant membership from 6,217 to 38,941. During those eighteen years the Methodist Church increased 526 percent, or at the rate of 177 percent DGR. During the next thirty years, however, it plateaued, growing from 38,941 to 58,725 communicants, at a rate of only 15 percent DGR. The graph shows the length of the stoppage and—because of the three surges of conversion growth in the preceding eighteen years—leads one to consider what caused it and whether it was really necessary or not.

A cause that began about 1925 and continued throughout the thirty years is required. Such a cause was the massive emphasis on education that began in the early twenties and continued throughout the period. The Methodist Church, becoming responsible for most of the education done by the British in the Methodist areas of Gold Coast, and receiving large government grants, relied more and more on converting schoolchildren through education and less and less on converting pagan adults by preach-

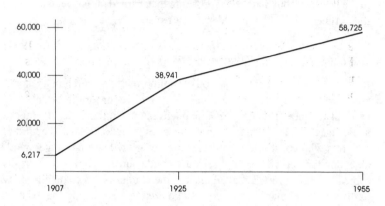

COMMUNICANTS IN GOLD COAST METHODIST CHURCH

ing. There were other causes for the standstill in growth, but the emphasis on education was no doubt the main one.

The near-monopoly on education held by the churches in West Africa made this kind of growth attractive to missions—as seen earlier in the case of Rhodesia (Zimbabwe) and Zambia—but one wonders whether the leaders were acutely conscious of the fact that the school approach was delivering very little church growth. It was Christianizing the leadership of the country, but it was permitting the masses to remain pagan. The theory was that once the leaders were Christian, the people would turn to Christ; but the theory was not working out—as the graph for the Methodist Church in Ghana clearly shows.

The British Methodists had planted a church in both Ghana and Nigeria. After 1925 the policies followed in one country differed little from those followed in the other. Consequently what Deaville Walker writes in *A Hundred Years in Nigeria* (1942) has more than passing interest as we consider the slow growth that occurred in Ghana. He concludes his book with a statement that sums up Methodist mission and church policy in West Africa in 1942:

> For the present, the supreme task is that of thorough training—larger and more efficient provision for training teachers, pastors, evangelists, and ministers; the training of boys and girls in our schools, and the careful training of Christians in our churches. Until in the not distant future, the whole Methodist Church in Western Nigeria, strong and devoted to its Redeemer and Lord shall be mobilized for the su-

preme task—the evangelization of the yet unreached multitude within its borders (Walker 1942:138).

Grimley and Robinson in *Church Growth in Central and Southern Nigeria,* quoting Walker's conclusion, add: "Twenty years later (in 1962) the Methodist Church has still to break out of its educational fortress in a campaign to evangelize the 'yet unreached multitude'" (1966:339). They go on to sum up causes for the stoppage as follows: "The failure to grow was mainly a result of over-emphasis on humanitarian service and spreading enlightenment, and underemphasis on evangelizing. Education became the doorway to the Church, and thus limited the potential and slowed the process" (Grimley and Robinson 1966:337).

The line graph by itself does not, of course, say all this, but it does display with startling clarity the long plateau, and that in turn, illuminated by policies, actions, people, and conditions, makes possible exact thinking about growth.

HOMOGENEOUS UNIT GROWTH

Graphs of homogeneous unit church growth contribute greatly to the understanding of causes. Since the figure easiest to obtain is the field total, copied out of the denomination's printed annual report, the most common graph is that which portrays the growth of a whole denomination in one country. Since, however, the denomination is very frequently made up of several clusters of congregations, each growing in some segment of the population, the graph of the field total can be deceptive. It can hide the real causes of growth. Graphs of homogeneous unit church growth are essential.

A classic example of this is given by Roy Shearer in *Wildfire: Church Growth in Korea* (1966). Shearer photographed the membership records of the Presbyterian Church in all Korean presbyteries and, carefully refining the statistics, drew nine graphs of growth, one for each presbytery. These, reproduced below, show conclusively that the great growth of the Presbyterian Church in Korea took place chiefly in the two northwest provinces—North and South Pyongan.

In his fourth chapter, "Comparison of Geographical Sections of Presbyterian Church Growth," Shearer takes up the ordinary conclusions about church growth in Korea (based on the general fact that the church there has grown greatly) and, examining them in the light of the graphs of growth in each presbytery, finds most of them inadequate. His analysis is essential reading for any student of church growth. After Shearer's work, any conclusion based on a field total alone will be suspect. Time will not permit us to examine here his rich and varied argument, but two examples must be given.

A. W. Wasson (1934) did a notable pioneer study entitled *Church Growth in Korea,* which threw a flood of light on the subject, but was seriously handicapped by the fact that he studied only field totals. These showed a marked slowing down of growth from 1911 to 1919, which Wasson ascribed to loss of security of life and property under Japanese government, and to the persecution of Christians which broke out when a hundred and fifty persons, mostly Christian teachers and students, were arrested in Sunchun in North Pyongan on the charge of conspiring to kill the Japanese governor general as he passed through. After showing that these causes did affect churches in the more southerly provinces, Shearer says:

> Had the Conspiracy Case been an important factor in the growth of the Church one would expect that the area immediately affected with the harshest persecution would have slowed in its growth. But look at Figure 11 [an enlargement of the graph of North Pyongan province]. This is the area worked from the mission station of Sunchun. One searches in vain for any slowing of communicant membership growth there . . . (Shearer 1966:140).

Again in discussing the revival of 1907 and its outcome in church growth, Shearer addresses himself to the common opinion that the revival was *the* cause for the great growth of the Korean church. He says:

> It is true that in those areas of Korea where there had been little church growth, the rate of growth shows some increase directly following the revival. . . . However, the revival, which should have been a more important factor in the northwest because of its huge breakout there, was not. [According to the graphs] the Church shows significant growth *before* this revival and *very* little change of growth rate following the revival. Therefore, we must conclude that in the northwest the revival was not the original cause of the growth of the Presbyterian Church and probably not even a major cause (Shearer 1966:136).

The importance of graphs of homogeneous unit churches would become crystal clear if it were possible to take the graph of the Presbyterian Church in Taiwan during its first thirty-five years, given a few pages ear-

COMMUNICANT MEMBERSHIP OF THE PRESBYTERIAN CHURCH IN
KOREA, BY PROVINCE, 1885–1930

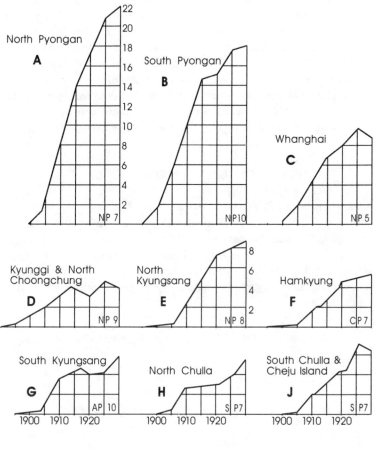

AP   Australian Presbyterian Mission
CP   Canadian Presbyterian Mission (now United Church of Canada)
SP   Southern Presbyterian Mission
NP   Northern Presbyterian Mission (now United Presb. Church USA)

Lower right-hand corner figure is number of ordained missionaries
in each area in 1911.

lier, separate the figures for the Pepohwan Christians from those of the Chinese, and present two graphs. The first would show the growth and decline of the Pepohwan people movement to Christ and the second the growth of the Chinese membership. Unfortunately, church figures are seldom reported by ethnic or other units (unless these happen, as in Korea, to be geographical units also). Consequently, clusters of congregations growing in homogeneous units often cannot be accurately reported. Full allowance for their presence should nevertheless be made whenever possible. One can hope that, as church growth comes to be taken with greater seriousness, homogeneous unit growth will be recorded separately. This small addition to routine procedures would enable leaders of the churches to see which clusters of congregations were growing and which were not. The reasons for growth would then become clearer.

GRAPHS OF SUPPLEMENTARY FIGURES

Causes of growth will also be clearer when supplementary information is portrayed graphically, such as number of adherents who have declared themselves Christian but have not yet been baptized; gains from biological, transfer, and conversion growth; losses from deaths, transfers out, reversions, and exclusions; and data obtained from family analyses and school enrollment. Figures for these elements give depth to the reasons for growth and nongrowth.

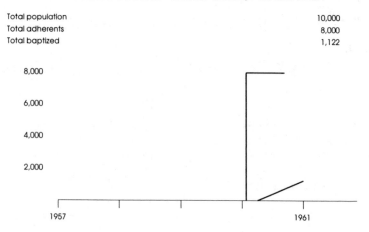

DANI CHURCH GROWTH—BALIEM VALLEY, PYRAMID AREA

Total population	10,000
Total adherents	8,000
Total baptized	1,122

In Irian Jaya (formerly West New Guinea) on February 14 and 15, 1960, 8,000 Dani tribesmen declared for Christ, piled their fetishes on a pyre fifty feet long and four feet wide, and burned them. Missionaries of the Christian and Missionary Alliance put the 8,000 adherents under instruction, trained indigenous leaders for them, and as men and women came to know enough about Jesus Christ to put their faith intelligently in him, baptized them. By 1961, 1,222 had been baptized and by 1967 about 6,000 had been. The above graph of adherents and baptized believers portrays the situation in 1961 exactly. The vertical line shows 8,000 Christian adherents in 1960. The lower rising line shows the gradual increase in full members or communicant Christians (Sunda 1963:28). The increase in baptized believers was taking place out of a community of 8,000 who had declared themselves Christian.

A WORD ON THE CONSTRUCTION OF GRAPHS

Single congregations or clusters of them in all American and European cities can easily construct meaningful graphs. So can many congregations in other continents. The following rules will be useful everywhere. As I have previously mentioned, Waymire and Wagner's *The Church Growth Survey Handbook* will prove helpful.

1. Portrayal of reality by graphs is convenient and dramatic, but it is not exact. The width of the line itself frequently covers scores or hundreds. Consequently, in exact research, tables of the figures on which the graphs are based should be carefully preserved and presented along with the graphs in any report.

2. Proportions in graphs may be managed to convey a message. The message is greatly affected by the proportion chosen, that is, by the relation of the vertical to the horizontal scale, or, in other words, of the number of members to the years.

In choosing proportions, two aims should be borne in mind. The graph should tell the truth and should tell it meaningfully. Showmanship in the construction of graphs is legitimate, but never outranks exactness.

3. In presenting a series of graphs, the proportions or relative scale in each should be kept the same wherever feasible. Otherwise, while the graphs may be exact and convey the truth if read separately, in sequence they mislead readers, because readers assume a consistent scale. Even if they read more carefully, the first impression conveyed by the general size of the increase outweighs the later exact knowledge conveyed by reading

the scales. Or, on the other hand, readers will experience annoyance at what seems almost an attempt to misrepresent.

4. If, on one sheet, churches of great growth (above 5,000) are compared with those of a few hundreds or thousands, the lines portraying the small churches will hug the bottom, their increases will be discerned with difficulty, and they will suffer by the comparison. Therefore, it is good procedure to use two main proportions: (a) for churches above a certain figure, let us say 5,000, and (b) for churches whose membership is below that—and on one sheet to present only one category of churches. If the first proportion is always portrayed in green and the second in red, greater clarity results.

As engineers know, this may also be done on semilogarithmic graph paper, but several years of experimentation have showed that the relatively low aptitude of the average church growth researcher for logarithmic concepts reduces its usefulness across the board.

5. In a preliminary study, or for the sake of speed, membership figures at intervals of five or ten years are sometimes gathered; but for accuracy figures should be obtained for each year. What happens particularly during the most recent ten-year period is frequently of vital importance.

8

SOURCES TO SEARCH FOR CAUSES OF GROWTH

WHERE SHOULD CHURCH LEADERS look to find the reasons why cells of Christians (churches) have proliferated throughout a city ward, a country district, a tribe, or other segment of society?

Some may feel the question is rhetorical and the answer obvious. Evangelistic campaigns, they think, bring people to Christ and establish new churches. Church leaders should find what evangelism has been done. They need look no further. This line of thinking fails, however, to take into account the fact that evangelistic campaigns have very different results. In some places thousands are won and in others only dozens. Many city-wide campaigns add only a few new responsible Christians to existing congregations and not a single new congregation.

We who would understand the ways in which the Holy Spirit, through establishing thousands of new communities of the redeemed, is spreading abroad the sweet savor of Christ, must ask why evangelistic crusades issue in conversions in some populations and not in others. Why do conversions in some cases set off a chain reaction resulting in a multitude of new congregations, while in others the few scattered converts scarcely strengthen the existing ones? Why does a given church grow vigorously during one period and stagnate in others? What environmental and missionary factors condition church growth?

Where do we look for answers to these questions? They are not rhetorical and the answers are not obvious. They must be diligently sought in the right places.

PASTORS AND MISSIONARIES WHO WERE THERE

Unquestionably the best sources of understanding of growth are the men and women who saw it happen. They knew what was going on. They knew every inquirer and baptized every convert. They met the opposition, enjoyed the victories, and grieved over the defeats. They were part of the community in which growth was occurring. The pastors and missionaries who were there when growth, plateau, or decline was happening are the ones to ask.

They know more than other persons who were present. They are educated, accustomed to discriminating thinking, and have wide experience. They know the language spoken by the Christians and talk with them freely. Few persons are as intimately related with new churches as pastors and missionaries. They have thought much about church growth. They want it, have worked at it, and prayed for it. They have been alive to it.

However, they also frequently suffer from being too close to the situation. They are inclined to credit what they have done toward church growth with too much influence in bringing it about, and are often insufficiently aware of social structures and the considerable part they play in growth or stagnation. Fog obscures their vision just as it does that of administrators and others. Despite these handicaps, the pastors and missionaries who were on hand during the period in question are the best sources of insight. Researchers can allow for their weaknesses and help those they interview to overcome them.

When asking for information about church growth, they should ask about specific cases and obtain light on their extent. A graph of growth of the church in view helps to prevent irrelevant talk and elicit pertinent information. You see the sudden upturn of the line? In 1961 something happened that caused your denomination to double in six years. I am looking for the causes of that sudden surge of growth, which gradually subsided and ended about 1976. I would like to know also why it diminished. You were there during those years. Please tell me what really happened.

Retired persons are sometimes good informants, but unless they were interested in church growth while active, they may have little to contribute.

Searching for reasons for the surprising growth of the Christian Church (Disciples of Christ) in China, I interviewed two retired missionaries. The problem was this. During the years 1880 to 1940 a large number of missionaries had built up a small church of 1,198 members, increase being at a snail's pace throughout the six decades. Why then in 1942 did this church revive and surge forward to *add* 1,867 members in six years? Both missionaries had been there during the critical six years.

O. J. Goulter gave two reasons. First, after the Japanese invaders had been repelled with the aid of American arms, American missionaries for the first time in sixty years appeared to the general populace as "our friends and allies." Instead of hostility, indifference, or suspicion, friendliness greeted them. The gospel could be "heard"; it no longer appeared as itself the spearhead of a foreign invasion. Second, the Bible school instituted a new form of training for evangelists. They were taught evangelism *and* agriculture. They went out able to teach peasants not only the way of salvation but also ways to increase their yields of rice and pigs. Wherever these evangelists went, small rural churches sprang up.

James McCallum, who had been the field administrator of the mission, taking one look at the figures said, "During those years several independent congregations in Nanking decided to affiliate with our church."

The example illustrates several traits of the information to be derived from pastors and missionaries. It will usually be partial. The field administrator knew part of the reason. Living at Nanking, he had helped to unite the independent congregations with his own and remembered them. The head of the Bible school, living in a corner of the field, knew about the growth he had seen. Information from church leaders usually exhibits the enthusiasms and biases of the informants.

Executive secretaries of missions are not likely to contribute much to an understanding of church growth. They usually administer several fields and do not become intimately acquainted with the people in any one of them. They converse with missionaries and church leaders in English, and since they are responsible for many kinds of work, automatically guard against undue interest in particular ones. Their chief duty is the recruitment of missionaries and the raising of the budget in the sending land, and for this they need and specialize in not diagnostic but promotional materials.

Nevertheless, some executives are becoming students of church growth, and more of them will. Accurate, extensive knowledge of how churches grow is helpful for any administration that intends to carry out the Great Commission. The day is coming when knowledge of the science of church growth will be part of the qualifications for office of any church or mission administrator. As soon as this happens, executives will be a good source for learning the reasons for growth. Few others have the opportunity to know firsthand so many instances of growth, plateau, and decline.

LAY CHRISTIANS

A rewarding mine of information may be found in the laity. Church growth is the sum of many baptized believers. No one knows better what caused it than those who make it up. Granting this, it is not easy to extract the gold from this vein of quartz. Interviewing demands skill, and interviewers need special training. They must not suggest answers. They should be at home in the language, for interpreters retard the process and color answers with their own convictions. They should select with care those interviewed so that they constitute a random sampling of the whole unit being studied. This last point is frequently neglected, and those interviewed are apt to be the most devout, most easily reached, or most educated. Very great patience is required with rural people and illiterates. They take a long time pondering a simple question and, if one is to have a true answer, must not be hurried. They are likely to give answers they think will please their distinguished visitor.

Despite these drawbacks, lay Christians furnish a valuable source of information. They are realistic. They recount the reasons that impelled them and their intimates to become Christians. Their answers are not distorted by theological considerations and Western cultural overhang. If researchers want the whole truth, they ought to interview hundreds of lay persons who have been an integral part of the growth under study. The historical treatises and statistical summaries which are all that researchers working from books can manage are good; but new light will shine on the complex processes of growth when older members of a church, and the common people who make up its bulk tell why they became Christian.

For example, a researcher was investigating a fifty-year growth that had created a remarkable church of about 7,000, with 147 congregations, which met regularly for worship and had many educated members. As he chatted with the older men, illiterates all, he directed the conversation to the early days when they first became Christians. Again and again they mentioned police persecution.

"We were a rough lot before we became Christians," said a grizzled old man. "Because of our bad name, the police harassed us continually, much more than we deserved. They jailed our youth. They insulted our women. They made us give them rice and vegetables and forced us to carry their burdens to the next village without any pay. We had no recourse. After we became Christians, when we were innocent our pastors spoke up for us. Even our missionary sometimes pleaded our case. Then, too, we became better people and gradually got a good name. The police do not trouble us any more" (McGavran 1956).

Interviewers will use only some of the many lines of inquiry they know. They approach every new case with preconceived ideas as to why growth did or did not occur. These hypotheses form the basis of the questions. Some lines of inquiry will speedily prove useless; they do not fit the situation. They are not productive and should forthwith be dropped. Other angles of questioning, not contemplated at the beginning, will emerge and prove rewarding. These should then be continued and expanded.

For example, in doing a study of the United Church of Christ in the Philippines, I interviewed lay Christians in more than a hundred congregations. I soon stumbled across the fact that some congregations consisted largely of half families in which only one partner was Christian. Compared with those consisting mostly of full families, the half-family congregations were much less vigorous. As soon as I discerned this, I made finding out the number of full and half families in each congregation a prominent part of my research. The new line of inquiry yielded much understanding of the dynamics of growth.

RECENT CONVERTS

Recent converts are a rich source of insight. Within the past few years they have turned from the world to the Savior. What brought them is vivid in their minds. Whenever possible, I ask the pastor or missionary to arrange interviews with recent converts. The ideal way is to talk to them one by one, lest what the first one says influence subsequent informants. "Tell me how you became a Christian. I want the whole story. Take your time." Or "Tell us how your people became Christians. What were the main reasons?" As the narrative unfolds, the researcher should probe likely spots and follow up promising leads. "Do you have many non-Christian relatives? Well, what do they think about your becoming Christian? And what about becoming Christians themselves?"

When interviewing recent converts in Orissa I asked a young married woman what her parents thought of her being baptized.

"Last week, before the baptismal ceremony," she replied, "my husband and I went to see my parents fifteen miles east of here to tell them we intended to become Christians and to ask their permission. They granted it readily and said, 'After you are baptized come and tell us about Christ. We are thinking of following you in this way.'"

This one remark revealed volumes concerning the attitude toward Christianity of many in the caste that God had prepared for the journey to the promised land.

There is no better way of judging the vitality of a congregation than to ask its members how many non-Christian relatives they have and what these relatives think of the Christian religion. On one occasion we were visiting congregations that for some eight years had shown only biological growth. We felt the Christians were cold and the churches static. Then one day we asked a group of men whether they had any non-Christian relatives.

"Many," they replied promptly.

"And what do they think about becoming Christians?" we asked.

After a moment's surprised silence, they began to tell of cousins, uncles, in-laws, and others who in the past few weeks had spoken quite favorably about seeking baptism. Finally one man jumped to his feet. "In a village three miles from here," he said, "are a number of my relatives, who have been asking me about the Christian religion. Will you come with me and talk to them?"

On arrival we were surrounded by a crowd of about seventy-five who listened to the gospel intently, and ended up by enrolling as inquirers. Whenever relatives of Christians are talking among themselves about becoming Christians, no matter what the past record of the church, the harvest is ripe.

In short, information about church growth is common. In every land it lies all about us in the people we meet. Any pastor or missionary who searches for the factors that caused it will find out much about it.

SCRUTINIZE WRITINGS

Books furnish less information about church growth than people, and different kinds of books give different yields.

History and ethnography describe the matrix in which churches grow. They inform the reader about culture, customs, racial characteristics, and governments that condition those to whom the gospel is presented. Reading such books enables the Christian to speak intelligently to others. If well written, they are fascinating; but they say little or nothing about church growth.

Church and mission history and biography yield information of a different sort. They recount what missions and leaders have done. Yet because of the promotional bias of most such books and the fact that many missions have seen little church growth and have been engaged in doing things other than planting churches, such writings are not the mine of information one might expect.

Since understanding of church growth is being sought, background books of all kinds should be read, *with graphs of growth in hand.* Only when we have clearly in mind the real magnitude of the growth that has occurred, and its dates and changes, do we know what to look for and the times in which to search.

Unless one knows that between 1776 and, say, 1796 the enormously influential Anglican Church in the United States was suffering severe reverses because of its close connection with Britain, it is difficult to assess aright the remarkable growth of Baptist churches in those years. However, the political factor was not the only one. During those very years the Methodists were growing tremendously, despite the fact that Asbury and Coke were British missionaries.

Unless one knows that between 1907 and 1912 the churches in Gold Coast had a phenomenal growth, the cocoa boom, which opened up the back country at just that time, will not be seen as a likely contributing cause. Only when one sees the Pentecostal graph of growth shooting skyward for the cities of southern Brazil will it be possible to separate the great immigration into the cities of which history tells us from thousands of other occurrences, and see it as a growth factor. Only when one observes the slow growth obtained after 1916 by most old-line evangelical missions in Latin America, does their great swing to education starting at that time and recounted in their histories take on a sharp meaning.

We should apply our existing church growth knowledge as we read. With its aid we will see implications we would otherwise miss. What we read will in turn correct our existing knowledge and add to it. When we read of the Seventh Day Adventist people movement to Christ around 1920, led by Camacho from among his fellow Aymara Indians living near Lake Titicaca in Peru, we will recognize how important it is for Aymara Indians under their own Aymara leaders to turn to Christ in social units, and will thus add to our understanding of the way in which the social situation affects growth. When we read of the considerable initial growth of the church that has been won by the school approach in Africa, our previous opinion, based on experience in India, that mission schools very seldom lead students to become Christians, will be modified. We will conclude that under some African circumstances the Christian school is a good beginning for the Christianization of tribes.

Articles in church magazines have limited value. Their promotional bias is overwhelming, and save in reporting great growth in progress, they seldom mention the subject. Nevertheless, articles should be scanned. There is a small amount of gold in these sands also.

Letters are an excellent source of understanding—an original source, very close to the actual happening. Their historical value is high. Some missionary societies have microfilmed all their correspondence from the field and will make it available to responsible researchers. In many cases letters show to what an extraordinary extent missionaries and field administrators deal with secondary matters—personnel problems, disagreements between staff members, finances, new buildings, repairs, and the like. Nevertheless, here and there letters yield shining nuggets and are worth careful perusal. They are our chief source for knowledge of clashes of opinion as to vital policies. Letters from Korea, for example, in the first decade of the twentieth century document the determination of missionaries in northwest Korea, when the church was growing apace, to concentrate on church growth. They actually fought against accepting funds to build a big hospital, feeling it would shift the main emphasis from discipling Koreans to healing their diseases.

Denominational and mission minutes are readily available and furnish a rich source of information concerning policies and people that have affected church growth. Frequently surging growth has followed church or mission action in occupying a new area where a few hundred have already become Christian. Conversely, moving a pastor or missionary who has led hundreds to Christ to a "more important" post in administration or seminary has frequently damaged and sometimes arrested a promising movement.

Budget distributions in congregations, denominations, and missions should be scrutinized. They reveal true long-range goals and indicate where the actual emphasis of the church or mission lies. At a glance the researcher can discern both the philosophy and the main drives of the organization being studied. The inner meanings of budget headings should be taken into account. "Student work" is commonly listed under evangelism; in some cases correctly so. In other cases, however, student work is simply shepherding Christian students and wins no one to Christ.

DISCOUNTING ERRONEOUS OPINIONS

Many pronouncements about church growth are rationalizations. These are normal in any walk of life, but should be recognized and discounted in soberly assessing the increase of the church.

In Japan in 1889 when the government, disappointed in its efforts to secure treaty revision, made an about-face and took a hard line toward the West, the wonderful Presbyterian and Congregational church growth stopped short. The communicant memberships of these two churches remained for many years at about 10,000 each. Missionary writings after the standstill are full of defensive thinking. They see "elements of encouragement in the situation." Earlier gains were not entirely lost. The rolls were purged of the half-hearted. A higher conception of the Christian life evolved. Great caution was exercised in admitting applicants. Missions gained a more realistic conception of the task and perceived that the church had entered a more mature stage of its existence! (Thomas 1959:209).

All these are rationalizations. The Christian cause had suffered a disastrous reversal and leaders were looking around for crumbs of comfort.

Methodological reasons for growth, when unduly stressed, should be questioned. For example, A. W. Wasson in the last chapter of his fine study *Church Growth in Korea* (1934) ascribed growth in the early thirties to the agricultural emphasis of Methodist missions. Yet when we observe that Methodist growth was relatively small, while Presbyterian Pyongan growth—where there was no agricultural emphasis at all—was large, we suspect that the agricultural emphasis (which, being the latest thing in missions, was sweeping around the world at the time) was at best a minor cause of whatever growth occurred among the Methodists.

Theological reasons *by themselves* should often be questioned. For example, a missionary writes, "The church in that district has never flourished. Faith in Christ and willingness to stand persecution for his name seemed high in the first thousand converts, but must really have not existed at all because many reverted to their former faith." A theological reason for reversion is adduced: their faith was not deep and sincere. This may have been the case, but a conversion that separated from race and kin, lack of skill in shepherding, environmental pressures, and downright

neglect have so often played dominant parts in reversions that one hesi-
tates to believe that the theological reason was the only one.

A pastor in Texas wrote, "Among the Pentecostals, joyous abandonment to the Lord and unquestioning obedience to the Bible have been the
means whereby thousands have come to a living relationship with him."
One may rejoice that these Christian graces have been found in considerable measure among Pentecostal Christians and yet observe that many
environmental or contextual factors have also played significant roles in
their growth.

If we would understand church growth we must always assume mul-
tiple causes for each spurt of growth or period of retardation. When we
have discovered one cause we should search for others. That is why this
chapter has described many causes and sources, each likely to add further
understanding. Keith Hamilton (1963:138) points out that the reasons for
church growth not only vary from case to case but are combined in different proportions in each. Hamilton, borrowing from the art of cooking,
says that ingredients of growth are mixed in different proportions in each
case. This is true, and the principle applies not only to different denominations and missions, but also within the same church or mission, to its
different periods and homogeneous units.

The principle of ingredients combined in varying proportions may be
clearly seen in the New Testament churches. During its first expansion—
from Pentecost until about A.D. 48—it grew mostly among Palestinian
Jews. The intense people-consciousness of this population, its conviction
of being the chosen people of God, the firm belief in (Old Testament)
Scripture, personal knowledge of Jesus of Nazareth, common Aramaic
language, and longing for release from the Roman yoke were dominant
human factors on which the Holy Spirit breathed to create, all through the
hill country, a multitude of Christian congregations that continued strictly
to obey the Jewish law.

During the second expansion—from about A.D. 48 to the death of the
apostle Paul—the church grew vigorously in the synagogue communities
of the Diaspora. In this population, in addition to some of the factors mentioned above that operated in lesser measure, new factors came into play.
For example, God fearers in multitudes became Christians. These syn-
agogue-attending Gentiles were strongly attracted to the high morality
and monotheism of Judaism but repelled by circumcision, food taboos,
and other externals of the law. When they learned they could be saved by
faith in Jesus Christ without assuming the burden of the law, and saw that
in Christ men and women become new creatures who manifest the fruits

of the Spirit, they became ardent members of the church and joyfully propagated the gospel among their non-Christian—and non-Jewish—relatives and friends. It was the same church that was growing, but the factors in the second expansion differed from those in the first and were combined in different proportions. The source for this understanding of church growth is the New Testament itself.

9

HELPS AND HINDRANCES TO UNDERSTANDING

CANADIAN, AMERICAN, and European readers should study this chapter with care. It will be most rewarding to them. They will discover many helps and hindrances to understanding that dog their footsteps and cloud their perceptions. As they read, however, they should resolve to translate these insights from the world of mission into thought forms that fit the Western scene. In this chapter all the illustrations are from the Third World. Because of this let no one say, "These have no meaning for me. I work in Chicago or Berlin."

The principles are universal. They apply in every continent and almost every culture. Take, for instance, the first illustration below. The principle there presented is that rapid growth is often considered disreputable by those not getting growth. To illustrate this I quote the remark of a missionary to China to the effect that 100 percent growth a decade would create not a church but a madhouse. American readers will at once recognize that such self-justifying judgments are constantly being made by notable leaders about their static or declining congregations and are a serious hindrance to understanding, in Europe and America as well as elsewhere.

Again the illuminating lessons illustrated by the Baptist/Mennonite case history will focus the American reader's attention on the large receptive units of society in a particular city or state. A little work is being done among these. Slight growth—when worked for—is granted. More would be if the church counted this receptive society as a pearl of great price and . . . single-mindedly did those things which multiply churches in it.

The point need not be labored. Illustrations from the mission field may indeed help Western readers make far more applications than could possibly be printed here.

GROWTH-ARRESTING CONCEPTS

Many concepts current in the missionary world inhibit the discipling of the nations. They sound plausible, but they hinder and damage the only growth the churches are achieving or are likely to achieve. They cloud the issues, sap the will to ingathering, and impose on the entire missionary enterprise methods and theology generated in static areas. As nationals and missionaries are exposed to these concepts, the passion of Christ for the salvation of the world, which once filled them and thrust them out to disciple the nations, grows cold. Resolute action gives way to debate. The will to heal is supplanted by the will to polish the surgical instruments. This noxious miasma spreads equally to liberals and evangelicals and weakens the ability of both to bring people to faith and obedience. To recognize these half-true and hurtful ideas and see how they have become influential is necessary if we are to break their grip on the missionary mind.

GLORIFYING SLOW GROWTH

Growth-arresting concepts arise in several ways. First, churches in their amazing spread all over the world have carried on work in many areas where people have not believed, and where inch-by-inch progress has been the only sort achieved. Evangelistic methods congenial to slow growth have developed. Theologies have been formulated, ostensibly built on Scripture but actually arising from the debris of decades of rejection, which demand that mission be carried on in the expectation that the church will grow very moderately. To look askance at rapid growth is orthodox in areas of inch-by-inch operation; rapid growth is regarded as more or less disreputable.

A noted leader whose experience had been in a Chinese church growing at a DGR (decadal growth rate) of 13 percent exclaimed, "If growing
at the sound conservative pace we are, we have such terrific difficulties
developing a real church among these people, a galloping 100 percent a
decade increase would create not a church but a madhouse." In areas
where growth has been slow, whether because of the resistance of the
population or the mistakes of the church, opinions like the following are
often voiced:

1. We do sound work and are not interested in shortcuts.

2. It takes decades to grow an oak. A pumpkin grows in a single
summer.

3. God takes his own time to make a sound church.

4. The field, maintained at great cost and agony over many years,
often proves to be the seedbed from which a rich harvest is finally reaped.

5. Soundness of growth, not rapidity, is the criterion.

These concepts *assume* that good growth is necessarily slow and that
length of labor guarantees the excellence of the product. Nothing in the
Bible or the growth of the New Testament churches supports this assumption. Modern industry or education would laugh at it. That these concepts
have achieved almost the sanctity of Scripture in many Christian circles
may be credited to a prolonged experience of rejection—not to their accuracy. For it does indeed take courage to hold on in the face of rejection,
a courage that instinctively needs reassurance as to its own rightness.

Sentiments such as item 4 above are frequently expressed by those
whose labors have brought few to Christ. For example, Baptist missiologists know that their South India missionaries, whose story we told previously, after hanging on for twenty-five years during which very few
believed, baptized 2,222 converts in a single day! The church increased
by 10,000 in a few months! Yet when the facts are known, this remarkable outcome does *not* support the theory that "the field maintained at
great cost over many years often proves the seedbed of rich harvest." On
the contrary, the Baptist field maintained for twenty-five years in the face
of minute church growth was that of the high-caste Hindus in and around
Nellore. The harvest came only when young John Clough, leaving this
field in the hands of the older missionaries, pressed on to Ongole, and
started a new field by baptizing Madiga Untouchables.

The fallacy in the common inhibiting concept that length of occupation automatically brings growth at last is that of supposing that the church
grows in a geographical area, when as a matter of fact it always grows in
people themselves—usually a homogeneous unit of society. The upper-

caste homogeneous unit worked by the first Baptist missionaries was precisely the one where length of labor did *not* bring forth a rich harvest, nor would it have, had they remained there a hundred years. The Madiga homogeneous unit, which had not been worked for long years at great cost and agony, was the one where Clough reaped a rich harvest.

However, a measure of truth underlines some of the opinions arising in areas of slow growth. It is true that after seed has been sown, time for germination and maturation must be allowed. In the world of farming, harvest usually comes four months after sowing. In world evangelization, it need cause no surprise that some years should elapse between sowing and harvest. But this must not be used to justify continued tiny growth in populations where other churches are increasing by leaps and bounds, while secular ideologies and pagan religions also flourish. There is nothing biblical or spiritual about very slow progress in itself. Sometimes it must be endured, but there is no reason to canonize it.

Remnant Theology

Second, concepts inhibiting to growth arise where Christian missions have suffered not merely slow growth but decades of defeat. Failure is always difficult to bear. How can they neglect so great a salvation? How can they reject the one who died for them? When decade after decade they do, God's obedient servants, believing in his sovereignty and finding it hard to see themselves at fault, wonder whether God himself wants church growth. In the history of Israel, they ask, do we not see again and again the crucial importance of the remnant? Was there not a time when the real "church" was the paltry seven thousand who had not bowed the knee to Baal? Did not our Lord say that many are called but few are chosen and ask whether, when he returned, he would find faith on the earth?

Remnant theology proves attractive. A glorification of littleness prevails, in which to be small is to be holy. Slow growth is adjudged good growth. Concepts and slogans such as the following are born in these beleaguered outposts of the church:

1. The tiny minority suffering for its belief is the true church.

2. To create this minority is the highest success known to missions.

3. The persecuted church, the church under the cross, is the true church.

4. The power of a small group of believers, with God, must never be underestimated.

5. The creative minority is what the church must ever strive to be.

Under some conditions, for some churches, and in certain ways these concepts are surely true and helpful. Our Lord did say that his disciples were yeast—just a tiny pinch of yeast hidden in a large lump of dough; but the force of the metaphor is precisely that the yeast multiplies exceedingly. The virtue of the yeast lies not in its littleness but in its amazing ability to grow. The yeast cells multiply and ramify into every part of the dough. The minority, if it is to be creative, must not only generate productive ideas but convert the majority to them. It must grow.

Furthermore, even if we were to take the passages from the Bible to which I have alluded, without, for the time being, balancing them against many others which affirm that God desires the salvation of multitudes—still, is it not fallacious to assume that the 1,000 Christians in our congregations are exactly *the* few chosen? Our field has, let us say, a population of 7,000,000 souls. Out of these might not perhaps a church of 200,000 (only one thirty-fifth of the population) be the few our Lord was referring to? If so, should we not seek the remaining 199,000 who have been chosen by the Lord, and induct them into his church? How can we possibly maintain that our thousand constitutes all of God's elect?

All Christians agree that they should be passionately concerned that the church be a real church—made up of committed Christians; but if we make a *small* company our goal, are we true to him who preached the gospel to multitudes? And if we make a *select* company the goal, is there not some danger that we become pharisaical and holier-than-thou? Is to be a Christian an ethical achievement—or a redemptive relationship to Jesus Christ? In view of the three billion who have yet to believe, do we do well, in unbiblical fashion, to exalt littleness?

True, when a church is suffering for Christ's sake or is hemmed in by an overwhelming multitude of gospel-rejectors, it can correctly take comfort in the thought that, under persecution, its chief duty is to remain faithful, confident that such faithfulness is not measured by numbers. This truth, however, ought not to be stretched to affirm that when the Lord commands sheaves to be brought out of ripe harvest fields, the chief duty of Christians is to pray in a shady corner of the field. It would have been a great pity had the churches in Indonesia in 1966 and 1967 permitted their will to share salvation with their Muslim and pagan neighbors to be eroded by growth-arresting glorifications of littleness.

Discipling and Perfecting

Third, antigrowth concepts arise from confusing perfecting with discipling. This confusion has been compounded by a sudden proliferation of meanings for the verb *to disciple*. Standard dictionaries do not list *disciple* as a verb; but I started using it as a verb in 1955 in *The Bridges of God*. There it meant helping a people (a segment of *non-Christian* society) turn from non-Christian faith to Christ. Discipling was to be followed by perfecting, that is, by the whole complex process of growth in grace, ethical improvement, and the conversion of individuals in that first and succeeding generations.

The new English verb *to disciple* proved attractive. Shortly after 1970 it began to be used for the process by which individuals in any society (Christian or non-Christian) first became Christian. And then it was used for the entirely different process by which existing Christians become illuminated, thoroughly dedicated followers of Christ.

To clarify these three meanings the May 1979 issue of *Church Growth Bulletin* printed a lead article, entitled "How About that New Verb *To Disciple*?" In that I set forth three meanings of the verb: D-1, D-2, and D-3. D-1 would mean the turning of a non-Christian society for the first time to Christ. D-2 would mean the turning of individuals from nonfaith to faith in Christ and their incorporation into a church. D-3 would mean teaching an existing Christian as many of the truths of the Bible as possible.

Stages in the growth of a church are as distinct as stages in the growth of a child, a fact frequently missed by those educated in the West. They themselves see only one stage—perfecting (D-3)—and advocate policies suited to it as if these were applicable at every point of the church's development and in every society and culture. The church that stands on the edge of a great D-1 opportunity where tens of thousands of its kindred are friendly to the idea of becoming Christian, has a God-given duty to disciple. In such a situation, any perfecting done must above all inculcate that mind of Christ which sought—and seeks—the salvation of all. A premature perfecting that lifts educational attainments, increases earning ability, heightens conscience as to social justice, and decreases concern to win kindred to eternal life, betrays the gospel. High secular and social attainments must not be mistaken for dedication to Christ.

The constant improvement of the existing church (D-3) is mandatory on all Christians. God commands it and the church will languish without it. No one should minimize the importance of perfecting. At the same time, all should be certain that undiscipled pagan multitudes must be added to

the Lord before they can be perfected. The church exists not for herself
but for the world. She has been saved in order to save others. She always
has a twofold task: winning unbelievers to Christ and growing in grace.
While these tasks overlap, they are distinct. Neither should be slighted.
Today's great vision, which calls the churches to rectify injustices in their
neighborhoods and nations, is good; but it must not supplant the vision
that calls them to make disciples of all nations.

Confusion at this point gives rise to many ideas that are antagonistic
and stunting to growth. Let us consider a few. A missiologist writes, "A
church may grow in numbers, and yet has the church grown—as a
church?" Of course it has. Its churchhood arises from its relationship to
Jesus Christ and does not vanish simply because it is deficient in some
duty or other.

For many years the church of Jesus Christ coexisted quite comfort-
ably with slavery. This social evil cannot have been pleasing to God. It
has brought incalculable sorrow and loss to human beings. Yet, despite
that, the church existed and spread abroad. Indeed, only because it spread
enormously and gained tremendous political power was it able for the first
time in history to end slavery. Wherever non-Christians believe in Jesus
Christ, are baptized in his name, accept the Bible as their rule of faith and
practice, and manifest the fruits of the Spirit, there a new branch of the
real church is born. The power of Jesus Christ becomes available to its
members. They live on a higher plane. That they may not live in some respects as we think they ought is regrettable, but in no way vitiates the fact
that the church *as a church* has grown.

"The scandal of third world churches is that the lives of their members are a constant stumbling block to their non-Christian neighbors.
They cannot grow in size till they grow in holiness. They cannot go
further till they go deeper." There can be no question about the need of
all churches to go deeper. The statement, therefore, sounds plausible,
but nonetheless is simply not true. The least perfected church is superior to its non-Christian origins. Congregations as they are—so imper-
fectly showing forth glories—are constantly going further. Indeed, in
many cases the congregations that grow best are those that have most
contact with their kindred and neighbors—are most solid with the
world—though they as yet neither have as much knowledge of the Bible
nor manifest as many fruits of the Spirit as favored congregations of
highly sanctified Christians.

What of the Motives?

As the gospel is proclaimed, people sometimes seek to become Christians from unworthy motives. Particularly when the preacher is an affluent Westerner, supposed to be making a living by getting people to become Christians, it is natural that some should confess Christ through love of money rather than love of Christ. Having no spiritual thirst, nor belief in the Savior, nor experience of sins forgiven, such "converts" get what they can from the missionary and then, when they can get no more, cease claiming to be Christians. Every church leader does well to beware of such frauds.

On the other hand, those who proclaim the good news and welcome women and men to salvation must also beware lest their suspicions deter those groping their way toward salvation. Our Lord took twelve whose chief motivation for three years was that of sharing in his glory when he drove the Romans into the sea—and turned them into apostles. Furthermore, while the physical needs of the poor and oppressed are more clamant, their spiritual needs are more basic. We dare not give rice freely for the belly and withhold the pure milk of the gospel from the soul. It is hard to know whether to list examination of motives among would-be converts as a help or hindrance to church growth.

Waskom Pickett in *Christian Mass Movements in India* devotes a chapter to this important subject. Among many valuable emphases are these:

> The subject of motives is always difficult. . . . Its consideration encounters much prejudice and excites strong feeling. Many Christians think it necessary to examine with great care the motives of all who seek entrance to the Christian Church. . . . Others fearful of placing themselves in the position of a judge, take the attitude that whosoever will may come, and while trying to stimulate motives that they consider proper, scrupulously refrain from prying beneath the voluntary declaration of the inquirer (Pickett 1933:155).

He goes on to point out, however, that

> the gospel often awakens in the mind of the receptive hearer a desire for self improvement and a fuller, as well as a better life, appreciation of kindnesses shown him, hope of escape from century-old wrongs previously endured without question, and ambition for his children. . . . Some of us see in the desire of Sweepers . . . to be treated like respectable people, to secure for their children some other work than the cleaning of cesspools and privies, and to obtain help against oppression, not

evidence of unworthy motives, but, rather, support for their claim that they have admitted Jesus to their midst (Pickett 1933:157).

Pickett's most startling finding about motives, however, and one that relates most to church growth, concerns the bearing that motives have on Christian achievements. He interviewed 3,947 individuals, examining them closely about their reasons for becoming Christian and ascertaining their attainments in the Christian faith. Four kinds of motives were distinguished, and respondents were placed in four groups according to their answers.

In Group 1 (spiritual motives) are placed all those whose answers had been recorded under the heads: "seeking salvation," "convinced by the preacher," "to know God," "to find peace," "because of faith in Jesus."

In Group 2 (secular motives) are placed all those giving answers such as "sought help of the missionaries," "in hope of education for children," "for improved social standing," "because landowners oppressed us," "to marry a Christian girl."

In Group 3 (social reasons) we put all those giving answers such as "family was being baptized," "My people told me to do so," "I did not want to remain a Hindu when my relatives were Christian."

In Group 4 (natal influences) we put those whose replies were entered as "child of Christian parents," i.e. who were brought up in the Christian faith . . . (Pickett 1933:164).

Attainments were measured in eleven areas: knowledge of the Lord's Prayer, Apostles' Creed, and Ten Commandments, Sabbath observance, church membership, church attendance, frequency of services, support of the church, freedom from idolatry charms and sorcery, nonparticipation in non-Christian festivals, freedom from fear of evil spirits, Christian marriage, and use of intoxicating beverages.

Pickett points out that, as might be expected, those who became Christians from spiritual motives had slightly higher attainment than those who came from secular and social motives. The great surprise in his findings, however, was the small degree of difference between the Christian attainments of those who came from spiritual, secular, and social motives. Whether they had good postbaptismal training made more difference in their attainments than the motives from which they became Christian.

Possibly the result most worthy of emphasis . . . is the encouraging attainments of converts listed in Groups 2 and 3 (those who came from secular or social motives). The smallness of the margin between Groups 1 (spiritual motives) and 2 (secular motives), we venture to say, will surprise many who have not supposed that *a purely secular motive* such as the desire for help against oppression, *may lead to conversion* and a wholesome productive religious experience. Likewise the nearness of Group 3 (social motives) in many of these tests to Group 1 (spiritual motives) will surprise people who have not discovered how *God uses social forces to bring men under the influence of the gospel.*

We find that 70 per cent of the men who say they became Christian for some motive not accounted spiritual and 75 per cent of those who declare that they became Christians because others of their family or caste did so, have become regular attendants at church services. We also find that the homes of 93.2 per cent of the former and 94.8 per cent of the latter are free from all signs of idolatry; that 90.5 per cent of the former and 91.2 per cent of the latter contribute to the church . . . (Pickett 1933:168).

In any revival or expansion of the church, leaders asking themselves, "Should we admit these converts who know so little of Christ and yet have determined to follow him?" should know of Pickett's findings. The more spiritual the motive the better, but when groups turn to Christ, the care they receive after baptism and the excellence of the shepherding have more to do with Christian attainments than the motives that operated to bring them to follow Christ.

THERE COMES A TIDE WHICH TAKEN AT THE FLOOD

Connected with motives is the important question of when to allow the decisive act that breaks a convert's connection with the former religion and admits them to the Christian community. This may be a burning of fetishes, cutting of hair, throwing away of charms, or performance of some other symbolic act. Baptism, according to the rules of the church in that place, may take place immediately (and *it* may be the decisive act), or it may take place at the close of six months or a year after an examination testing sufficiency of knowledge.

I am not asking when baptism should take place or how long prebaptismal instruction should last. I am asking when the church planter should allow the decisive act by which a person renounces his or her former faith and declares for Christ. If the evangelist is indecisive at this point and does not know what to do, opportunity to reconcile men and women to God may pass.

We have seen the decisive act by which 8,000 Dani tribespeople in Irian Jaya burned all their fetishes and decided to follow the new Jesus way. James Sunda in recounting it remarks that many missionaries of the four missions concerned did not know whether to permit the fetish burning or not. One in fact "tried to dispel the crowd and run off 'the false teacher.'" "Some opposed, some approved, and some did not understand fully what was going on." Fortunately the Dani knew what they were going to do! They understood the meaning of a power encounter. "A notable thing about the whole affair is the fact that while the missionaries debated the issue, large groups of Dani continued to burn their charms" (Sunda 1963:31).

A different and tragic drama (for the details of which I am indebted to Bishop Pickett, who knew the persons concerned) was enacted at Mirzapur, an ancient Indian city near Benares. The London Missionary Society had maintained missionaries there from the first half of the nineteenth century, but the church had not grown. Mirzapur was a typical mission station in resistant territory; converts were few and far between, and most Christians were employed by the mission or the missionaries.

In the early years of the twentieth century, three unusual missionaries found themselves at Mirzapur. A. W. McMillan, an educator and a splendid Urdu speaker, who later went to Fiji as head of the Indian Educational Service there. Robert Ashland, a physician, established clinics and dispensaries and spent himself treating malaria, smallpox, typhoid, and other diseases. John Grant, a minister, was a specialist in cooperative credit societies.

During the incumbency of these three, the notable receptivity that had enabled thousands of Indians belonging to the depressed classes to hear and obey the gospel, reached Mirzapur district. For the first time, following Christ became a real option to the Chamars there. They had been exposed to the gospel for years, but God had now touched their ears and they were hearing it. In short, the Holy Spirit had moved upon the *biradari* (the Chamar brotherhood).

Their leaders came to the missionaries and said, "We want to become Christians in groups, as a caste, by clusters of families, and by *mohullahs* (wards). We are tired of Hinduism. We will abandon our idols. What power is there in these stones? Christianity is the true religion. We believe on Jesus Christ. We do not know much about him, but are willing to learn. Will you accept us as Christians, teach us, baptize us, and help us?" These Chamars were ready for the decisive act. They wanted to declare for Christ.

The three missionaries spent hours with the leaders and satisfied themselves that these men spoke for considerable numbers of Chamars. They were leaders and would be followed. However, they knew pitifully little about Christ and were undoubtedly motivated by desire for education for their children and emancipation from their deplorably low status.

McMillan, Ashland, and Grant, talking the situation over, came to the conclusion that the Chamars wanted to become Christian because they were poor, sick, and ignorant. They were heavily in debt. Their children could not attend the town schools. They had no hope. These are not good reasons to become Christians. Let us first minister to their needs and then let them decide for spiritual reasons to become Christians.

So they built schools to which untouchable boys and girls could come. They established dispensaries in their midst and made them welcome at the mission hospital. They organized cooperative credit societies and redeemed many Chamars from perpetual indebtedness to the rapacious moneylenders.

After some years the lot of the Chamars improved noticeably, and the missionaries said words to this effect: "Now you see what Christianity is and what it is doing. Now you are not driven by hunger, sickness, and debt. It is time now for us to admit you to the Christian faith. Let us talk about the next step in advance, discipleship to Jesus Christ and adherence to the true religion."

"Oh," replied the Chamar leaders, "we did not know that you knew anything about religion. You are wonderful in education, medicine, and cooperative credit societies. We are deeply indebted to you. You are our saviors; but about religion, we have our own untouchable religious leaders, you know, and they would not be happy if we became Christians. To tell the truth, we have changed our mind about becoming Christians."

Some years after this the London Missionary Society withdrew from Mirzapur and turned the station over to the Bible Churchman's Missionary Society, which was still working there in 1960. Thus two missionary societies carried on work in that ancient city for more than a hundred years, and at the end of a century of work the congregation in Mirzapur was still a gathered-colony church of about two hundred, many of them employed by the church (which used to be called the mission).

Had the decisive act been allowed, indeed encouraged, Mirzapur, like hundreds of Indian towns, might today be the headquarters of a church numbering thousands, living in their ancestral homes in a hundred towns and villages round about. Such a church would have continued whether the mission remained or not. If McMillan, Ashland, and Grant had allowed this numerous caste to opt for Christ, had fed the catechumens on the word, and shepherded them in the way, Mirzapur might have proved to be the seedbed of a rich harvest. Church growth often depends on when harvesting fields are ripe.

COMPARATIVE STUDY OF GROWTH ACROSS THE CHURCHES

In these days, study of the growth of churches other than our own is not merely possible but highly desirable. No one can afford to neglect the comparative study of church growth. It uncovers a rich vein of knowledge concerning how churches grow, and increases understanding of God's purposes for his church and the methods he is blessing to their increase.

The basic methodology for study of other churches is the same as that used in studying one's own. Secure accurate figures for communicant membership and other pertinent data across the years. Refine the data to eliminate statistical errors and redefinitions. Make sure all figures are for the same geographical unit. Draw accurate graphs portraying growth histories. Dig out from histories, biographies, interviews, and reports the reasons for growth or decline shown in the graph for each denomination. More accurate findings are obtained if one gets figures for the separate homogeneous units in each church. Check all thinking about church growth against the graphs.

Compare churches growing in the same kind of population—not those in different kinds. Churches in African Muslim tribes cannot be fruitfully compared with those growing in African pagan tribes; but churches and their assisting missions evangelizing animist tribes are quite comparable. If they are evangelizing sections of the same tribe, the comparison will be even more fruitful. This principle should always be observed, but within reason, for no two populations are ever exactly the same.

For example, Loren Noren's figures for the churches at work in Hong Kong show that during the fifties Anglicans were growing at 90 percent, Baptists at 120 percent, and Lutherans of the Missouri Synod at 420 percent (Noren 1963:6). Before this interesting information can convey much church growth meaning, we shall have to know which of the many populations in Hong Kong each denomination was working with. Were Baptists working in one or several populations? Did Anglicans grow among the middle class while Lutherans grew among refugees? Noren does not say, but when his fine beginning is carried further, the information should be given. Only for churches working in similar populations can significant comparisons be made.

Two very useful findings result from comparative study. First, we can form objective judgments about the responsiveness of populations. Estimates of responsiveness are of crucial importance to church planters. If the population to which God sends missionaries is stony hard, then they should properly do those things that will enable them to hang on, bearing whatever limited witness possible. If the population is warmly responsive, it is sinful merely to hang on. The task is to disciple.

How does one know whether a population is responsive? The science of cultural anthropology has learned much about societal conditions in which people are restless for change. The developing technology relating to diffusion of innovation and marketing research is providing helpful clues. The experience of the church indicates that immigrants in a new country, migrants to a city, societies suffering from deprivation or shock, and the oppressed hear and obey the gospel more readily than contented beneficiaries of the social order.

But the surest and simplest way to know whether a population is responsive is to observe whether others working in it are enjoying church growth. Has God blessed the labors of any group here to the growth of his church? If so, the population in which that mission labored is responsive. In the last century Bishop Thoburn of India, observing that Baptist, Lutheran, and Anglican churches were growing greatly from among the untouchables, advised Methodists as he traveled among them on his episcopal duties to pay special attention to these victims of the Hindu social order. The subsequent growth of Methodist churches in several provinces of India is directly traceable to Thoburn's correct observation that the untouchables were responsive.

To be sure, when a segment of society is large, there is no guarantee that all parts of it will be equally responsive. Degrees of responsiveness vary. For example, among the four million Hispanics in the Los Angeles area, those recently arrived are much more responsive than those whose grandparents came here seventy years ago.

Second, comparative study tells us what methods God is blessing to the increase of his church. We do not have to guess. Finding a denomination or even a cluster of congregations that is growing, we observe what Christian leaders there are doing. Theorizing about causes of church growth can be eliminated. Estimates of what ought to work can be dismissed. We can see what has been done and measure the degree of growth that has followed.

J. B. A. Kessler in his fine study of the Protestant churches in Chile and Peru feels that the great growth of the Adventists in Peru is in large part due to their excellent program of indoctrination of catechumens and second- and third-generation Christians (Kessler 1967:225). Herbert Money, noted authority on Peru, agrees with him.

Many missionaries, deterred by honest reservations about the soundness of Adventist theology, might hesitate to seek growth "in the Adventist way"; but if Kessler and Money are right, and Adventist growth in Peru can be credited in large part to effective teaching of what they consider essential to salvation, why could not any Christian, copying this part of the Adventist program, *teach effectively* what *they* considered essential to salvation? It will be found that, contrary to the presuppositions of many, many causes of growth are nontheological. Anyone can use them.

Protestant diversity in all six continents constitutes a rich source of insight. The hundreds of different missions and thousands of different homogeneous unit churches are in reality God's vast laboratory, in which those with eyes can see numerous experiments in church growth going on. Some procedures are accompanied by no growth. Others multiply cells of Christians under certain conditions. Still others propagate the gospel very satisfactorily. The church leaders should train themselves to see the many different varieties of growth and the many factors that play a significant part in each. Then they should resolutely seek the people whom God has prepared, and use those methods of proclaiming and persuading on which God has put his seal of approval.

10

REVIVAL AND CHURCH GROWTH

WHAT IS REVIVAL?

REVIVAL BEARS a close relationship to church growth; yet exactly what that relationship is, particularly where the church is growing on new ground, is not clear to many. Under certain conditions revival may be said to cause growth. Under others, its relationship to church growth is so distant that apparently revival occurs without growth and growth without revival. Careful consideration of the subject is necessary if we are to understand the function of each in God's purpose of redemption.

To begin with, revival is a word that has many connotations. To the elite it may signify a distasteful trait of frontier life and lower-class denominations. Some, who understand reality chiefly through their intellects, think of it as an emotional orgy that creates an illusion of spiritual well-being and leaves congregations much as they were before. Many social action partisans tend to feel that revivals are the antithesis of responsible Christian conduct. To many, the word means merely large accessions to the church, or a period of increased interest in religion. Whenever large numbers are converted, they would say that a "revival" has occurred. To most Christians a revival means primarily purifying and vitalizing the existing church. For certain thoughtful historians, it is one of God's principal means for vivifying his church and carrying out his program of justice, mercy, and world evangelization.

No one knows more about revivals or has studied them across the world and written more extensively about them than the late J. Edwin Orr. He equates revivals with evangelical awakenings and defines them as follows:

> An Evangelical Awakening is a movement of the Holy Spirit in the Church of Christ bringing about a revival of New Testament Christianity. Such an awakening may change in a significant way an individual only; or it may affect a larger group of people; or it may move a congregation, or the churches of a city or district, or the whole body of believers throughout a country or continent; or indeed the larger body of believers throughout the world. Such an awakening may run its course briefly, or it may last a whole lifetime (Orr 1965:265).

This history of revivals has shown that two principal preconditions of revival or evangelical awakening are prayer and feeding on God's word. Let us look at them.

1. Prayer

While an evangelical awakening is a movement of the Holy Spirit in the church of Christ and thus depends on the initiative of almighty God, it is usually granted to those who pray earnestly for it. In hundreds of instances, prayer has brought revival. The pattern is the same: first intense prayer, often long continued, then revival. Orr illustrates the point:

> Early in the year 1858 the wave of revival (which originated in the east) passed over the crest of the Appalachian system of mountains and poured down the Ohio Valley following the line of settlements established by the pioneers. . . . Union prayer meetings were soon launched in Kentucky's big city [Louisville], secular journalists observing that the meetings were growing so that it was impossible for the Y.M.C.A. premises to accommodate the crowds. . . . In early April, four popular prayer meetings attracted the crowds to the Masonic Temple, the Mechanics Library, the Key Engine House, and the Relief Engine House. A report on April 5th stated that "an immense concourse" had entirely filled the Masonic Temple. . . . Revival had already commenced in Lexington, Covington, Frankfort, and other towns throughout the state. . . .

In Cincinnati, attendance at the daily prayer meeting became so large that the venue chosen was unable to accommodate the crowds. . . . In Cleveland, in population forty thousand, the attendance at the early morning prayer meetings throughout the city churches was two thousand. . . . Noonday prayer meetings were begun in Indianapolis. . . . (Orr 1965:119ff.).

Prayer for revival is no mere American phenomenon. All through the British Isles on numerous occasions prayer has brought revival. Here is an illustration from Scotland:

In the middle of August 1859, the Revival became news in Glasgow with all the suddenness of a summer thunderstorm. . . . The noon prayer meetings gave rise to prayer meetings and preaching services in the various evangelical churches on week nights, and in these meetings there were scores of reported conversions. After a year of the movement, Glasgow was still enjoying "times of refreshing" (Orr 1965:134).

Prayer for revival is the essential first step. Time would fail were examples from country after country to be presented. One from the great 1907 revival in Korea will suffice:

It paid well to have spent several months in prayer, for when God the Holy Spirit came, He accomplished more in half a day than all of us missionaries could have accomplished in half a year. In less than two months more than two thousand heathen were converted. It is always so as soon as God gets first place; but, as a rule, the Church which professes to be Christ's, will not cease her busy round of activities and give God a chance by waiting on Him in prayer (Goforth 1943:12).

Revival is God's gift. Human beings can neither command it nor make God grant it. God sovereignly gives revival when and where he wills. It "breaks out," "strikes," "quickens a church," "comes with the suddenness of a summer storm," "makes its appearance," "inaugurates a work of grace," and "blesses his people." But God responds to sincere continued prayer. Prayer is what God wants his people to offer. "Ask and it will be given to you, seek and you will find, knock and it will be opened to you."

2. Feeding on God's Word

Knowledge of the Bible is also necessary. It does not invariably lead to revival; but unless it is there, revival in the classic sense does not usually occur. Revivals in the churches of Europe and America were preceded by long years of careful reading of the Bible in homes and churches. The Korean revival owed much of its power to the thorough Bible study that formed an integral part of the Presbyterian Church's regimen from the days of its inception in 1895. Elder Keel, whose story is related in the next section, would not have known that he was Achan, nor would the congregation have felt the impact of his confession, if both had not been familiar with the biblical account. The God of righteousness and love, prayer for revival, ethical heights reached by the revived, concern to share salvation with those for whom Christ died, reality of the Holy Spirit, and many other aspects of Christian revival would be impossible without knowledge of the Christian Scriptures.

OUTCOMES OF REVIVAL

When God grants revival to his people, the usual pattern is that holy living increases, fresh power is experienced, and the gospel is proclaimed with new fervency.

1. Revival Leads to Holy Living

Though it is often accompanied by powerful emotions—trembling, weeping, agonizing prayer, and feelings of great joy and peace—revival is no mere emotional binge. It is restoration of New Testament Christianity. Humility, brokenness, and yielding of self to God our righteous heavenly Father result in confession of sin and restitution to those sinned against. An evangelical awakening results in holy living. The following account from Korea is a typical happening in revivals.

It had now come to the first week of January 1907. All expected that God would signally bless them during the week of universal prayer. But they came to the last day, the eighth day, and yet there was no special manifestation of the power of God. That Sabbath evening about fifteen hundred people were assembled in the Central Presbyterian Church. The heavens over them seemed as brass. Was it possible that God was going to deny them the prayed for outpouring? Then all were startled as Elder Keel, the leading man in the church, stood up and said, "I am Achan. God cannot bless because of me. About a year ago a friend of mine, when dying, called me to his house and said, 'Elder, I am about to pass away; I want you to manage my affairs; my wife is unable.' I said, 'Rest your heart; I will do it.' I did manage that widow's estate, but I managed to put one hundred dollars into my own pocket. I have hindered God, I am going to give that one hundred dollars back to that widow tomorrow morning."

Instantly it was realized that the barriers had fallen, and that God, the Holy One, had come. Conviction of sin swept the audience. The service commenced at seven o'clock Sunday evening and did not end until two o'clock Monday morning, yet during all that time dozens were standing, weeping, awaiting their turn to confess. Day after day the people assembled now, and always it was manifest that the Refiner was in His temple. . . . [Sin] hindered the Almighty God while it remained covered and it glorified Him as soon as it was uncovered; and so with rare emotions did all the confessions in Korea that year (Goforth 1943:8).

Confession and restitution is sometimes the key to revival, sometimes the result of it. Often the first initiative seems to rest with believers. Until Elder Keel determined to confess his sin, the heavens seemed as brass. But when revival comes and the Holy Spirit is outpoured, then conviction of sin sweeps the audience and men and women accomplish what of themselves they would be powerless even to attempt.

2. Revival Gives Tremendous Power

The supreme good of an evangelical awakening is that it gives tremendous spiritual power to do Christ's will. Thoroughly Christian conduct becomes practical for ordinary people when they earnestly seek and God graciously grants revival. When the Holy Spirit comes, he accomplishes the impossible in the lives of believers. Sins that a person hides are openly confessed and renounced. Evil habits of mind and body— covetousness, hate, lust, addiction to drink, idolatry, race prejudice—that had for years enslaved women and men are broken. The Holy Spirit gives new standards of justice and mercy to the revived, and they begin to advocate advanced social righteousness.

Christ's will for the world covers all spheres, individual and corporate. Body, mind, and spirit; political, economic, social, and intellectual life; interpersonal, interracial, and international relationships; black, brown, yellow, and white races—Christ's will concerns all these. All of a Christian's activities in any of these spheres—worshiping, learning, working, playing, holy living, and evangelizing—have some relationship to the growth of his church.

3. Revival Drives Christians to Proclaim the Gospel

Revival implants Christ's Spirit in believers and forthwith they, like their master, make bringing salvation to the world a chief purpose of their lives. A holy anxiety that their neighbors and loved ones share the redeeming power of the gospel seizes the revived. Like those indwelt at Pentecost, they go everywhere preaching the word. They seek to win men and women to Christ. The good life they now enjoy they ardently wish others to experience. As Jonathan Goforth reports:

> A missionary in Manchuria sent two evangelists to Ping Yang, Korea, to find out all about the revival. When they returned he asked if the missionaries had opened many street chapels. The evangelist replied, "None at all. They do not need them because every Christian is a street chapel." Christian workmen have been known to spend a summer in a country where there were no Christians in order to evangelize it. Merchants as they travel from place to place are always telling the wonderful story. A hat merchant, converted in a revival on the east coast, when we were there, had within a year afterwards started up little Christian communities in about a dozen places. . . . A student spent a month's holiday in an unevangelized district and won a hundred souls for God. Another resolved to speak each day to at least six persons about their soul's salvation. At the end of nine months he had spoken to three thousand (Goforth 1943:24).

In summary we may say that when, driven by their own powerlessness, believers turn to God and devote themselves to prayer, he pours out the Holy Spirit on them. Filled with the Holy Spirit, they sometimes experience feelings of great joy and exaltation. Sometimes the chief effect appears to be in mind and conscience. Without emotional accompaniments, the revived dedicate themselves to be Christ's people and do his will. The gift of the Holy Spirit enables them to confess sin, make restitution, break evil habits, lead victorious lives, persuade others of the available power, bring multitudes to Christ, and cause the church to grow mightily.

WHAT DOES REVIVAL MEAN TO CHURCH GROWTH?

To call ingathering of unbelievers into churches "revival" prevents understanding. To make possible clear thought we must distinguish between the various kinds of growth that churches are experiencing.

By the very structure of the word, revival means revivification of an existing church or existing Christians. There must first be tired believers before they can be revived. All accounts tell of cold, indifferent, or sinful congregations that, by revival, are kindled to new consecration. For instance, the American colleges in which the revivals took place were founded by churches and staffed chiefly by minister-teachers. The president of the college was almost always a minister. Students were frequently children of church members, and the little bands who gathered to pray were composed of Christians. In Europe the Irish, Welsh, Norwegians, and others whose revivals have been recounted were mostly baptized persons. Such as were not would nevertheless have called themselves Christians rather than pagans. As Orr says, "It can be clearly demonstrated that great numbers of actual church members are professedly converted in every revival movement" (Orr 1964:51).

In the Fiji Islands, where practically all the original population became Christians in a series of people movements, the early missionaries distinguished two stages in Christian growth. In the first—a most meaningful stage that cost many converts their lives—whole communities declared for Christ, destroyed their fetishes, were instructed and baptized, built churches, heard the Bible several times a week, learned hymns and Scripture portions, and sent their children to Christian schools. After several years of this, deeper consecration became possible and the second stage began. Revivals broke out in the churches. Old cannibals who had been Christian for some time broke down and wept bitterly at the thought of their sinful, cruel, and fear-ridden lives. They had been nourished on the Bible for years and had learned how to pray; a revival that lifted the churches to new heights became possible. Revival generally takes place in existing churches.

It is essential to avoid calling every turning to Christ, every ingathering, and every accession to the church a revival. If the significant meaning of the word—vitalizing an existing church—is to be preserved, it must not be used for the original turnings of non-Christians to Christ. And indeed, these disciplings seldom partake of the nature of revival. Non-Christians do not ardently pray God to revive them. They do not have the biblical background to make dedication result in ethical conduct. The Holy Spirit certainly moves them, but he moves them to take the steps which at that time are most essential to them—to renounce all other gods, believe on Jesus Christ as Savior, and accept the Bible as sole Scripture. Once these fundamental steps have been taken and converts have been baptized and organized into churches, other advances will follow as the day follows the night.

The revival I have been describing has a distinct pattern.

1. Prolonged exposure to the Bible and knowledge of its teachings.

2. Persistent prayer for revival on the part of a group or congregation whose members are in kin-contact with a generally Christian population.

3. Descent of the Holy Spirit on that group or congregation.

4. Confession of sin and restitution in open meeting under circumstances where these acts can be seen and known by many nominal Christians and unbelieving relatives and friends.

5. Vital, convincing witness and consequent inflooding of converts from among the homogeneous unit of which the Christians are an integral part.

In contrast with these, conversion on new ground follows radically different patterns, of which I will describe two.

1. The very first spread of the gospel in a new non-Christian population frequently brings individuals one by one, against the will of their kindred, into conglomerate congregations at or near the mission station. The congregation consists of rescued persons and orphans, converted schoolboys and girls, and an occasional adult convert. All these are uniquely dependent on the pastors, missionaries, and teachers at the station for spiritual guidance and schooling. Sometimes, in addition, they depend on them for food, clothing, and shelter. Laborious formation of such congregations over a period of several decades is a far cry from revived persons winning multitudes of their fellows to Christ; but it is often a prerequisite. It painstakingly gathers Christians who will later be revived.

2. The spread of the gospel on new ground frequently occurs through people movements to Christ. The causes, nature, and cultivation of this important means of communicating Christ will be taken up in a later chapter. Here it is sufficient to point out that, though these are often called revivals, since they involve the turning of multitudes of non-Christians to Christ, they *should not be*.

People movements have some superficial resemblance to revivals. They bring in large numbers. Converts are enthusiastic Christians with deep conviction of the truth of Christianity and the benefits of becoming Christian. They seek out relatives and friends (within their own homogeneous unit) and persuade them to become Christians. They receive Bible teaching and, though often illiterate, learn the key stories of the drama of salvation and commit to memory sections of Scripture such as the Ten Commandments and the Lord's Prayer. They are frequently not baptized until they pass an examination proving that they grasp a minimum of Christian truth.

Yet people movements have great dissimilarities to revivals. They begin on their own timetable. Unlike European revivals, they are not triggered by news of revivals in other lands. Among the means God uses to ripen a given population, news of distant revivals plays a minor part. Local cultural influences of all sorts—dissatisfactions, wars, oppression, deprivation, shock, hostility, erosion of belief in the old gods, and a thousand others—bring a given population into a condition where it can hear the good news. Information that whites in Baltimore, Edinburgh, or Stockholm are being greatly blessed by God does not affect them in the least. Since they care nothing for what another caste or tribe of their own color a hundred miles away is doing, why should they care what whites on the other side of the globe are doing?

But, it will be protested, did not the revival in Wales trigger that in the Khassi Hills in Assam? And did not news of the Khassi Hills ingathering set off the great Korean revival?

To understand what happened, one must recognize that in 1905 hundreds of bands of missionaries were working in thousands of populations. It is a safe assumption that most missionaries heard about the Wales revival and many besought the Lord to grant them similar blessing and power. In the Khassi Hills and Korea (and a few other places) God had ripened populations. In *them,* when the missionaries and congregations they had raised up heard the news from Wales and asked God's blessing and turned single-mindedly to reaping, great church growth followed. We hear about such instances. But in hundreds of mission stations whose populations were not ripe, the news of distant Wales did not lead to ingathering. We do not hear about these. News of revivals activates church leaders. It does not and cannot activate non-Christians who are not in kin-contact with Christians.

SEVEN BEARINGS OF REVIVAL ON CHURCH GROWTH

The dynamic of revival is so great and the potential for church growth so tremendous that all concerned with world evangelization must be deeply interested in it. The more ministers and missionaries know about the growth of churches, the better stewards of God's purposes in revival they will be. The same God brings both revival and great church growth. It must grieve him when a revival in the midst of receptive peoples remains shut up among a few churches. He has given his people power, and they have not used it to reap the harvest he has ripened. With this in mind, I shall venture to set forth seven basic ways in which revival bears on church growth. These are not exhaustive but will, I hope, prove suggestive.

1. Revival in the church can bring great ingathering if Christians are in living kin-contact with a non-Christian population, provided that the spiritual power is channeled into witness with the purpose of winning to Christ. If activity is directed toward other members of the homogeneous unit in which the revival has broken out, greater growth will occur than if it is diverted to other peoples.

2. Revival in the church brings growth when a constant stream of converts is flowing into it. It is many times more likely to lead to great growth in an already growing congregation than in a blocked church.

3. Revivals in conglomerate congregations in towns have more chance of issuing in reproductive conversions outside the existing church if:

a. Individual pastors have church growth eyes—that is, if they know which are the receptive units in their general population; which congregations are growing greatly and why; that group conversion is a valid form of conversion; and that the rich services rendered by church and mission are no substitute for Christ.
b. Individual pastors carry out a consistent program over the years, single-mindedly dedicated to church growth.
c. Churches and missions form their policies in the light of whatever means the Holy Spirit has already used to multiply churches in their kind of societies.

4. Revivals within people movements and web movements have far more chance of issuing in great church growth if:

a. Focused on the winnable elements of their own population.
b. Leaders from among the new converts are discovered and trained.
c. As much biblical training as possible is given to entire congregations, as well as to leaders.

5. Revivals issue in church growth when leaders of revival are taught all we know about how God has brought about great ingatherings:

a. The various kinds of readiness and how to discover and serve them.
b. Right methods, which do not hinder the Holy Spirit and do not put a ceiling on church growth.
c. Known revivals that have led to great church growth.
d. The priorities in mission and church work that help or frustrate, respectively, the spread of churches throughout the world.

6. Revivals issue in church growth when revival is counted of great importance. If the choice has to be between revival and knowledge, Christians should choose revival.

7. Revivals issue in great church growth when *revival plus knowledge* is counted of even greater importance. Christians should learn all God has to teach us about church growth, and pray without ceasing for revival.

Revival is like a head of steam in a railway engine. Without it the engine remains motionless. With it, plus rails, pistons, water, oil, timetables, engineer, and other elements, the engine travels widely and fast. Great growth of the church following revival will come where all the conditions are *right*. So right, in fact, that people are not conscious of them. This was the case at Pentecost, which is the prime example of the bearing of revival on church growth.

11

DIVINE HEALING AND CHURCH GROWTH

T HE ROLE OF THE HOLY SPIRIT in the growth of the church is supreme. Only God, not human forces, builds the church. Jesus said "I will build my church" (see Matt. 16:18). The apostle Paul acknowledged that while he plants and Apollos waters, only God gives the increase (see 1 Cor. 3:6). The sovereign power of the Holy Spirit often surprises us by overriding ordinary contextual factors or institutional factors and granting vigorous growth under the most unpromising circumstances. In the last chapter I discussed how the Holy Spirit often works through revival. Now I would like to look at divine healing.

EVIDENCE IS THERE

As I have reviewed church growth around the world, I have seen that it frequently correlates with great healing campaigns. That is why I am including this brief chapter on divine healing and church growth. Where the church is up against an insuperable barrier, there, no matter what you do, how much you pray, how much you work, how much you organize, how much you administer for church growth, the church either does not grow, grows only a little, or grows from within, not from without. Under such circumstances we need to lean heavily on that which is so wonderfully illustrated in the New

Testament, namely the place of healing in church growth. I think of two villages of Lydda and Sharon where it is recorded in the book of Acts that all Lydda and Sharon turned to the Lord. Two whole villages in a day! When did it happen? When Aeneas was healed by Peter. This great ingathering was preceded by a remarkable case of divine healing.

American missionaries, who have grown up in a highly secular society, usually take a dim view of divine healing, considering it mere charlatanism. After long years of sharing that common opinion, I now hold that among vast populations, divine healing is one of the ways in which God brings men and women to believe in the Savior. Missiologists ought to have a considered opinion on the matter. They should not brush it off cheaply and easily. Administering for church growth in part means arranging the stage so that divine healing can take place. Look at the evidence of divine healing. Withhold judgment until the evidence has been reviewed. There is much more evidence than I am able to present in one short chapter.

My considered recommendation is that missionaries and Christian believers in most populations ought to be following the biblical injunction to pray for the sick (James 5:14-15). When notable healings have taken place in your denomination, when some Pentecostals mount a great healing campaign, then say to yourself, "This is the time to strike, while the iron is hot."

Presbyterians in India

Let us examine a few cases of divine healing that have come to my attention from various sources. The first is a case of healing carried out by American Presbyterian missionaries. I quote a report from India about the operation of these ministers, visiting India for a brief period:

"Every day there was preaching in the evening and teaching in the morning. They lived with us as brothers. They visited and preached in 24 of the 278 churches we have. The work of the Holy Spirit was experienced throughout the preaching ministry. Dick Little was blessed with the gift of healing power. All those who came to the gospel meetings with a real longing for healing were wonderfully healed. Every night Little had to minister for more than four hours. People who were healed came forward and witnessed about their healing. Hundreds of people were healed. Thousands were able to accept Jesus Christ as their Lord. People were made whole physically, mentally, and spiritually. Some of our pastors were healed from serious illnesses. Those who were suffering from chronic diseases were healed. A woman who was suffering from asthma for twenty-one years was healed. A man who was deaf for more than forty years was healed. So many blind people were able to see. Lame people were healed. People who were suffering from bleeding were healed. Wilson shared how more than two weeks after Little had departed, he would visit a church and find people still praising God for the healing they had received. He discovered that a number of Hindus had received Jesus Christ as their Lord and Savior. It was customary for Dick Little to ask the people to renounce their gods before repenting and accepting the Lord Jesus into their lives. Apparently a number received their healing as Christ Jesus came into their hearts."

Anglicans in Tanzania

The second comes from the CMS newsletter. This is written by the general secretary of the famed Church Missionary Society whose headquarters are just across the Thames from the Parliament Building in London. Here is what was published:

"Perhaps there is no more impressive example in recent years of healing than Edmond John, younger brother of the archbishop of Tanzania, with his great healing missions over a three-year period of ministry from 1972 to 1975. Not only were vast numbers of people healed, exorcised, moved to open repentance, led to or brought back to Christ in great gatherings, but also in quiet, ordered proceedings. All that happened was related to the central apprehension that Jesus is Lord; an amazing response for the lax Christians and the newly drawn Muslims alike. John's death at the end of the astonishing blaze of ministry to his people left behind in many places a church spiritually and numerically strengthened."

Methodists in Bolivia

The third is from Bolivia, from a United Methodist. This man studied at our School of World Mission and went back to Bolivia a convinced church growth advocate. His letter is addressed to me personally. In it he says:

"It is most striking that the district of our church which has really broken new ground in growth is our very own Lake District where we have worked for sixteen years. This is the rural Aymara Indian district. This growth really began to gather momentum during our absence and has been strongest during the last year. So new is this that we do not yet have proper statistics on what has taken place. The mother church of the district in Ancoraimes, our mission station, has increased its Sunday morning attendance six-fold. They hold weekly meetings that have usually averaged 250, and this year we have averaged over 600. For the first time in the history of our work, a majority approaching consensus has turned to Christ in a single community; practically the whole village became Christian. This was shown dramatically on May 31, 1973, the traditional fiesta date, when the community celebrated their first community Christian Fiesta. Of the 170 families, 160 have turned to Christ, five out of six zones of the community, which is called Turini. The lay pastor of the Ancoraimes church, Juan Cordero, was the key man in this movement.

"Now mum's the word on the following factor: preaching has been accompanied by healing! Over and over this has been the case. The lay pastor has been practically mobbed on occasion, but he has stood his ground and has virtually obliged interested persons to hear him out on the gospel before he will pray for healings."

India and Ethiopia

The fourth case of healing followed by growth is one in which the gift of healing was exercised by a layperson, a recent convert, not by the pastor or missionary. In Tamilnadu, India, the Evangelical Church of India, planted by OMS of Greenwood, Indiana, has grown from a few hundred in 1966 to more than 15,000 in 1982. Currently this denomination is planting a new church every week.

After 1970 growth was accompanied by healings and exorcisms. What convinced multitudes to follow Christ was that with their own eyes they saw men and women healed by Christ's mighty power. Evil spirits were driven out in his name. The Holy Spirit was at work.

The fifth is from the Mekane Yesus Lutheran denomination in Ethiopia, the fastest-growing Lutheran church in the world. A report says that, "Eighty-three percent of our congregation give healing from illness and exorcism as reasons for their growth."

In summary, it is clear from these five cases and much more evidence that the growth of the church has often—not always, but often—been sparked by healing campaigns.

THE MISSIONARY DOCTOR

During the last 100 years, Western Christians have been heavily secularized and saturated with scientific thinking. They believe diseases are caused by germs. And these diseases are cured by drugs; malaria by quinine, colds by

Contac, atherosclerosis by open heart surgery. As Christianity has spread throughout the world, missionary physicians have proved enormously more effective than the mumbo jumbo of witch doctors, herbalists, faith healers of the animist world. The missionary doctor gave the patients penicillin and offered prayer to God for their cure. They were cured.

The Christian doctor would say that it was not by unaided prayer but by using the medicine that God has graciously given to humankind. This Christian interpretation of the healing process and the part played by unaided prayer and faith differs from the rationalist's view, and yet it holds that, as a matter of fact, God does not act independently of physical means. That is the atmosphere in which we all live. Secularists believe that there is no God; the causes of illness that can be measured and manipulated by humans are the only reality. These causes can be physical, chemical, or psychological.

To such twentieth-century thinking, faith healing is at best mistaken and at worst charlatanry. The faith healer is either a self-deluded enthusiast or a clever manipulator. If people claim to be cured, maybe they were not really sick in the first place, or have temporary feelings of well-being induced by the excitement of the moment due to crowd psychology. The "healed" may even be planted by the faith healer to build up his or her reputation. The power of hundreds of thousands who believe alike and express their belief vividly is a well-known psychological factor in human affairs and has been used by politicians, merchants, priests, and magicians from time immemorial. Westerners and Eastern secularists alike are highly skeptical about any power available other than what human beings themselves generate by one means or another. Faith healing causes lifted eyebrows and superior smiles.

CAN SPIRITS CAUSE DISEASE?

To most people in Asia, Africa, and Latin America, however, disease is inflicted by spirits. It is cured by superhuman power, regardless of what people in America think.

People in the Third World are convinced that witches eat up the life force of other people. An angry neighbor casts an "evil eye" on a woman and she grows weaker day by day. A wandering evil spirit devours a baby and the baby dies. A demon causes an illness that no medicine can cure. Western medicine may help some people, but Africa is full of mysterious powers that the white person does not know, and only those who know the secret source of black power can heal African affliction. These evil powers must be overcome by superior powers.

In Spanish America curanderos have great power. Their incantations, potions, sacrifices, and medicines marvelously heal the sick. In Asia, Africa, and Latin America, perhaps ninety-eight out of every 100 persons believe that superior power drives out inferior power. Even in Europe and North America the impersonal, mechanistic system of scientism fails to satisfy millions. Therefore, they, too, eagerly believe in the occult, extrahuman powers. Satan-worship flourishes. The mysterious influence of magic words, rites, robes, stars, yoga, and gurus fascinates many people in Europe and North America. But Christians in North America and Europe have a special problem with faith healing. Why? Because their religion wars with their science.

HEALING IN THE NEW TESTAMENT

Faith healing unquestionably occurred in biblical times. The New Testament church rode the crest of a tremendous, continuous manifestation of faith healing. One of the many passages reads as follows:

> And through the hands of the apostles many signs and wonders were done among the people. . . . And believers were increasingly added to the Lord, multitudes of both men and women, so that they brought the sick out into the streets and laid them on beds and couches, that at least the shadow of Peter passing by might fall on some of them. Also a multitude gathered from the surrounding cities to Jerusalem, bringing sick people and those who were tormented by unclean spirits, and they were all healed (Acts 5:12-16).

Divine healing was an essential part of evangelization as churches multiplied across Palestine and the Mediterranean world. What are we Christians to make of all this? Is there something here that we can use?

Many educated Christians have been more secularized than they realize and are antagonistic to divine healing. They write it off as superstition and fraud; it leads people away from sound medicine and counts many as healed who are still sick. They say divine healing is a massive deception. They think that divine healing is using God for our own ends.

Some educated Christians say that, in addition to the human mechanism and material means God uses, he sometimes acts with sovereign power. He retains the right to act outside his laws, which we know, in order to use higher laws that we do not know. He ordinarily operates through his laws, but he is not bound by them. When it pleases him, he intervenes. Such Christians hold that the best possible world is one in which most of the time a just and loving God rules through natural laws. But occasionally, when he sees fit, he uses the higher law. Such Christians view healings in the name of Christ as demonstrations of the power of God.

Some would add that since the healings are a mixture of God's acts and human acts, we see many incomplete healings, and failures of healings, due to lack of faith or sincerity.

SEEING IS BELIEVING

Some hard-headed Christians, who would normally be highly skeptical about divine healing, have gradually come to accept healing campaigns on seeing the great numbers who throw away crutches, plus those healed of deafness and blindness and cured of heart disease. They have seen large numbers of recent nonbelievers rejoicing at Christ's power, singing his praises, hearing his work, and praying to him. The *facts* overwhelm the hard-headed.

Finally, some Christians believe that God has called them to engage actively in healing the sick, exorcising evil spirits, and multiplying churches. They deliberately use the vigorous expressed faith in Christ that abounds in a healing campaign to multiply sound churches of responsible Christians.

All Christians ought to think their way through this matter and realize that here is a power for church growth that a great many of us have not sufficiently used.

EDITOR'S NOTE: This chapter represents some of Donald McGavran's later thinking on a vital subject. It was in the late 1970s that he began to introduce this lecture on divine healing in his advanced church growth classes at Fuller Seminary, and he continued giving it until his retirement from teaching in 1981. This summary of the lecture is taken from *Signs and Wonders Today,* C. Peter Wagner, ed., Altamonte Springs, FL, Creation House, 1987, with permission of the publisher. That book tells the complete story of the introduction and implementation of the controversial MC510 course on signs and wonders into the Fuller School of World Mission curriculum by Peter Wagner and John Wimber in the early 1980s.

PART IV

THE SOCIOLOGICAL FOUNDATION

12

SOCIAL STRUCTURE AND CHURCH GROWTH

SINCE CHURCH GROWTH takes place in the multitudinous societies of the world, essential to understanding it is an understanding of their structure. People exist not as discrete individuals, but as interconnected members of some society. Innovation and social change, operating in particular structures, play a significant part in determining the direction, speed, and size of the move to the Christian religion. This is as true in America as in Asia or Africa.

Normal people are not isolated units but part of a whole that makes them what they are. For instance, individuals do not choose what language they will speak. The society where they are born, the mothers who nurse them, and the children with whom they play determine it. Moreover, society either determines or strongly influences every aspect of what they say, think, and do. Consequently when we comprehend the social structure of a particular segment of the total population, we know better how churches are likely to increase and ramify through it.

SOME COMPONENTS OF SOCIAL STRUCTURE

Social structure is a broad reality comprising many factors, each of which has bearing on how the church can reconcile men and women to

God among the more than three billion who have yet yielded no allegiance to Jesus Christ. A few typical elements of social structure will be considered.

The Unique Self-Image

Each society, finding itself in certain physical, economic, and political circumstances, develops a characteristic culture and self-image, as anthropologists have pointed out, that makes it different from every other society. The physical base has much to do with this. All rice-planting societies that depend on hand labor share a complex of customs that arise from working barefoot in rice paddies. Since the culture of each society, however, is the combined outcome of many different forces—racial, military, religious, climatic, and other—rice planters in coastal valleys of Buddhist Japan will have a different self-image from Christian rice planters in the mountainous country between India and Burma.

The rugged individualism of the American people a hundred years ago was developed by the frontier. Baptist, Methodist, and Christian churches, because their system of creating leaders and certain other traits fitted the frontier temperament, grew better than Episcopal and Presbyterian churches. The highly regimented mentality of Americans today has been developed by a number of years of compulsory schooling, intricate traffic regulations, national press and television networks, and other similar influences. American denominations are trying out many different activities and methods to find those which, in this particular culture with its particular self-image, really communicate Christ and build up the church.

In Latin America, the structure of society among hacienda owners is radically different from that of hacienda serfs. The former think of themselves as the conquerors, the latter know they are the conquered. The first not only own vast estates, but until recent times held the power of life and death within them; the second lead a safe life only if they obey the master of the big house and his overseers. If peons work five days on the master's thousand acres, they are allowed to work two days on their own few. They can keep five sheep—if they give the dung to the field of the *hacendero*. The structure of both societies differs again from those of independent mestizo peasants and free Indians who own a few acres of their own. The church grows differently in each of these four Latin American structures.

People Consciousness

A homogeneous unit of society may be said to have people consciousness when its members think of themselves as a separate tribe, caste, or class. Thus the Orthodox Jews have high people consciousness, as do the castes in India, the Indian tribes in Ecuador, and many other societies in many lands.

The degree of people consciousness is an aspect of social structure that greatly influences when, how, and to what extent the gospel will flow through that segment of the social order. Castes or tribes with high people consciousness will resist the gospel primarily because to them becoming a Christian means joining another people. They refuse Christ not for religious reasons, not because they love their sins, but precisely because they love their neighbors.

In India, Brahmins and many others whose people consciousness is very high discipline their members rigorously. They ostracize those who marry non- Brahmins and read the funeral ceremony over them. They have debased the blood and must be excluded.

It may be taken as axiomatic that whenever becoming a Christian is considered a racial rather than a religious decision, there the growth of the church will be exceedingly slow. As the church faces the evangelization of the world, perhaps its main problem is how to present Christ so that unbelievers can truly follow him without traitorously leaving their kindred.

The resistance of most Hindus, Buddhists, and Muslims to the Christian faith does not arise primarily from theological considerations. Most of the adherents of these faiths, being illiterate, know very little about their religious system. Most Hindus are more animist than Hindu, and the same may be said for each of the other major religions. Their resistance arises primarily from fear that "becoming a Christian will separate me from my people."

It is often affirmed that primitive peoples and low-caste folk become Christians easily, whereas Christianity has not appealed to followers of the great ethnic religions; but this is to distort the truth. In many cases, tribes resist Christianity quite as effectively as advanced peoples. The Egons of Badagri in the southwest corner of Nigeria solidly refused the gospel for a hundred and fifteen years, though it was ably presented first by the Methodists and then, when these retired from the area, by the Roman Catholics. The Maasai of Kenya—a primitive tribe if there ever was one—have been entirely indifferent to Christianity. Most of the low castes of India have proved just as resistant to Christ's appeal as the high castes. The fact is that men and women, high and low, advanced and primitive, usually turn to Christian faith in numbers only when some way is found for them to become Christian without leaving their kith and kin.

The great obstacles to conversion are social, not theological. Great turning of Muslims and Hindus can be expected as soon as ways are found for them to become Christian without renouncing their loved ones, which seems to them a betrayal. Confirmation of this can be seen in the 1966 and 1967 turning to Christ of perhaps fifty thousand Muslims in Indonesia. Whole communities became Christians together. It was reported that in one place twenty-five mosques became twenty-five churches. The principle need not be labored. It is patently true that among societies with high people consciousness those methods of propagating the gospel which enable individuals to accept Christ without renouncing their peoples are blessed of God to the growth of his church.

Marriage Customs

Where men get their wives is an important element in social structure. In rural Mexico men find wives within their own rancho (village) or those immediately adjacent. In the Gangetic Valley of India, each caste is made up of many *gotr* (exogamous clans). A man must get his wife outside his *gotr* but inside his caste. All girls of his own *gotr* are his sisters even if there is no blood connection for ten generations. Some castes take daughters-in-law from the east, give daughters to the west. Where men get their wives determines where their maternal uncles, fathers-in-law, and sisters' sons live. This, in turn, influences where the Christian will normally visit, in which villages his or her intimates will be found, and consequently where the gospel will spread.

The Elite, or Power Structure

I am not speaking now of the elite of a whole country or city, but of those in a given *ethnos* or homogeneous unit. Every university faculty has its power structure—its elite, whose opinions have great weight. So does every labor union.

Each segment of society has its own power structure or aristocracy, as I found to my great surprise when I discovered that among the latrine-cleaning caste of Jubbulpore there were certain elite families. The Dumars of that city were organized into twenty-nine associations, each of which was ruled by a *chaudhari* and his assistant, the *sakidar*. Thus the sweepers—the lowest of low castes—had an aristocracy of these fifty-eight families and their relatives.

The power structure of a community sometimes consists exclusively of these born into the right families. Often wealth has something to do with it. In many societies a light skin gives prestige. Religious talents, too, such as shamans, sorcerers, and priests are supposed to possess, elevate their owners to the elite. In the villages where I worked, the wise man *jis ki baat nahin kut-thi* ("whose decision cannot be controverted") was part of the power structure. He knew village and caste law by long observation, had a judicious mind, and patiently listened to the ins and outs of each dispute until, sensing an unspoken consensus, he would announce a decision that carried the day.

When members of the elite become Christian, the faith is likely to spread among their blood and marriage relations.

Land Rights

Land-owning rights are complex and a most important aspect of social structure. In Madhya Pradesh, India, most peasants own merely the cultivating rights to land. They can neither buy nor sell the land itself, which belongs to the feudal lord of the village. If he permits them to sell it, he does so after "graciously accepting as a gift" a third of the price at which it is sold. If he does not like the person wanting to buy, or wishes to prevent that person's becoming part of the village, he simply refuses "the gift," that is, refuses to sell. If the feudal lord is hostile to Christianity, and Christians own only cultivating rights, it is impossible to get land for a church building.

In Puerto Rico the low fertile coastal lands belong to the sugar barons, but in the interior, coffee growers own their own patches of the hillside. These independents can become evangelicals if they want to, whereas landless labor on the sugar estates can be ordered off if by becoming evangelicals, or in any other way, they displease the owner.

Where people live, their geographical location, is an obvious part of the social structure and greatly affects church growth. Throughout Hindu India, the depressed-class ward has been separated from the rest of the village by physical distance—often a hundred yards or more. As people of these wards became Christian and pastors were appointed to shepherd them, the separate location posed a problem to missions. Should the pastor—an educated, respectable Christian—live in the untouchable ward or seek quarters in the upper-caste section of the village? Arguing that it would help Christians more if their pastor lived in a respectable part of the town, missions in North India located their pastors there. Arguing that the pastor's place was with his people, missions in South India located him in the untouchable ward itself. Pickett observes that the South India procedure (its use of the social structure) was much more successful in terms of creating a genuine Christian church (1933:228).

Sex Mores

The degree to which sex mores affect the growth of the church has not commonly been recognized in Western nations. There, because for long centuries the state enforced the sex code taught by the church, ideals of monogamy and faithfulness until recently have been part of the common life of the people. Since practically no divorce was permitted, lifelong marriages became the rule. Among the truly converted, faithfulness was commonplace. Adultery, mistresses, premarital sexual intercourse, and the like were, of course, found but were recognized as sin. To be converted meant leaving the abnormal for the normal, the illegal for the legal.

In some countries, however, non-Christian sex mores are the dominant variety and militate heavily against the growth of the church. For example, in Jamaica, where the great bulk of the population is descended from slaves freed in 1838, two patterns of marriage obtain. Marriage Pattern I—Christian marriage—is that used by the higher classes: the wealthy, educated leaders of Jamaica. The masses, however, who comprise more than 85 percent of the population, practice Marriage Pattern II. In this, temporary unions outside marriage are formed from middle adolescence on. Some last a week, many a few months, and some for years. Either party is free to leave when he or she tires of the other. A succession of temporary unions is the rule.

As long as couples are living together out of wedlock, no church will accept them as members. However, they count themselves as, in a vague way, belonging to the community of this or that church and bring their babies to the ministers to be baptized or dedicated. If, in a revival meeting, fifty such persons were converted, the first question asked them in the after-meeting would be, "Are you married or willing to be?" If the answer were no, then they could not be baptized or added to the church. Many pastors, sure that adolescents of the masses will fall away and have to be removed from the roll, do not encourage them to join the church.

After the age of forty, many women and some men, through with sex, decide to live alone. They then become eligible for church membership.

Older men of the masses who have made money and want to step up in the world get married. Their children and grandchildren attend the wedding, which—a costly affair with suitable clothes, rings, wedding feast, and the like—is a status symbol and proclaims that this man and wife, who have been living together for years, have now arrived. They have also become eligible for church membership.

Consequently the church in Jamaica is comprised mostly of members of the upper classes and some of the elderly among the masses. In research done there in 1957, I came to the conclusion that fourteen out of fifteen adults of the masses between the ages of sixteen and forty could not join the church (McGavran 1962). They were living in Marriage Pattern II, which they called "our Jamaican way," and intended to continue in it. The slow growth of churches in Jamaica is largely due to the adverse effect sex mores have had on growth.

In Africa, the system of polygamy keeps very large numbers from confessing Christ. Churches rule that men who have married two or more women according to tribal custom must give up all but one on becoming Christians. For several reasons, churches are not happy with this rule and are discussing whether it is really Christian. Most churches agree that polygamy cannot be allowed in the church for those who have been brought up as Christians or who come in with one wife. That is not the issue. The issue is whether converts with two or more wives whom, while pagans, they have married according to tribal law, may be baptized with their wives and continue living with them, on the clear understanding that (1) while they will be members in good standing they may not be deacons or elders, and (2) they will cleave strictly to monogamy as a system. If a wife dies they will not replace her, and they will arrange monogamous marriages for their sons and daughters.

A few mission-derived denominations have ruled that, on this understanding, they may be baptized. Many others have ruled they may not. Most independent African denominations not only allow men and all their wives to become Christian but permit polygamy to those reared in the church. Their great growth of recent years is at least partly due to their open attitude toward polygamy.

Language

Hundreds of millions live in two worlds. The first, of great importance to them, is that of intimates who speak the same language; the second, of relatively slight importance, is that world of a strange tongue in which we trade and work with outsiders. In the first the medium of *communication* is the language of the heart; in the second, the medium of *confusion* is a trade language or standard language, good enough for buying and selling, taking orders and finding one's way, but pitifully inadequate for the things that really matter. People fight, make love, and mourn in their mother tongue.

Because the only way most modern nation-states think they can function is to create a citizenry all of whose members speak one language, governments and education departments work ceaselessly to propagate standard languages and to eliminate what they call dialects. Nations with more than one official language such as Canada or Switzerland are exceptions to the rule. For most, the standard language is the key to unity.

Nevertheless, the language of the heart is difficult to stamp out. It is learned from the mother's lips and spoken in the home. It is an inner sanctuary where the outside world cannot penetrate. It is jealously guarded because it enhances a sense of peoplehood. In Mexico, eighty-eight Indian languages have survived four hundred years of Spanish dominance and are heart languages for hundreds of thousands today.

Not four hundred miles from where I am writing, for instance, many missionaries from half a dozen boards of missions are working among the Navajo Indians, but winning few to Christ. In Arizona and New Mexico, English is the standard language and Navajo the "dialect." A knowledgeable informant assured me that of all the missionaries in Navajoland he knew, only one was fluent in the Indian tongue. On the entirely untenable assumption that "the Navajos all know English," most missionaries had not even tried to learn it.

Today educated nationals who lead the churches of Africa, Asia, and Latin America know and love the standard languages of their nations and scorn languages spoken by small segments of the population as "dying vernaculars" or "corrupt forms of the national language." They usually believe that the welfare of the nation demands eradication of the dialects. They are not sympathetic with the argument that the people could hear the gospel better and obey it more readily if it were presented in their heart language and insist that "everyone understand our national language." They also feel that the best interests of existing Christians demand getting them away from the dialects and making them proficient in the national language. Hence church services, they think, should be in Spanish, Hindi, Swahili, Amharic, or other national languages. Probably unconsciously, they subordinate discipling to a cosmopolitan civilizing process.

The basic reform needed in those fields where missions are evangelizing speakers of dialects is to cease spreading one team of workers over several dialects or languages and to begin assigning single teams to one homogeneous unit at a time—preferably those believed to be responsive. Each member of the team would then learn the heart language of that people. Transfers could be made *within the one language area* as the good of the young church required. The Wycliffe Bible Translators have demonstrated that as a mission procedure this is quite feasible.

THE CASE OF JAMAICA

In 1820, the population of Jamaica was composed of three homogeneous units. (1) The English and Scottish estate owners were members of the Anglican and Presbyterian churches. (2) A considerable mulatto population, which had arisen in towns and estates through miscegenation, was culturally somewhat advanced. Some mulattoes had been educated by their natural fathers. Some had been freed. Many were foremen of the sugar plantations. (3) The black slaves formed by far the largest part of the population.

Until the early 1800s, Anglicans and Presbyterians, fearing unrest among the slaves if they permitted them to become Christians, had discouraged Christianization. True, some Baptist slaves of Tory planters, who left the thirteen states after the Revolutionary War, had before 1800 started a few churches among the slaves in Jamaica. Though Baptist sectarians were in great disfavor with the plantation owners, who often burned down the slave chapels, Baptist churches began to increase among the third homogeneous unit.

Then about 1800, Baptists and Methodists from England, in the first flush of their missionary zeal, came to Jamaica and a tremendous turning to Christ took place among the slaves. Baptist churches multiplied among the blacks and the Methodist churches among the mulattoes. Not that no mulatto ever became a Baptist or that Methodists resolutely refused to admit blacks, but rather each church prospered in its own segment of the social order.

Baptists found it hard to extend their churches among the mulattoes. Their gospel was sound, but their congregations, made up very largely of the blacks, did not attract the mulattoes. Mulattoes said to themselves, "Our friends are in the mulatto community. We want our children to marry people of their own color, and these Baptist services are not up to the standard of language or thought that we like." Methodists could have extended their churches among the blacks, but the existing mulatto Methodists did not encourage it. They did not want too many black men and women, boys and girls in their churches. They did not want black leaders and ministers. The mulatto community was relatively more cultured, educated, and free of voodoo. It formed a separate subculture. Methodists did not want to debase their church by bringing in lower-class people. They wanted churches that appealed to their kind of people and in which they felt at home.

When we see clearly how much social structure contributes to personal and group dignity and self-esteem we will cease to pass it off as so much of a nuisance and harness its positive dynamics for the spread of the gospel.

13

WITHOUT CROSSING BARRIERS

PEOPLE LIKE TO become Christians without crossing racial, linguistic, or class barriers.

This principle states an undeniable fact. Human beings do build barriers around their own societies. More exactly we may say that the ways in which each society lives and speaks, dresses and works, of necessity set it off from other societies. The world's population is a mosaic, and each piece has a separate life of its own that seems strange and often unlovely to men and women of other pieces.

UNMELTABLE ETHNICS

Michael Novak, in his perceptive book *The Rise of the Unmeltable Ethnics,* ably defends the right of each ethnic group to remain itself. He sees the barriers each group builds around itself as normal and desirable parts of the human scene. His list of ethnics in the United States shatters the notion of "one American people."

> When I say "ethnics" . . . I am speaking mainly of the descendants of the immigrants of southern and eastern Europe: Poles, Italians, Greeks and Slavs . . . Armenians, Lebanese, Slovenes, Ruthenians,

Croats, Serbs, Czechs (Bohemians and Moravians), Slovaks, Lithuanians, Estonians, Russians, Spanish, and Portuguese (1971:46).

Novak does not deal with the English, Scottish, Irish, Danish, Norwegians, Swedes, Germans and French, the Chinese, Japanese, Filipinos, Pakistanis, Indians, Arabs, Africans, Koreans, and Vietnamese.

Like the United States, most nations are composed of many unmeltable ethnics. India, for example, has more than 3,000 ethnic units (castes and tribes) each of which practices endogamy. Highly educated and politically powerful Indians are members of tightly structured segments of humanity, each of which has a stout wall built around it. Afghanistan, often thought of as one country and one people, is in fact composed of many different peoples, with different languages and customs.

In this vast mosaic, how does the Christian faith spread from piece to piece? Does it invite members of all pieces to leave their own people and become parts of the people of God? Or does the church form inside each piece?

The mosaic is a useful figure of speech but can easily convey an untruth. The many colored pieces of the mosaics in the beautiful Renaissance buildings in Italy have changed neither shape nor color in four hundred years. The human mosaic is not like that. Its pieces are constantly changing, merging with, swallowing, and being swallowed by other pieces. The languages they speak change. The clothes they wear change. They used to walk; now they ride cycles or drive cars. They were solidly illiterate; now they are highly educated. Their cultures change radically. In view of this great readiness to change should we think of the propagation of the gospel as a process of change by which all peoples and cultures are gradually transformed into a new and beautiful Christian culture? Or, does the Christian faith enter each changing, yeasting culture and transform it from within while it yet remains itself, and separate from other cultures that have become Christian?

The biblical teaching is plain that in Christ two peoples become one. Christian Jews and Gentiles become one new people of God, parts of the one body of Christ. But the one body is complex. Since both peoples continue to speak separate languages, does not the oneness cover a vast and continuing diversity?

This chapter describes the obvious fact that human beings are born into thousands of very different societies, separated from each other by many barriers. It also explores the ways in which the Christian faith, while making all Christians one in Christ Jesus, can be communicated across the barriers, over the ditches, and thus built into the other societies, classes, castes, tongues, and segments of humanity.

HOMOGENEOUS UNITS

For the sake of convenience, we talk about these as homogeneous units. Some are linguistically, some ethnically, some economically, and some educationally different from the others. The term homogeneous unit is very elastic. Scandinavian Americans might be considered a homogeneous unit; but since there are many kinds of Scandinavians, so might the Swedish Baptist denomination in 1930. The Brahmins in India are a homogeneous unit, but so is each of the scores of Brahmin castes.

James C. Smith, impressed by the universal applicability of the homogeneous unit principle, in 1976 wrote his doctoral dissertation on "Without Crossing Barriers: The Homogeneous Unit Principle in the Writings of Donald McGavran." He discovered that this aspect of human society had intrigued me from the beginning, noting that in *The Bridges of God* (1955) I had written, "Peoples become Christian fastest when least change of race or clan is involved" (Smith 1976:23). After that I had very frequently called attention to ethnicity as a significant factor in propagating and arresting the flow of the gospel.

During recent decades church growth thinking has been enriched by the writings of Lyle E. Schaller, who has explored thoroughly the part played in growth and decline by diversities (different groups) within seemingly homogeneous congregations.

Schaller, more than anyone else, has studied the various parts of congregations and denominations. For example, on the basis of face-to-face conversations with thousands of Christians and extensive returns on questionnaires, he explored questions such as this: Why did those who have joined the church during the past ten years take that step? He found that:

- 3 to 8% walked in on their own initiative
- 4 to 10% came because they liked the program
- 10 to 20% joined because they liked the pastor
- 10 to 25% joined in response to visitation evangelism
- 3 to 6% came because of the Sunday school
- 60 to 90% were brought by some friend or relative.

One of his most telling illustrations of homogeneous units *within* seemingly homogeneous wholes is this: Young marrieds looked at one way are a single group. They are quite different from the senior citizens or the high schoolers. Looked at from a different angle, the young marrieds themselves have several groups within them. There are significant differences among the members of this one group that older members refer to simply as "the young married couples." Each of the following subgroups has different needs and schedules. (a) Many 22-year-old couples with no children feel nearly a generation younger than the 28-year-old husband with the 26-year-old wife and two children; (b) the couple with both husband and wife employed outside the home and the couple with only the husband employed; and (c) the couple born and reared in this community and the couple living 1,000 miles from "back home."

Note that none of these homogeneous units on which Schaller focuses our attention is an ethnic or linguistic group. Yet they are important for church growth. The same kind of subgroupings affect the growth of churches in all continents. In many countries of Africa, for example, the early growth of the church has come from older school boys; but the *great* growth did not come until the mature started becoming Christian in groups of like-minded persons.

Men and women do like to become Christian without crossing barriers.

LANGUAGE AND CLASS BARRIERS

This universal principle is readily seen when we think of the linguistic barrier mentioned in the last chapter. In Los Angeles or San Francisco, English-speaking Anglo-Americans are not likely to become Christians in Spanish- or Japanese-speaking congregations. When they become Christians it will usually be in English-speaking churches. American Protestants living for a short time overseas seldom worship in the Protestant churches there, partly because the service in Urdu, Mandarin, or Portuguese is unintelligible to them. How much more difficult it would be to leave one's ancestral faith and *join* a congregation whose members spoke a different tongue!

In the 1870s hundreds of Pepohwans in Taiwan were burning their memorial tablets and fetishes and declaring for Christ. They built chapels and were put under instruction by the English Presbyterians. Those who passed the examination were baptized. But the instructors spoke only Chinese, and while some Pepohwan men knew a little Chinese, the women and children knew practically none. The result was that out of a whole village that declared for Christ, only a few would be judged eligible for baptism. The movement eventually failed. It was hard for Pepohwans to become Christian across the linguistic barrier.

The principle is also readily discerned when it comes to pronounced class and racial barriers. It takes no great acumen to see that when marked differences of color, stature, income, cleanliness, and education are present, unbelievers understand the gospel better when expounded by their own kind of people. They prefer to join churches whose members look, talk, and act like themselves. Although apartheid laws in the Union of South Africa apply to Indians as well as Africans, the differences between these dark-skinned peoples are so great that it is difficult for Indians to join African churches. Few Indians were becoming Christians. But once a church made up of Indians started to grow (so that Indians could become Christians without having to cross a pronounced race barrier), thousands of Indians became Christian in one denomination in a relatively short period of time.

In Denver, Colorado, a Presbyterian congregation was declining because its members were moving out to the suburbs. The new whites moving into that part of the city did not join this congregation in any but the smallest numbers. The class barrier (which would have been vehemently denied by the congregation), while not high, was there. It was inconspicuous but powerful.

In the nineteenth century, the high, cool plateau of Mexico was the site of many haciendas that originated in sixteenth-century land grants given by the king of Spain and therefore ultimately by the Pope himself. In each hacienda, villages—called ranchos—had grown up where water and arable land lay close at hand. The Spanish-speaking population was at least nominally Roman Catholic and was composed of the exploited masses and the upper classes. The latter—beneficiaries of the social order—lived chiefly in the towns and were close allies of the Roman Catholic Church (McGavran, Huegel, and Taylor 1963:38).

The revolutions of the early twentieth century—and in particular that of 1927, when the central government was breaking up the haciendas and giving the land to the peasants—divided the peasantry into two parties: *agraristas* who were ready to fight for land distribution, and *cristeros* who had been persuaded that, since the land had been given to the hacienda owners by the Pope, taking it away from them was stealing and would be punished by God. *Cristeros* fought to keep the feudal lords in power.

The peasants of both parties looked very much the same. All spoke Spanish, counted themselves Roman Catholics, had the same culture, cultivated the same kind of land, and wore the same kind of clothing. Yet for the propagation of the gospel the difference between the two had crucial significance. For the establishment of evangelical congregations, the *agrarista* ranchos were of great importance and the *cristero* ranchos of none. True, *agraristas* did not rush to become evangelicals, but, freed from the control of the feudal lords, thinking of the Church of Rome as an ally of their oppressors, and having divided up the land despite the fact that it was given to the feudal lords by the Pope, they could "hear" the gospel. For the first time becoming evangelicals became a live option to them.

Yet this minor difference was not seen by most evangelical pastors and missionaries working in the high, dry heart of Mexico. To them, the people of the ranchos were all rural Mexicans, poor, illiterate, and indifferent to the gospel. Suspicious of revolution and cultivating friendly relations with the business and professional leaders of the towns, evangelical leaders did not concentrate on planting churches in the revolutionary ranchos. A few churches did arise there—eloquent testimony to a crucially important minor difference. Had a movement been initiated that gave agrarian reform a biblical base and thus enabled *agraristas,* while remaining ardent *agraristas,* to become evangelicals, it might have swept the revolutionary ranchos of the plateau.

ESSENTIAL FACTORS IN CHURCH PLANTING

Biblical Requirements

Church planters who enable unbelievers to become Christians without crossing such barriers are much more effective than those who place them in their way. But biblical barriers must not be removed.

The offense of the cross is one basic barrier to becoming Christian. To accept the truth that we are sinners whose salvation depends not at all on what we do but entirely on accepting what Jesus Christ has done on the cross, affronts the ego. To repent of our sins and turn from them is another basic barrier to discipleship. Openly to confess Christ before others, be baptized in his name, and join the church is a third obstacle. To those who accept the authority of the Scriptures, these barriers must remain, to be accepted and surmounted as part of the test of a Christian.

But the church and its emissaries are constantly tempted to add others. In most cases of arrested growth of the church, people are deterred not so much by the offense of the cross as by nonbiblical offenses. Nothing in the Bible, for instance, requires that *in becoming a Christian* a believer must cross linguistic, racial, and class barriers. To require that they do so is to take the spotlight off the three essential biblical acts and focus it on human requirements. The Scriptures affirm that in Christ there is "neither Jew nor Greek, there is neither slave nor free, there is neither male nor female" (Gal. 3:28); but this is true only for those who, being baptized into Christ, have put on Christ. It is a fruit of the Spirit, not a prerequisite for salvation.

During the first fifteen years of the church's history, almost all believers became Christians while remaining members of the Jewish community. Unless we are foolhardy enough to say that members of the early church, because they "preached the word to none but Jews" and maintained intact most of their Jewish antipathy to Gentiles, were not really Christians at all, we must go on to add that fruit often takes a long time to mature. Furthermore, the last phrase in the text (that in Christ "there is neither male nor female") must be taken into account. It certainly does not mean that in order to become a Christian one must adopt a manner of life as if sex differences did not exist, or that churches that deny ordination to women are no part of the true church. Nor must the first phrase be made to mean that, to become a Christian, one must act as if class and race differences do not exist.

New Testament Churches

Nineteen hundred years ago the church found that Jews liked to become Christians without crossing racial barriers. The Jewish caste was a tightly knit society. It had effective control. It insisted that Jews marry Jews. It ostracized women who went wrong with men of other races. It took seriously the command not to take women of the land to wife.

The Jewish caste had no dealings with the half-breed Samaritans. In foreign cities, Jews lived in their own wards. Distant Jews sometimes married back into Jerusalem families, as in the case of Paul's sister. This gave the community marked commercial advantages. Jewish families became banking families, and money could be transmitted by letter and a double-entry system of bookkeeping.

All this provided a broad avenue for the expansion of a *Jewish* church. As long as Jews could become Christians within Judaism, the church could and did grow amazingly among Jews, filling Jerusalem, Judea, and Galilee. When the gospel spread among the half-breed Samaritans, there is no reason to believe that Christian Jews started to interdine and intermarry with them. When the church began to grow in the synagogue communities around the Mediterranean, the first to become disciples of Christ were devout Hellenistic Jews who had been eagerly expecting the Messiah. These, becoming Christians within the synagogue, could do so without crossing racial and class barriers.

As soon as numerous Gentiles had become Christians, however, to be a Christian often involved for a Jew leaving the Jewish people and joining a conglomerate society. Admitting Gentiles created a racial barrier for Jews. Indeed, it is a reasonable conjecture that as soon as becoming a Christian meant joining a house church full of Gentiles and sitting down to agape feasts where on occasion pork was served, would-be Jewish converts found the racial and cultural barriers too high and turned sorrowfully away. Jews have been largely resistant to the gospel ever since.

The Conversion of Europe

It is difficult to comprehend that it took a thousand years to win the peoples of Europe to the Christian faith. Two hundred years passed during which Ireland was Christian and England pagan. The British Isles were Christian for a hundred years before that great Englishman, Boniface, led North Germany to turn from her pagan gods. France was Christian for at least six hundred years before Sweden was evangelized. During each of these long periods, the natives of the pagan country knew something about Christianity. Travelers and traders passed to and fro. An occasional missionary labored in the land. Northern mercenaries in southern armies became Christian and returned home. Christian women were carried off by pagan marauders and became parts of their harems or households or communities. Yet during this two hundred years, or that five hundred, the natives of the adjoining pagan land did not become Christian. They were highly resistant. This resistance consisted chiefly of linguistic and cultural barriers.

The time came when some military change, political realignment, conquest, or Spirit-filled missionary of genius opened up a way for the pagans of a given territory to become Christian without crossing these barriers. Then pagans flooded in. Since church and state were one, Christian law became the law of the land, the monastic system of education and the holy life were established, churches were built, and the land became "Christian."

When gathered churches arose, they insisted that only the intelligently committed individuals, consciously subordinating their will to that of the Lord Jesus and deliberately feeding on God's word, could rightly be called Christians. It then became popular to decry the initial turning from paganism to the church. Yet had it not occurred, the gathered churches would never have been born.

In the initial turnings to Christian faith in northern Europe, the principle that people like to become Christians without crossing barriers kept whole countries out of eternal life for centuries, and then when a way to become Christian within the social unit was found, a whole country would speedily declare for Christ.

India

The principle is well illustrated in the growth of the Baptist Church among the Panos and Kuingas in the Kond Hills of India. From 1918 to 1957, British Baptists carried on work at Udaigiri in the hills. Two-thirds of the hill population was made up of the aboriginal Kuingas and one-third of the low-caste Hindu Panos. The Kuingas considered themselves superior.

The goal of the mission was the conversion of the land-owning Kuingas. But soon after 1918, the Panos began to turn to Christian faith. The more they turned, the more others of them wanted to turn. By 1956, 1,700 were communicants in good standing. They liked to become Christians without crossing caste (racial) barriers. They continued to interdine and have marriage relationships with non-Christian Panos, and lived on in the Pano section of the villages.

About a hundred Kuingas—the steady objects of mission work—by ones and twos became Christians, mostly around the big mission station of Udaigiri, where the schools and the hospital were located and all the missionaries lived. Many of the Kuinga converts, alas, had married Christian Pano women. To Kuingas in general, becoming Christian began increasingly to look like becoming Pano. Thus, since Kuingas could not choose Christ without crossing racial lines, very few others followed him.

Then, about 1955, about thirty miles from Udaigiri in a little-worked section of the hills, a series of group conversions brought in hundreds of Kuingas, who became Christian while remaining Kuinga. As conversions continued, enough came in so that Christian Kuinga youth could marry within their own race. When village congregations met for worship, Kuingas met with other Kuingas. At meetings of all Christians in that section, thousands of Kuingas looked around and saw their own people. Between 1955 and 1961 ten new churches a year were established and in 1962 twenty were started (Boals 1961:67).

Brazil

Around the turn of the century, great waves of Italian immigrants were flooding into Brazil. These

> settled in certain districts of Sao Paulo, being attracted to their fellow countrymen already "in transition" into the Brazilian culture and national life. The barrio of the Bras was an Italian colony in the growing city of Sao Paulo. The adults spoke Italian exclusively while the children quickly picked up Portuguese. . . . The process of integration took two or three generations and the arrival of Louis Francescon (the Italian immigrant to Chicago who, converted there, went to Brazil as a lay missionary) was timely. He was able to enter, move, and work in a community of Italians that was in evolution into the new culture, but at the same time was receiving new immigrants regularly from the old country (Read 1965:23f.).

For the first twenty years or more, the churches Louis Francescon started grew entirely among the Italians, because the only language known to the founder and the first Christians was Italian. Starting from no members at all in 1910, the Congregacao Crista—for such is the name of the denomination—grew until by 1962 it numbered 260,000 full members. From zero to over a quarter million members in fifty-two years is unusual growth for any church. Most Italians in Brazil are now in comfortable circumstances and some have become citizens of wealth and position. When I visited the mother church of the Congregacao Crista in 1965, the streets were lined with cars in which members had come to the service.

None can imagine that the Congregacao has grown among a primitive people. Yet here too the principle that people like to become Christians without crossing class and language barriers is clearly a factor in the amazing growth. It must be emphasized that in Sao Paulo, during the years 1910 to 1962, the Methodists, Baptists, Lutherans, and Presbyterians were strong. Only a very small number of the responsive Italians, however, became evangelicals in these well-established, Portuguese-speaking denominations, each with notable mission schools and colleges buttressing it. Among other reasons, unquestionably one was this: that to become evangelicals in any of these four churches, Italians would have had to cross linguistic and class barriers and leave their own community.

OTHER ESSENTIAL FACTORS

Mere ability to become Christian without crossing linguistic, racial, and class barriers never made anyone Christian. By itself it provides no incentive to follow Christ. To realize this, one has only to look at middle-class white Americans in any university community. In them anyone can confess Christ without this deterrent; yet large numbers remain outside the church. Other factors are essential to the growth of the church: the Bible must be taught (and often translated), the word must be proclaimed, and—constrained by love—Christians must seek to persuade their intimates and relatives that it is a wonderful thing to become a follower of the Lord of life.

How Does the Process Begin?

Right at the beginning, when there is no church in the new segment of society, when no one from that segment has ever become a Christian, the principle I have been setting forth would seem to inhibit all movement. When each would-be convert says, "Becoming a Christian means leaving all my kith and kin," how do enough converts act together so that they do come in without crossing class or linguistic barriers? The hard fact of history is that most sizable movements to Christ have begun with the conversion of an individual—or at most a few families. How then can the individual—or the group—avoid being ostracized? How can they avoid feeling that they are leaving their own folk to join another people? The answer is that right from the beginning the few converts who start large group movements deliberately continue on as part of their own folk. They refuse to be mentally excluded. They continue to love their people, identify with them, serve them, spend as much time with them as possible proving to them that though they have become Christians they are still good members of the society—indeed, better members than they were before.

The Battle for Brotherhood

A major reason the element of peoplehood is commonly ignored by Christians is that the church in America has been fighting a great battle for brotherhood. To many Christians, the establishment of brotherhood among the races is the supreme goal of the church. They are opposed to segregation in any form. They doubt the validity of any principle that en-

courages Christians of one class or race to worship together or form congregations for their particular kind of people only. In 1976, an eminent
white Christian, on reading for the first time the sentence that heads this
chapter, wrote me indignantly saying, "Of course they like to become
Christians without crossing barriers, and they must not be permitted to."
Let us consider this position.

Dedicated Christians in discipled populations, where most persons
consider themselves in some way Christian, for the most part think exclusively in terms of "What should Christians do?" rather than "How do non-
Christian populations accept Christ?" They are particularly critical of al-
lowing one kind of people (one subculture) to form congregations of its
own. They erroneously call this segregation, and say that Christian mission should never promote or condone it. It is better, they think, to have
a slow growing or nongrowing church that is really brotherly, integrated,
and hence "really Christian," than a rapidly growing one-people church.

Such a position is natural for Christians today engaged in the battle
for brotherhood. When they see the injustices perpetrated on blacks in
the United States and ethnic minorities in many lands, what other position can they take? Furthermore, black Christians in the Third World, revolting against white imperialism, add a powerful voice to this demand
that the American church in no way countenance discrimination against
black citizens.

We must, of course, cordially endorse these sentiments. The principle I am setting forth, which plays such a large part in the growth of
the church, should not be understood as condoning white racial pride.
Nothing I have said justifies injustice and intolerance, or the strong enforcing segregation against the weak. My own considered opinion is that,
in the United States, the refusal of any congregation to admit blacks as
members is sin. The church, I hold, is rightly engaged in a great battle
for brotherhood against all such non-Christian behavior. In the battle, it
is ranged on God's side.

Part of that battle, however, is to lead non-Christians to Christ. Simply
becoming Christian is the greatest possible step toward brotherhood that
most people can take. All nations have their classes. Human nature encourages the formation of exclusive groupings. Many religions encourage
their adherents to feel that they alone are the superior people. Hinduism
gives its caste system not merely legal but religious justification. When
unbelievers become Christians they adopt a faith teaching the fatherhood
of God and the universal brotherhood of humans. They espouse a religion
whose Scriptures demand brotherhood. If class distinctions continue, they

do so in spite of the Christian faith, not because of it. Brotherhood is part of the basic theology of the Christian church.

The Christian in whose heart Christ dwells inclines toward brotherhood as water runs down a valley. True, Satan occasionally throws some great dam across the valley and the water does not flow. Such a dam was the iniquitous system of slavery that intertribal warfare in Africa and plantations in the Americas made possible. The tearing down of such dams requires, in addition to the natural inclination of the Christian heart, special action on the part of the church, and this social action is part of the church's work. But it must never be considered the whole work. If Christ in the heart did not impel toward brotherhood, no amount of social action would help the situation. The church's real business is the proclamation of the gospel. Her real business is also to obey her Lord's command to love one another, as well as to worship fervently. The church needs to get on with all of the above.

While the church is properly engaged in the battle for brotherhood, it must always remember that the rules for that battle are not the rules for a prior discipling that brings men and women of various subcultures, minorities, tongues, and ethnic units into the church and makes the development of true brotherhood possible. Christ is indeed "our peace, who has made both one, and has broken down the middle wall of division between us, having abolished in his flesh the enmity, that is, the law of commandments contained in ordinances, so as to create in himself one new man from the two" (Eph. 2:14-15). But it must be noted that Jesus creates one new man in place of the two *"in himself."* Jews and Gentiles—or other classes and races who scorn and hate one another—must be brought to Christ before they can be made really one.

As the debate in America raged concerning the rightness of the homogeneous unit principle, C. Peter Wagner determined to write his doctoral dissertation at the University of Southern California, maintaining that properly understood the concept is thoroughly ethical and very helpful in the discipling of *panta ta ethne* commanded in the New Testament. His dissertation was published in 1979 by John Knox Press—a landmark book entitled *Our Kind of People.* Anyone who wants to probe the depths of the radical turnaround in theory of evangelism and mission that the concept has caused must read this book.

Puerto Ricans and Yakima Indians

A few years ago Puerto Ricans, among them many Protestants, were migrating to Bridgeport, Connecticut, for work. The churches there said,

"We shall not establish segregated Puerto Rican churches. That would be wrong. We shall open our Anglo churches to these brothers and sisters, make them welcome, and count ourselves fortunate to have our fellowship broadened and enriched by their coming." The Puerto Ricans were invited, came a few times, and were treated most cordially. But they felt more at home in their own Spanish worship services. More importantly, unconverted relatives and friends came more readily to those than to the stately New England churches where the services were so orderly and no one shouted *Amen!* or *Gloria a Dios!* when they approved of something in prayer or sermon. So the Puerto Rican Protestants established congregations of their own in rented halls and vacant stores, and grew. They wisely avoided premature integration that would have blocked church growth.

In the Yakima Valley of the state of Washington is an Indian reservation. Between 1860 and 1880 many Yakima Indians became Christians and members of the Methodist church at White Swan. In the 1890s the government allowed Indians to sell their land, and white settlers bought up farms throughout the reservation. To protect the Indians, the government then forbade Indians to sell their land. This left many whites within driving distance of the Methodist church. They joined it, making it an integrated congregation. Soon leadership drifted into white hands. They sang better, read the Bible more, came more regularly, gave more, and knew more about how churches operate. The Indians found themselves attending a church run by whites.

At just that time a nativistic movement called the Shakers began to spread among the Indians, and many Indian Methodists, wanting a church of their own where they could function under their own leaders and in their own ways, became Shakers. The Shaker church that Yakimas could join without crossing racial and cultural lines prospered, while the Methodist (unquestionably the more Christian and orthodox congregation) became less and less Indian. Integration, before both groups of Christians are ready for it, is often the kiss of death to the weaker party. The issue is not theological but social.

DISCIPLING OUT TO THE FRINGES

Whenever people-consciousness is high—when classes and races think of themselves as distinct, and Christian churches are starting to multiply in one or two groups—the correct policy of evangelism is to disciple each homogeneous unit out to its fringes. To attempt to plant congregations in several homogeneous units at once, arguing that Christian ethics demand this, and insisting on integration first, whether the church grows or not, is a self-defeating policy and, with rare exceptions, contrary to the will of God.

When several homogeneous units of a society turn responsive at the same time, the policy should be to disciple each out to its fringes. In these societies, "loyalty to our people" becomes the chariot in which Christ rides to the hearts of unbelievers. If each homogeneous unit is completely discipled, nothing can prevent God from merging them into one fellowship; but if, before two percent of each unit has become Christian, churches and missions devote their energies to building up one Christian brotherhood, then most non-Christians (98 percent, to be exact) will be forced to leave their own folk and cross class and race barriers to become disciples of Christ. If this stumbling block is put in their way, the movement to Christian faith will usually falter and stop. Christian brotherhood is a *result* of the operation of the Holy Spirit in the lives of Christians—not a prerequisite for baptism.

Common Sense Assumed

In applying this principle, common sense must be assumed. The creation of narrow churches, selfishly centered on the salvation of their own kith and kin only, is never the goal. Becoming Christian should never enhance animosities or the arrogance common to all human associations. As members of one class, tribe, or society come to Christ, the church will seek to moderate their ethnocentrism in many ways. It will teach them that persons from other segments of society are also God's children. God so loved the world, it will say, that he gave his only Son that *whosoever* believes in him might have everlasting life. It will make sure that its people are in the vanguard of brotherly practices. The one thing the church will *not* do—on the basis that it is self-defeating—is to substitute kindness and friendliness for the gospel. It knows that brotherhood is the fruit and the gospel is the root.

And the church, I am sure, will not deify the principle I am describing in this chapter, whether it brings people into the way or not. Knowing that growth is a most complex process, it will humbly recognize that God uses many factors as yet not understood by us, and will not insist that he use just this one. If in a given instance, congregations neglecting the homogeneous unit principle grow better than those observing it, the church will not blindly follow the principle. It will be open to the leading of the Holy Spirit.

The church will remember that many factors contribute to church growth, and a suitable combination is more important than any one factor. It must not press the homogeneous unit principle emphasized in this chapter disproportionately nor allow it to obscure others. Good judgment and a humble dependence on God who alone gives growth is assumed in this discussion.

The homogeneous unit principle is certainly not the heart of church growth, but nevertheless has great applicability to many situations in America and other lands all around the world. Apply with common sense is the rule.

14

THE RECEPTIVITY OF INDIVIDUALS
AND SOCIETIES

OUR LORD SPOKE of fields in which the seed had just been sown and those ripe to harvest. Sometimes people who hear the word do nothing. The field appears no nearer harvest after receiving the seed than it did before. Sometimes, however, people hearing the word leap to obey it. They receive it with joy, go down into the waters of baptism, and come up to Spirit-filled lives in self-propagating congregations.

Our Lord took account of the varying ability of individuals and societies to hear and obey the gospel. Fluctuating receptivity is a most prominent aspect of human nature and society. It marks the urban and the rural, advanced and primitive, educated and illiterate. It vitally affects every aspect of world evangelization, and must be studied extensively if church growth is to be understood. I turn, therefore, to consider the fact of receptivity, its common causes, and its bearing on church growth in every country. Arthur F. Glasser explains that

> there is a time when God's Spirit is peculiarly active in the hearts of men. They become ripe unto harvest. . . . When this empirical factor has been deliberately made determinative of strategy, God has abundantly confirmed with good harvests. . . . In seeking to win those whom God has made winnable, we have not unnaturally gained new

insight into what it means to be co-laborers with God in the building of His Church (1976:38).

The receptivity or responsiveness of individuals waxes and wanes. No person is equally ready at all times to follow the way. The young person reared in a Christian home is usually more ready to accept Jesus Christ at twelve than at twenty. The skeptic is often more willing to become a disciple after serious illness or loss than before. This variability of persons is so well known that it needs no further exposition.

CHURCH GROWTH IS UNEVEN

Peoples and societies also vary in responsiveness. Whole segments of society resist the gospel for periods—often very long periods—and then ripen to the good news. In resistant people groups, only small single congregations can be created and kept alive, whereas in responsive ones many congregations that freely reproduce others can be established.

Unevenness of growth has marked the church from the beginning. The common people, the Gospels tell us, received our Lord's message better than the Pharisees and Sadducees. For the first three decades of the Christian era, the Jews responded far more than the Gentiles. When Judea had been Christian for a hundred years, Philistia on one side and Arabia on the other still remained solidly pagan.

Western nations display the fact that segments of the population ripen to the gospel at various times. Following the Revolutionary War, as immigrants kept pouring into the United States, the population was remarkably responsive. The Episcopal Church failed to see this and would have denied it. Heavily handicapped by its connection with the Anglican Church, it declined. Its system of creating ministers (priests) did not fit the free scattered settlements of the frontier. Baptist and Methodist churches, however, multiplied exceedingly. The immigrant population, when approached the right way, was remarkably responsive.

Missions in Asia, Africa, and Latin America also abundantly illustrate the fact that societies ripen to the gospel at different times. During the century 1850-1950 at least 500,000 in the Chota Nagpur area in India became Christian, whereas in nearby Mirzapur the century ended with less than 300 in the church. The aboriginal tribes of the first area were much more responsive to the gospel than the castes of the second. Southern Baptists between 1950 and 1960 maintained major missionary units in Thailand and Hong Kong. In 1960 they had 42 missionary forces in Thailand and 38 in Hong Kong. The outcome in terms of people "added to the Lord," to use the Lukan phrase, varied enormously. At the close of the decade, in Thailand the membership of churches planted by Southern Baptists was 355; in Hong Kong it was 12,527.

About 1949, the province of Apayao in the extreme north of Luzon in the Philippine Islands was largely occupied by the Isnegs—a pagan aboriginal tribe. The country is exceedingly mountainous, and they lived by the slash-and-burn method of cultivation. A few had become Christians in the small town that was the capital of the province and very difficult of access. The United Christian Missionary Society sent an agricultural missionary and his wife to teach this one congregation of Isnegs the cultivation of irrigated rice. Just as the couple, who had no children, arrived, pagan Isnegs all across the province turned highly responsive. They were not interested in growing more rice. They wanted baptism. The missionary was called to villages all through the mountains whose inhabitants had decided to become evangelical Christians and wanted instruction. He would scramble up a two-thousand-foot ridge and down the other side, slosh up a creek bottom for five miles, and spend two weeks instructing one group. In his absence a call would often come from some other hamlet, and his wife would hike off in the other direction to instruct its residents. In four years several thousand became Christians in the United Church of Christ.

The Roman Catholic Church, hearing of the great turning, sent in its missionaries and also won several thousand. The evangelical missionary told me that if the United Church had sent in three more couples in 1952, Apayao could have become an evangelical province, the only one in the Philippines.

Sudden ripenings, far from being unusual, are common. No one knows or has counted the ripenings of the last decades, but it is safe to say that they total hundreds if not thousands. Those which have been effectively harvested are, alas, smaller in number. One wonders why a single one of them should have been neglected.

How long does receptivity last? It is impossible to foretell. One thing is clear—receptivity wanes as often as it waxes. Like the tide, it comes in and goes out. Unlike the tide, no one can guarantee when it goes out that it will soon come back again.

CAUSES OF RECEPTIVITY

Myriads of factors affect responsiveness; I cannot attempt to list them all. A few, however, are so common and influential that they should be set forth.

New Settlements

When Bishop Rodriguez of the United Church of Christ in the Philippines was conducting me through Mindanao in my 1956 study of church growth, we came to a well-watered plain cut up into sections by dusty roads. Everywhere palm trees eight to ten feet tall were visible.

"See these small palms?" he said, pointing them out. "Churches can grow here."

I replied, "I see the palms, but what do they have to do with church growth?"

"Everything," he answered. "These young palms proclaim that this is a new population, recently moved in, broken loose from old associations, and not yet hardened into new patterns. These settlers are making new friends, entertaining new ideas, and are free from the social and religious bondages of the old barrios. They can become evangelicals."

A Methodist minister in Lima, Peru, bore similar testimony when he said that country folk who moved to the squatter settlements of that great city remained winnable for a decade or so; but when they began to earn well, built a brick house, and educated their sons and daughters, they grew hard of heart and dull of hearing. The nub of the matter is that immigrants and migrants have been so pounded by circumstances that they are receptive to all sorts of innovations, among which is the gospel. They are in a phase of insecurity, capable of reaching out for what will stabilize them and raise their spirits. It is no accident that the tremendous growth of Pentecostals in Brazil took place in the early days largely among the migrants flooding down from the northeast to the great cities of the south.

Returned Travelers

Travel sometimes turns people responsive. African soldiers in World War II who had seen the world came back to resistant tribal areas of Africa and sparked movements to the Christian faith. The bleak paucity of pagan life repelled them. Since the soldiers had prestige and were "of our people," their revulsion against paganism spread. When they told what the outside world was like, the tribespeople believed. The climate became more favorable for change. Becoming Christian became a real option for many.

Mexican laborers, during the years 1940-64, flooded into the United States for six months each year, worked on Protestant farms, and frequently were invited to attend church with their employers. They were sometimes—not often, alas—given Spanish Bibles and New Testaments, and took these back with them to their fanatical ranchos in Mexico. Years later evangelical missionaries commonly found that *braceros* (returned laborers) were remarkably open to the gospel. Numerous beginnings of congregations can be credited to the *bracero* movement. In at least one case (the Otomi church) a man converted in the United States founded a whole denomination. Had evangelical mission in 1944 sensed the importance of *braceros*, the presence of 300,000 Mexicans on the Protestant farms of the United States each subsequent year could have had tremendous effect in spreading the biblical faith. Unfortunately, only in 1962 and thereafter was the importance of the *bracero* as a carrier of the gospel widely recognized—and by then the arrangements between the Mexican and American governments that made the *bracero* movement possible were being terminated (Taylor 1962).

Conquest Affects Responsiveness

Since they have not been invaded and defeated, Britishers and Americans do not realize the shattering effect of being conquered. Defeat means not merely deaths, brutalities, and hostile armies marching across the motherland, but also terrific shock to the entire culture of the conquered. Their pride is humbled, their values trampled underfoot, their institutions abolished, and their gods dethroned. Five hundred years ago, when Muslims conquered Hindu states, they defaced Hindu idols, knocking noses and breasts off gods and goddesses. Though physical insult is frowned upon today, conquest defaces the national image just as effectively. Brutalities characterize every war, and though rape, pillage, arson, and murder among civilian populations are no longer the automatic accompaniment of victory—still, to be conquered is a traumatic experience, which has great meaning for church growth.

Sometimes the conquered are bitter against the victors, and evangelization meets implacable rejection. This is likely to be true among the ruling classes. The steady resistance of the intelligentsia of India to the Christian faith may be credited partly to this cause.

Sometimes the conquered are favorable toward the conquerors, and evangelization meets with cordial acceptance. This is likely to be the re-action of the ruled. They have new masters and are disposed to learn from them. Sometimes conditions attending defeat conduce toward acceptance. For example, Japan's defeat in 1945 coupled with her amazement at the decency and humaneness of the occupation produced seven years of wonderful receptivity toward the Christian religion.

Sometimes a population is not conquered but merely comes within the influence of some expanding power and is rendered receptive. For in-stance, Latin Rite Roman Catholics in the province of Kerala (southwest India) number about 900,000 and are composed chiefly of the fishing castes along the coast. Their conversion dates from the time the Por-tuguese ruled Goa, five hundred miles to the north, and were the sea power in all that part of the world. A remarkable Indian Christian named De Cruz championed the fishermen against oppression by Arab Muslim traders, and about 20,000 became Roman Catholics within a few years. That com-munity has grown, by further conversion of members of the fisher castes and by the excess of births over deaths, to its present large size (Gamaliel 1967:9).

Nationalism

Nationalism exerts a profound influence, both for and against the growth of the church. In Korea, after nine years of small growth in most provinces (1910-18), there came five years of great receptivity (1919-24). The cir-cumstances were these. Following World War I and the proclamation of the Wilsonian doctrine of self-determination for small nations, Korean patriots in 1919 launched a movement of nonviolent noncooperation against the Japanese with the purpose of forcing Japan to grant self-government to Korea. "Of the thirty-three Korean signers of the Declara-tion of Independence, fifteen were Christians, some of whom were prom-inent Protestant ministers" (Shearer 1966:64). The church became the rallying point for the oppressed Korean people. Evangelism building on the pronational stance of the church produced a significant surge of growth in most provinces. Nationalism aided church growth.

In Mexico, in 1857 at the height of the Juarez revolution a great com-pany of priests walked out of the Roman Catholic Church. Finding no guidance and no allies, some married and became secularized, some sought pardon and went back into the church, and a handful became Prot-estants. Had evangelical missions in North America been afire to extend the biblical faith in Latin America, the Mexican revolution might have been given a sound New Testament base, with incalculable consequences. But in those days missions were just beginning, and were convinced that Latin American countries were tight shut. American churches had very few Spanish-speaking pastors and no idea at all of the speed with which nationalism turns populations responsive.

Religious Change

An extraordinary happening has gone almost unmarked in the world of missions. One of the four great non-Christian religions has died during the last half-century. In 1920 Confucianism, the religion of four hundred million Chinese, was a most powerful faith. The Communist conquest of China has radically altered the situation. The whole family system, so basic to Confucianism, has been uprooted. Inside mainland China, Confucianism has lost its power. True, it is still practiced by some Chinese of the dispersion and may continue in vestigial form for decades or centuries; but as a great faith, Confucianism is finished. Buddhism in China is greatly weakened, too.

As China opens to freer interchange of thought, the church will face at least nine hundred million who live in a faith vacuum. Some, of course, are convinced Marxists and many will be in love with the world, but many more will be hungry for sure belief. To be sure, any Communist government can heavily handicap and persecute Christians. The church always evangelizes within the limits of the possible. But nevertheless Christians all around the world should be expecting a new and remarkable receptivity of the Chinese toward Christ. Some fifty million have already responded. An unbelievable desire to learn English is sweeping mainland China. This would seem to offer considerable openings for sensitive and sensible evangelism.

What will happen in Islam, when Muslim scholars subject the Koran to the same intense examination to which Christian scholars have subjected the Bible? And when Muslim archaeologists share the generally accepted findings of Jewish and Christian archaeologists? When the Koranic versions of biblical events are seen—as they certainly will be—to be garbled reproductions of Old and New Testament records, what will Muslims do? The faith of Islam is uniquely dependent on the claim that the Koran is the true and the Bible the corrupt version. When the acids of modernity eat away the protective layers of ignorance and the light of learning exposes the falsehood in this claim, faith in Islam is likely to wane. After Muslims have tried substitutes of various sorts, they will become responsive—to Communism or to Christianity—in very large numbers. They, too, are human beings and cannot live in a faith vacuum.

Freedom from Control

Control inhibits responsiveness to the Christian gospel. Relaxing of controls encourages it. Most of the three billion who yield no allegiance to Jesus Christ live under rigid controls. When these disintegrate, people become free to consider the claims of Christ.

Controls are of several varieties. The most intimate is that exercised by the family and immediate relatives. Persons do not exist as independent entities who make decisions entirely on their own, but as parts of a social whole. Their thoughts and feelings are conditioned and determined to a very large extent by the control of the family. The elaborate mourning, with loud wailing and repeated address to the dead, common in the villages of India is carried on as much for the observer as to express the bereaved's own sorrow. Villagers are not conscious of the control that dictates their form of mourning, but it is real nevertheless. "What will others think of my conduct?" is a serious consideration in all societies where each member is truly dependent on the family for almost every aspect of life.

The control of the village, the rancho, the tribe, and the caste is also an objective fact of life. The welfare of the village requires that everyone sacrifice to the god who is causing cattle disease. Failure to sacrifice draws down the wrath of the whole village.

"Ah," they exclaim, "so you are no longer one of us. You want our cattle to die. You refuse to share in our sacrifice to the god who brings the hoof-and-mouth disease? We shall deal with you."

The tribe believes that those who become Christian anger its gods and thus destroy the fertility of the fields for the whole village. The tribe has effective controls which vary all the way from beating the innovators and grazing their fields to putting a curse on them.

The ecclesiastical organization, the hierarchy, also exerts control. As pastors and missionaries on furlough compare notes at the School of World Mission at Fuller Seminary, they find that whether the ecclesiastical machine be that of one religion or another makes little practical difference. In some territories, an illiterate leader of the pagan religion will visit villages that are considering becoming Christian to dissuade or threaten them. In other territories, a well-educated priest will do the same. When, for any number of reasons, this control is relaxed, receptivity can increase rapidly.

THE BEARING OF RECEPTIVITY ON OUTREACH

I have been analyzing receptivity not as an intellectual exercise but to obtain light on the complex process of church growth. The correct response to this chapter is not mental pleasure in understanding how receptivity fluctuates, but rather joy that through knowing these variations we may be more faithful in the discharge of our stewardship and commission.

Pastors and missionaries often ask, Are the factors that create receptivity measurable, so that with proper techniques of appraisal we can know that such and such a population is ready for the gospel or is on the way to becoming ready? One keen pastor asked, "Could measurements be fed into a computer so that the church would know exactly the degree of receptivity and whether it was increasing or decreasing?" The answers to these questions are in the distant affirmative. Someday this may become possible. Indeed, today a trained observer can judge with a fair degree of accuracy that a given homogeneous unit is in a state where its members will welcome change. But in practice, rather than carry on an elaborate program of measurement, the church or mission has at hand a quicker and more reliable method of ascertaining receptivity.

Are groups of persons becoming Christians? As Jesus Christ is proclaimed to this population and his obedient servants witness to him, do individuals, families, and chains of families actually come to faith in him? Are churches being formed? Is any denomination working in similar peoples planting self-propagating congregations? If the answers are in the affirmative, the homogeneous unit concerned is receptive.

Once receptivity is proved in any one segment of society, it is reasonable to assume that other similar segments will prove receptive. Evangelism can be and ought to be directed to responsive persons, groups, and segments of society.

Two creative thinkers have written influentially on the bearing of receptivity on church and mission policies. George G. Hunter has described how receptivity ought to guide the outreach of North American congregations and denominations. C. Peter Wagner discusses how it ought to guide missions and churches in the Third World.

In *Frontiers of Missionary Strategy,* Wagner entitles Chapter Six "Anticipatory Strategy." He declares, "To a large extent, missionary strategy must be based on predictions or at least on some intelligent anticipation of the future" (1971:106). This immediately raises the question as to whether in Christian work predictions should be made at all. Are they biblically justifiable? After examining the Scriptures, he concludes that while predictions are human wisdom and must be used with caution, they are nevertheless required of one who would be a good steward of God's grace. With that matter settled, Wagner goes on to explore how reliable predictions of church growth may be made. He points out that:

> Nongrowth is just as important to discover as growth. If no churches are growing in a given area, anticipatory strategy might lead to another more promising area (1971:111).

The central question is:

> Where is the church most likely to grow? Which countries have the greatest potential and which particular groups of people within those countries show signs of being receptive to the gospel? . . . by careful soil tests, missionary strategists should be able to advise sowers where they should plant the seed first (1971:115).

Wagner was for years field secretary of the Andes Evangelical Mission. As such he naturally thought in terms of getting the right resources to the right places. Receptivity demands strategic action and the rearrangement of priorities.

> What resources are needed for an efficient job? If the university student community in a socialist country turns ripe, one kind of worker will be needed. If a group of animistic peasants turns ripe, someone with different qualifications is needed. Part of good management is to look ahead and . . . determine where the needs will be and what kind of missionary should be recruited or reassigned (1971:116).

George Hunter, in his chapter "The Grand Strategy," discusses receptivity in the North American setting. He considers it enormously important and counts it "the greatest contribution of the church growth movement to this generation's world evangelization" (1979:104). The chapter is full of insights for American churches which, with rather small adjustments, would apply equally well to churches in other continents.

A particularly helpful section deals with guidelines for discovering receptive mainline Americans. Hunter lists indicators of receptivity and urges that congregational and denominational policy be set in the light of these. These, he says, have "a special potency for the Christian mission to America." In his chapter, he suggests that local churches give a high priority to targeting outreach toward (1) those who visit your church, (2) those who desire to join your church, (3) those who have recently lost faith (in anything), (4) those among whom churches or religious movements are growing, (5) those of the same homogeneous unit as your members, (6) those with conscious needs that your ministries can help, and (7) those who are in transition.

The *Church Growth Bulletin* for many years has been describing the receptivity of various populations in all six continents. One vast population very much on the hearts of Christians is the 900 million Muslims. This group is made up of thousands of separate pieces, each one varying in receptivity from the next. The general opinion that all Muslims are highly resistant is not true. Large Communist blocks that arise in Muslim countries bear witness that Muslims in considerable numbers are turning from the worship of Allah to an atheistic understanding of reality. If they can do that, they can also turn to the Christian faith. The *Church Growth Bulletin* has a perceptive article by Don M. McCurry on receptivity as it bears on the evangelization of the huge Muslim mosaic. He says:

> We need to use all the skills available to us in church growth think-ing to find the responsive Muslim units scattered all over the world and then move in with sufficient force to disciple those subgroups (1978:220).

Distribution of Receptivity

As church leaders regard the people with whom they work, they often ask, To what degree is becoming a Christian a real option to members of this homogeneous unit? How receptive is it? In answering these questions or estimating the receptivity of any population it is helpful to locate it on a resistance-receptivity axis.

The exact model for a resistance-receptivity axis has been undergo-ing some evolution over the past few years. At this point in time it seems that the most useful and widely accepted design for the axis comes from Edward R. Dayton's *That Everyone May Hear* (1983:47):

RESISTANCE / RECEPTIVITY SCALE

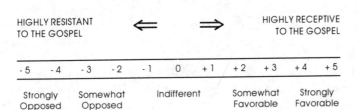

Let us suppose that different homogeneous units are represented by the numbers above at different positions on the axis. Populations at -5 would be pre-evangelized in a manner suitable to the highly resistant. Those at +5 would be harvested. At -5 the task of the church or mission is chiefly to hang on, sowing the seed and maintaining a loving Christian presence. In populations near +5, on the other hand, this kind of approach would be criminal. When the Holy Spirit has so moved on people that, resolved to become Christians, they press in to take the kingdom by violence, it is the height of unfaithfulness for the missionary simply to remain there demonstrating kindly Christian presence. Mere witness to the love of God is not what is demanded. At +5, the obedient worker must baptize multitudes in the name of the Father, Son, and Holy Spirit.

Two illustrations from the United States will help us see the situation. In the multitudinous new suburbs—which must surely be grouped toward the +5 end of the scale—the speedy establishment of adequate numbers of new congregations is clearly God's will. Also a much greater attention to first-generation immigrants is surely God's command. These fine people are intensely interested in becoming Americans, and we should make sure that they do not become pagan Americans.

Most populations today fall neither at -5 nor +5, but in between. To some degree they are winnable, but they are not storming the gates of Zion. In the mid-ranges of the axis, method is of supreme importance. Winnable men and women may be lost by one method and gained by another. For instance, heavy dependence on the school approach in Africa, south of the Sahara, makes possible the Christianization of 1 to 5 percent of populations left of center; but when these grow receptive and move to the right of center, excessive reliance on the school approach dooms the church to very slow advance. Proclaiming Christ to individuals only and taking them out of their society into Christian colonies may be the only mode of mission that will win any to Christ for populations grouped around -4 on the resistance-receptivity axis; but when increased responsiveness places these populations at +3 or +4 or other positions toward the right, it is fatal to continue the "one-by-one against their kindred" method of evangelization.

Occupying Resistant Fields

Recognition of variations in receptivity is offensive to some missiologists because they fear that, if they accept it, they will be forced to abandon resistant fields. Abandonment is not called for. Fields must be sown. Stony fields must be plowed before they are sown. No one should conclude that if receptivity is low, the church should withdraw evangelistic efforts.

Correct policy is to occupy fields of low receptivity lightly. The harvest will ripen someday. Their populations are made up of men and women for whom Christ died. While they continue in their rebellious and resistant state, they should be given the opportunity to hear the gospel in as courteous a way as possible. But they should not be heavily occupied lest, fearing that they will be swamped by Christians, they become even more resistant.

They should not be bothered and badgered. Generations should not be reared in schools where—receiving small doses of the gospel that they successfully reject—they are in effect inoculated against the Christian religion. Resistant lands should be held lightly.

While holding them lightly, Christian leaders should perfect organizational arrangements so that when these lands turn responsive, missionary resources can be sent in quickly. For some time now we have been hearing a great deal about the sudden new receptivity among Muslims in Indonesia. It is devoutly to be hoped that missionaries to Muslims in great numbers will be transferred to that part of the world. Some have, but not nearly enough. Reinforcing receptive areas is the only mode of mission by which resistant populations that become receptive may be led to responsible membership in ongoing churches.

The ways in which highly receptive populations may be filled with Christian congregations should be a subject of study in every seminary and theological training school. True, not every pastor will encounter a highly receptive population, but some of them will. Every minister in training therefore ought to have instruction as to how churches may be *multiplied* in the great receptive populations of Canada and the United States. The same is even more true of theological training schools in Asia, Africa, and Latin America.

In Europe, however, with its intrenched state churches, what church growth means is not yet clear. The state churches appear to believe that nothing more than renewal is called for. The population is already "Christian," that is, baptized. I myself am inclined to believe that renewal is not enough. Only the creation of multitudes of new vital congregations (either within or without the state denominations) will reconvert the myriads of European Christo-pagans. Much thought should be given to this.

FITTING METHOD TO RECEPTIVITY IN VIEW
OF THE CHIEF END

That receptivity should determine effective evangelistic methods is obvious. But readjustment of the total program of a church in America or a mission in Africa to enable it to fit a greatly increased responsiveness is difficult and rare. Few large populations change as a whole. When a community of 100,000 develops a mild degree of receptivity, moving let us say from -4 to +3 on the resistance-receptivity axis, this never means that all 100,000 have suddenly become winnable, but rather that among the total population *a few thousand* persons belonging to some homogeneous unit have become winnable, and then *only if approached in the right way.* If they heard the gospel from their own folk, they are winnable; but from strangers they are as resistant as ever. If they recognize the Christian messenger as "one who is on our side," they are winnable; but if those proclaiming Christ appear to them as disinterested professionals, they may remain resistant. If those who become Christian are really changed, the few thousand become winnable; but if the new Christians are as unhappy as ever, non-Christians remain indifferent to the gospel.

Unless Christian leaders in all six continents are on the lookout for changes in receptivity of homogeneous units within the general population, and are prepared to seek and bring persons and groups belonging to these units into the fold, they will not even discern what needs to be done. They will continue generalized church and mission work that, shrouded in fog as to the chief end of mission, cannot fit outreach to increasing receptivity. An essential task is to discern receptivity and—when this is seen—to adjust methods, institutions, and personnel until the receptive are becoming Christians and reaching out to win their fellows to eternal life. *Effective* evangelism is demanded. It finds the lost, folds those found, feeds them on the word of God, and incorporates them into multitudes of new and old congregations. That is why it is called effective evangelism.

PART V

SPECIAL KINDS OF CHURCH GROWTH

15

THE MASSES, THE CLASSES, AND CHURCH GROWTH

MORE THAN ANY previous century, ours is conscious of the masses and their claim to justice and equality of opportunity. The burden-bearers have always comprised the major part of society, but in the twentieth century they have gained more and more social and political power. Industrialism has created a huge proletariat in our ever enlarging cities. Labor organizations have achieved tremendous strength. The churches have called for social justice. An awakened conscience among national leaders has changed our tax structure in the direction of a more just distribution of wealth. Communism has established dictatorships of the proletariat in many nations, defending these as a necessary step toward a just society.

Scores of millions, through reading, study, lectures, the mass media, and indoctrination, have learned of both the needs of the masses and their might when organized and armed. Perhaps more powerful than books and speeches, however, managed events such as elections, victories at the Olympic games, space explorations, summit meetings, riots, and wars have strikingly focused attention on the masses and their right to education, health, leisure, and power. That the human race should be divided into beneficiaries and victims of the social order no longer seems right to thoughtful people.

What does this radically new element in human thinking, which dominates the world scene as the Himalayas dominate the plains of North India, signify for bringing nations to faith in Jesus Christ and obedience to the gospel?

CLASS/MASS SOCIETY DESCRIBED

While most Americans will agree with the first paragraph above, they understand it with their heads rather than their hearts. Though they have their poor, their exploited, and the underclass, most Americans are accustomed to a unified society and do not like to think in terms of the classes and the masses. The carpenter earns as much as the college teacher and the millworker drives a better car than the pastor. The idea of a privileged aristocracy is alien to our national ethos. So while they sometimes talk about the underprivileged masses, most Americans do not really know what it is to live as victims of the social order. It is hard for them to imagine countries where three-fourths or more of the population live below our poverty level.

In other parts of the world, the (privileged) classes as over against the masses are a vivid part of the scene. Economics, power structures, and religions are so arranged that the more comfortable classes remain high above the great mass of people. The distance can be measured in many areas of life. In income, the classes average 200 a month, the masses 20. In language, the classes speak the national language fluently and correctly. The masses speak many dialects and express themselves clumsily in the standard languages. In housing, the classes live in comfortable and permanent homes, with all modern conveniences. The masses live in shacks made of thatch and wattle, adobe and crude tile, odds and ends of lumber, and tin cans. As to health, the classes obtain competent medical service, buy sufficient food to keep well, rear their children to maturity, and enjoy old age. The masses depend on herbalists and medicine men of one sort or another, eat chiefly corn or manioc or rice, meal after meal, day after day, and year after year. True, their diet is fortified by a few beans, vegetables in season, and very occasionally meat or fish. The masses are lean. They do not count calories, their infant mortality is high, and they seldom live to have gray hair.

In the political arena, the classes are intimately related to those who run the country. The masses have little to do with those who rule them and care less. In religion, the classes are assured that they are God's special creation—recall the Hindu doctrine of castes. The masses are assured, in effect, that God created them "little people"—Shudras or inferiors in

India, Indians in Bolivia and Peru, blacks in North America—to be laborers forever.

In India the masses include not only 99 percent of the untouchable Shudras but most of the touchables, and great numbers of the upper castes also. In manufacturing cities and villages, the hungry are to be found in all castes, though the proportion grows less as one approaches the uppermost. In China, the Philippines, Indonesia, Africa, and all the countries of Latin America, as one adds disinherited, shirtless ones, sharecroppers, landless labor, and illiterates together, a vivid picture of the huge size of the masses and depth of their misery emerges.

We are indebted to Eugene Nida for popularizing a helpful diagram of the social order. The pear-shaped figure below shows proportions and classes:

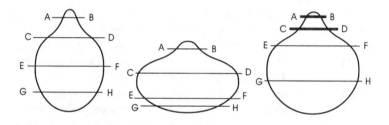

Any analysis to be meaningful must define accurately the terms used. Exactly who comprise the classes and masses? *Until sharp definition has been made of each segment of a given society, precise thinking about it is impossible.* Since society in each country, however, differs from that in other countries, and in a given country the definitions of thirty years ago will not fit society as it exists today, I shall not attempt precise definitions. Those made for Mexico would not fit Korea, those for Canada would not fit England.

Instead, for the sake of the illustration, I shall count the landed aristocracy as the upper classes (above *AB* in the pear-shaped diagram), the business community and professionals as middle classes (above *CD*), artisans, mechanics, mill foremen, and truck drivers as upper-lower classes (above *EF*), peasants and unskilled labor as middle-lower classes (above *GH*); and the unemployed, unemployable, serfs, drifters, and diseased as the lower-lower classes (below *GH*). Note the extremely small proportion the upper classes form of the whole—perhaps 1 percent of the total population. Note the small size of the middle classes, perhaps 6 percent of the population. The place of line *CD* will vary up and down depending on what country and what decade in that country is being considered. Note also how words mislead the mind. The middle classes are "middle" in no real sense at all; it is more realistic to call the "middle" and "upper" classes together "the classes." They are the beneficiaries of the social order. In many places they are the exploiters and the lower classes could more exactly be called the exploited. Consequently in this chapter I speak of only two main divisions: the classes and the masses. Any true picture of the population of the Third World must portray the small numbers in the tip and the very large numbers in the swelling bulb of the pear-shaped figure—everything below the line *CD*. Tiny classes and tremendous masses characterize most countries of the world today.

Tribal societies, where every member of the tribe has an equal right to the land, present an exception to class/mass society, but the exception will not be long-lived. As tribal societies break down, emerge into the common life of the world, and flood into cities, they join the masses.

As industrialization and education progress, the middle classes, particularly in favored nations, increase in size. However, middle-class growth does not decrease the tremendous numbers in the masses. Many nations publicize dramatic moves they make toward social justice, but one cannot help noting that by comparison to the size of the total problem, these changes are small. Christian leaders must not imagine that these moves toward justice, in which they rejoice, materially affect the discipling of nations. The glowering masses still remain. Their numbers grow with every passing year. The middle classes are still small and will remain small, if not proportionately smaller. Christians today should address themselves to the current problem.

The masses in the past have been resigned. They thought the kind of life they lived was the only kind possible. But resignation or what passes for contentment is disappearing. One should not overestimate the rate of its going, but it *is* retreating. The masses are learning that they do not have to live in perpetual poverty. Educated leaders inform them that they have a right to plenty, and organize and arm them to wrest a large share of this world's goods from the privileged. This is the revolution that seethes in every land.

Marxists are determined to ride this revolution to world domination. They believe Communism offers the only way by which the masses, through class struggle and the dictatorship of the proletariat, can wring justice out of the reluctant classes. Idealists among the students, groaning at the rank oppression that present systems impose on the multitudes, demand change. Patriots, seeing that nations composed of hereditary elites battening on a vast illiterate peasantry are weak, seek to enfranchise the peasants so that their countries may become powerful. Whoever does it—Marxists, idealists, or patriots—the masses are being roused, organized, and pushed into the battle for more of the good things of life.

THE BIBLE AND THE MASSES

The Bible shows a steady preference for the poor. It begins by declaring that all are children of Adam and hence equal. It ends by affirming that all, great and small alike, will stand before the great white throne and be judged. Wealth, learning, blue blood, power, and thrones count for nothing as people are judged. The sole criterion, equally possible to the masses and the classes, is: Have they washed their robes? Are their names written in the book of life? Have they confessed Christ before the world and, abandoning all sin and other allegiance, been faithful to death?

To Christians among the masses in India, the biblical account—that God created one man and one woman and all humans are their descendants—is particularly dear. It contrasts sharply with the Hindu account that the great god Brahm created the Brahmins from his head, the warrior castes from his shoulders, the merchant castes from his thighs, and the masses from his feet.

When God selected a people in Egypt and made a covenant with them, he chose not the learned, not the princes, not the aristocrats, not the students—but the slaves. Later when the Hebrews were settled in Canaan and wanted a king, the Bible records that God was not pleased with their thirsting after a more efficient aristocratic structuring of their society. In a remarkable passage he foretold the oppressions that the classes have always inflicted on the masses. The forms vary from age to age and land to land, but the oppression remains.

> This will be the behavior of the king who will reign over you: He will take your sons and appoint them for his own chariots and to be his horsemen, and some will run before his chariots. He will appoint captains over his thousands and captains over his fifties, will set some to plow his ground and reap his harvest, and some to make his weapons of war and equipment for his chariots. He will take your daughters to

be perfumers, cooks, and bakers. And he will take the best of your fields, your vineyards, and your olive groves and give them to his servants (1 Sam. 8:11-14).

When the aristocratic order flowered and came to fruit, and all these prophecies and more had come to pass, God sent his prophets to plead the cause of the poor and to demand justice for the common man.
Isaiah says:

Woe to those who decree unrighteous decrees, who write misfortune, which they have prescribed to rob the needy of justice, and to take what is right from the poor of My people, that widows may be their prey, and that they may rob the fatherless (Isa. 10:1-2).

Micah says:

And you rulers of the house of Israel: is it not for you to know justice? You who hate good and love evil; who strip the skin from My people, and the flesh from their bones. . . . What does the Lord require of you but to do justly, to love mercy, and to walk humbly with your God? (Mi. 3:1-2; 6:8).

Nathan, Jeremiah, Amos, and other prophets immediately join Isaiah and Micah when we focus attention on the rights of the masses and the oppression meted out to them by the upper classes. It is no accident that Communism arose in Christendom. The Communist ethical passion, so strangely distorted by its metaphysical framework, arises straight out of the biblical insistence that God is a God of righteousness and will not have the poor oppressed.

New Testament Emphasis

The New Testament tells us that, when it pleased God that the Word should become flesh and dwell among us, Jesus was born to a peasant girl of Nazareth and grew up in the home of a carpenter. The Son of God learned the carpenter's trade and carried heavy planks and beams on his head and shoulders. Like the masses everywhere, he ate his bread by the sweat of his face.
When at Nazareth our Lord announced the purpose of his coming, he said:

The Spirit of the Lord is upon Me, because He has anointed Me to preach the gospel to the poor, He has sent Me to heal the brokenhearted, to preach deliverance to the captives and recovery of sight to the blind, to set at liberty those who are oppressed, to preach the acceptable year of the Lord (Luke 4:18-19).

No one can miss Jesus' marked emphasis on God's will for the masses, a point that received added confirmation when later he included in the signs of the coming of the kingdom the significant one that "the poor have the gospel preached to them" (Matt. 11:5).

Of the twelve apostles, eleven were Galileans—country people who spoke with an accent. The rulers, elders, scribes, and high priests scorned them as "uneducated common men." The book of Acts tells us that the Christian religion spread through the masses in Jerusalem and Judea. The common people heard the apostles gladly. The rulers of the Jews were afraid to act against the apostles because they feared the people. The people, we are told, held the apostles in high esteem and, when the captain with the officers went and brought the apostles (Acts 5:18) to the high priest, they did so without violence, for they were afraid of being stoned by the people. It is no wonder that the masses were solidly behind the early church. It was made up largely of the common people and had common people for leaders. The church had only a few of the intelligentsia, and the great company of priests who later became obedient to the faith were perhaps those who were dependent on the masses who had become Christian.

When the church grew in the synagogue communities of the Roman Empire, it took in large numbers of the underprivileged, as is amply attested by the famous passage in 1 Corinthians—the only breakdown of the social standing of church members recorded in the New Testament:

> For you see your calling, brethren, that not many wise according to the flesh, not many mighty, not many noble, are called. But God has chosen the foolish things of the world to put to shame the things which are mighty . . . (1 Cor. 1:26-27).

The Masses Are Dear to God

These selected passages must not be distorted to mean that God loves the poor and not the rich. God is no respecter of persons, and the poor sinner is just as lost as the wealthy one. While the Old Testament prophets inveigh against the rich who sell the needy for a pair of shoes, the great weight of their judgment falls not on the rich but on those, rich and poor, who abandon God for idols. Wealthy women were disciples of our Lord, and Nicodemus and Zacchaeus were far from poor. All this must be held steadily in view. Nevertheless, it remains true that the common people are dear to God. The fundamental thrust of God's revelation demands a high valuation of the masses.

Facing the classes and the masses, the church and her emissaries may well pray the following missionary prayer:

> Almighty God our heavenly Father, who made of one blood all who dwell on the face of the earth, we worship you, we adore you, we bow in reverence before you. We yield ourselves to you and implore you to be born in us, take command of our wills, and make us yours in truth.
>
> O Lord Jesus Christ, we remember that you were born of a peasant mother in a poor carpenter's home and did surround yourself with disciples and apostles whom the educated of that day called ignorant and unlearned. You told the world that a sign of the coming of your kingdom was that the gospel was proclaimed to the poor.
>
> The common people heard you, Lord, gladly. Your blessed mother sang, My soul magnifies the Lord and my spirit has rejoiced in God my Savior, for he has scattered the proud in the imagination of their hearts, he has put down the mighty from their seats, and exalted them of low degree. He has filled the hungry with good things, and the rich he has sent away empty. And did not you, O Lord, invite all those who labor and are heavy laden to come to you and find rest?
>
> O Holy Christ, we lift up before you the poor of the earth, the masses of humanity, the rural multitudes whose backs are bent with toil, the urban multitudes who live in tenements and shacks and favelas and barrios and zongoes. We lift up the illiterate, the oppressed, the disinherited, the fishermen and the carpenters, the landless labor, the unskilled, the handicapped. We lift up the poor, Lord, the poor for whom you shed your precious blood and on whom you looked with compassion, for they were sheep without a shepherd. Grant us, Lord, your compassion, that we too may see the great masses as your lost children, and like you spend ourselves for them. In your blessed name. Amen.

MISSIONS FAVOR THE CLASSES

Missions from the wealthy West usually overlook the Bible at this point. Missionaries, particularly the non-Pentecostal variety, customarily place a high value on the educated, the wealthy, the cultured—in a word, the middle and upper classes. This is dictated and inspired, not by the Bible but, unconsciously, no doubt, by the extraordinarily affluent society of which most missionaries are a part. They thus devote themselves to maintaining cordial relationships with the business and professional leaders, seek to win the leaders of the coming generation, and believe one Brahmin convert is worth a thousand untouchable Christians. In a given congregation of 200 communicants there may be 10 from the middle classes and 190 from the lower classes; but if asked, "What classes are you reaching?" a typical pastor will reply, "Middle and high—and some low, of course." Part of the scorn that has, in days past, been poured on the Pentecostals in Latin America is due to the fact that Pentecostals are frankly churches of the masses.

From the human point of view, preference for the middle and upper classes is eminently reasonable. The masses, as Moses and Paul could testify, bring problems with them when they become the people of God. The wealthy can support a paid ministry much more easily than the poor. Having grown up with more to manage, they are much more experienced in managing things.

Anglicans, Lutherans, Presbyterians, and Catholics in Europe have largely lost the working classes. An Anglican priest remarked to me, "After the industrial revolution started, we never had the working classes, and the Methodists got only a small part of them."

Most missionaries are middle-class people. They have grown up with interior plumbing, electric lights, and plenty of books. They ride in cars and travel to the lands of their work in jet planes. Really, in relation to the masses of many of the lands to which they go, they are perceived not as middle-, but upper-class people.

Naturally they tend to create middle-class churches. There is nothing surprising in this, for the middle-class congregations in which they grew up have formed their standards. What are reverent worship, good singing, Christian treatment of wives, standards of punctuality, and proper use of leisure? What are efficient ways of conducting church business and educating one's children? Answers to these questions, given by missionaries and national pastors trained by them, cannot but be middle-class answers, unless leaders recognizing this part of their cultural overhang steel themselves against it.

Missionaries tend to identify with those leaders of younger churches who by virtue of their education are middle-class, and thus reinforce the image of the church as a middle-class organization. They frequently press middle-class clothes on a church made up of the masses. Then growth stops.

First the Upper Classes?

One of the key questions on which mission policy hinges is this: Should we seek to win the upper classes first, confident that if we do they will win the lower classes? Many missionaries and nationals, living in cities, working with students, and maintaining schools, believe the question should be answered in the affirmative. In part their answer is dictated by their own middle-class standing, but in part it is based on what seems a reasonable assumption: that the middle classes are the leaders and the masses are the followers. They believe in a trickle down theory of missiology.

Striking instances of the lower classes following the upper into the church can be found. The slaves in the United States became Christian largely because their masters were Christians—and would have become Muslims had their masters been Muslims. In the Philippines, the feudal lords of a large estate in Negros Oriental became evangelicals, and most of their peons followed them. A church of several thousand resulted, made up of many small congregations scattered over the vast holding.

But for the most part, the strategy of winning the upper classes first has not worked. They will not be won. The middle classes have it too good. Why should they risk losing it all to become Christians? For when they do, they are often disinherited and lose their position of leadership. No one has made a more careful study of this issue than Waskom Pickett. His findings should be carefully pondered before answering the question.

Movements to Christ, he says, "have not generally developed where missionaries were most closely associated with the government" and hence with the rulers of the people, nor "in areas where Western influence has been most strongly felt" through schools and colleges where the upper and middle classes were educated. "Nor have movements developed in areas where missionary forces have been most numerous or longest at work. . . ." Where movements did begin, they began almost in spite of the missionaries, for "the missionaries in practically every area were working primarily for the high castes hoping that they might first be won and might then take over the winning of the lower castes."

> The fear that reception of large numbers of the depressed classes into the Church would interfere with the winning of the upper classes seems to have restrained a section, at least, of the missionaries in every area when movements of the upper classes and the subsequent conversion, through their efforts, of those lower in the social scale, have not occurred (Pickett 1933:55f.).

Pickett's findings in India in 1933 can be duplicated in Brazil and Chile today. Far greater numbers of middle-class people are being won for Christ in those two lands where hundreds of thousands of poor people have become evangelicals in Baptist, Pentecostal, and other churches than are being won in Colombia, Costa Rica, and other lands where the chief effort has been to win the middle classes to Christ.

Arnold Toynbee has pointed out that, far from a new religion first being accepted by the classes and then by the masses, it is usually first accepted by the proletariat. Later, of course, as in the case of Christianity in the Roman Empire, the classes accepted it. He says:

> Higher religions make their entry into Society from below upwards and the dominant minority [the classes] is either unaware of these new religious movements or . . . is hostile to them. . . . [In the Roman Empire] the philosophies appealed to the middle class. . . . Christianity appealed to the masses (Toynbee 1956:37, 99).

The Masses Are Increasingly Responsive

Often the masses, groaning under centuries of oppression by the classes, regard their old religion as the instrument of their enslavement. Thus Ambedkar used to exclaim, "When I read the New Testament I find the very antidote my people need for the poison of Hinduism which they have been drinking for three thousand years!" The next fifty or a hundred years are certain to see the masses everywhere in the grip of a "steadily growing desire" to get the good things of life—and, if necessary, to overthrow the traditional social order to get them.

The Christian church has good news for the awakening masses—first that God the Father almighty is just, and second that he will give those who love and obey him power to treat others justly. Let us consider both parts of this gospel.

That God is just—the revolutionary impact of this simple statement should be grasped. It affirms that the very structure of the universe favors the common people. It proclaims that the vast mysterious power whom we call God the Father almighty intends an order of society in which each person can and will receive justice. Consider this ultimate fact in the light of the needs of the masses. Contrary to much superficial thinking, the greatest need of the masses and their leaders is neither aid nor kindness. Their greatest need is not handouts but a worldview, a religion, that gives them bedrock on which to stand as they battle for justice.

The highly valuable gifts of the Christian religion are: God the Father almighty who hates injustice, God the Son who died for each member of the masses, the Bible, and an ethical perspective that requires justice for all, thus endowing every human being with infinite value. Making people Christian, along with other things, means giving them a frame of reference that irresistibly, though often slowly, creates equality of opportunity and undergirds all strivings against entrenched privilege. With this wealth in hand, those of the masses can conquer all secondary poverties.

The second aspect of the good news is this: God gives those who love and obey him power to treat others justly. Those who accept Jesus Christ as God and Savior receive the Holy Spirit and his fruit—love, joy, peace, patience, kindness, goodness, faithfulness, gentleness, and self-control. They receive power to live the good life. They are able to live justly whatever the framework of their society.

The good news has a powerful corollary that appeals greatly to the masses today: that just people can build a just society. The just society of which I speak is the kinder, more humane order that by God's grace arises within family, neighborhood, city, or state as the number of Christians multiplies. Since a just society must be built, not by, but out of people who are profoundly interested in the welfare of others as such men and women and their churches multiply, the structures of society will become more and more righteous.

Because God is just, his mission maintains that every move toward justice is pleasing to him. It assures people that when they are fighting for justice he is on their side. Even more truly, in working for justice and brotherhood they are on God's side, and God will win. It is a message of supreme hope.

POLICY TOWARD MASSES AND CLASSES

As the church faces over three billion who know little or nothing about Jesus Christ, what should be the policy toward the classes and the masses?

Winning the Winnable

Policy should be formed on two assumptions: (1) that the masses are growing increasingly responsive and will continue to listen to the good news, just because every influence bearing on their lives will make them increasingly dissatisfied with their present status; and (2) that particular masses in certain countries and sections of countries fluctuate in response as they are played on by military fortune, economic forces, victories and defeats. In some places they will temporarily become highly resistant, in others highly receptive. Non-Christian classes, on the other hand, may be counted on to be generally resistant to the gospel, though their attitude also will fluctuate. Some sections may for brief periods become significantly responsive, and should be effectively evangelized.

Since the gospel is to be preached to all creatures, no Christian will doubt but that both the receptive and the resistant should hear it. And since gospel acceptors have an inherently higher priority than gospel rejectors, no one should doubt that, whenever it comes to a choice between reaping ripe fields or seeding others, the former is commanded by God.

Winning the winnable while they are winnable seems sound procedure. This is the strategic meaning of our Lord's words, "beginning at Jerusalem." While the Palestinian Jews were responsive, the Holy Spirit led the church to focus on them. The first fifteen years saw a powerful, one-race church built up among the residents of Jerusalem and Judea. When either masses or classes are winnable, they should hear the gospel, be baptized, and added to churches that immediately, without pause to consolidate, go out to win their still receptive fellows.

If in any given sector the masses turn indifferent or hostile, then efforts to win them should be transferred to other sectors where unbelievers will hear and obey. When our Lord gave directions to the twelve, he said, "Whoever will not receive you, when you go out of that city, shake off the very dust from your feet as a testimony against them" (Luke 9:5). When he instructed the seventy (Luke 10:10), he gave them precisely the same instructions. The indifferent of the masses have no more right to coddling efforts at persuasion than others. Those who stand with arms outstretched, whether of the classes or the masses, have a higher right to hear than those who stop their ears and turn away.

Time Is Short

This is not only the age of the masses, but the future belongs to them. Evangelistic policies should not be determined on the basis of the aristocratic feudal order that dominated the world a few years ago. What God requires of his church is based on the forms that society is going to take, not those that flourished a hundred years ago. Christian mission stands at one of the turning points of history. A new order is being born. Its exact form is hidden from us; the forces that combine to make the new world are far too complex to allow anyone a clear view of the outcome. Yet it seems reasonably certain that, whatever else happens, the masses are going to have a great deal more to say in the future than they have in the past.

It may be that the most significant movement in Christian mission is the discipling of the advance elements of the masses to the Christian faith—the people movements of India, the tribal movements of Indonesia, the hundred and fifty million and more who have become Christians in Africa, and the Pentecostal churches of Latin America. To win the winnable while they are winnable would, indeed, seem to be an urgent priority. The evangelization and incorporation of the receptive sections of the masses is the best gift we can give to them.

16

HALTING DUE TO REDEMPTION AND LIFT

OUT OF THE CLASS/MASS situation just described arises the crucial question: How can world evangelization avoid the halting of growth essentially due to the effect of redemption plus the socioeconomic "lift" of a program of educational, medical, and perhaps agricultural aid? As the church is established among the masses in the world, again and again it is stopped dead in its tracks. A Baptist denomination of 3,000 members has remained at about that figure for thirty years. A Lutheran cluster of 1,000 has grown at 1 percent for fourteen years. An evangelical denomination of seven congregations, planted by an interdenominational mission, has climbed from 400 to 500 in twelve years.

Many static denominations in America and Europe are classic cases of stoppage due to redemption and lift. They have benefitted so greatly from obeying Christ and having "all these things" added to them that they are gravely handicapped in propagating the gospel among their fellows. This is why the most respectable denominations in America and other lands are so frequently the least growing. While many illustrations in this chapter will be from Third World nations, the problem we are exploring is universal. It is well known in the West.

The Third World has so many arrested churches that church leaders commonly think of mission as aid in perpetuity to stopped little denominations on the other side of the world. A large percentage of the resources of missions is poured into these clusters of nongrowing congregations. They receive the rich services of a permanent staff of missionaries and much mission money; yet they remain encircled enclaves of a few hundred or a few thousand communicants.

For example, a mission with a college, high school, hospital, ten missionaries, budget of $200,000, and seven congregations whose aggregate membership remains less than a thousand year after year is no rare sight. It does not intend or expect to grow into a denomination of even twenty thousand. Its small size and stagnant condition are concealed in some cases by the fact that it has become part of a "large, united church"; but behind the facade, the fact is inescapable that this cluster of congregations continues to be aided and continues stopped. Clarity is so important here that again I ask the reader's patience for what may seem a blunt or staccato use of terms. Such a mission is typical of hundreds of others in and out of the united churches. Its problem—halting due to redemption plus lift that results in sealed-offness—is a major problem in the world today. Let us see how it arises and examine some suggestions for its solution.

THE REDEMPTION OF CHRIST

Every true church observes among its members a redemption due to Christ's saving activity in the human heart. When Christ comes in, they become new creatures. They repent and turn from their sins. They gain victory over pride, greed, laziness, drink, hate, and envy. They cease quarreling with their neighbors and chasing women. They turn from litigation to constructive activity. They educate their children. They learn what God requires of them, and worship regularly. They become more effective human beings.

The fellowship of the church buoys them up. Brothers and sisters in Christ gather at their bedsides to pray for them in sickness. They read or hear the Bible and realize that God is for them and is available to them. They realize they are children of God and begin to act as such. They begin to live for others. Their community, in which many others have accepted Christ, becomes a better and better place to live. All these aspects of redemption occur in imperfect measure, to be sure, but they occur. Church leaders from abroad may see much less advance than they hoped for, but then they are probably measuring converts against their Western background, not the converts'.

Redemption, depending solely on the Bible, the church, the Savior, the Holy Spirit, and prayer, is indefinitely reproducible. Wherever men and women trust Christ, read his Word, obey him, and gather round his table they are redeemed in this way, even when wholly independent of any aid from abroad.

LIFT DUE TO MISSION AND CHURCH ACTIVITY

A second kind of improvement, which I am calling "lift," is due to church and mission activities. The congregation and its members have the great benefit of medicine, education, loving friendship, and protection. The founding mission or church establishes schools, hospitals, agricultural centers, literacy classes, and many other institutions to serve and help the general public and especially the new brothers and sisters in Christ. If these are illiterate, they are taught to read. Their children, attending church and mission schools—or, increasingly, tax-supported schools—become grade-school, high-school, and college graduates. Perhaps they go to Christian vocational schools and become mechanics, radio technicians, or artisans. Perhaps, sent to nurses' or teachers' training schools, they are snapped up by the rapidly expanding government health and education programs and get good salaries. Able men and women rise to positions of international note in the churches. A few or many, depending on the country, enter government service and hold positions of influence. The wealth of Christians rises. They become middle-class people. Members of the Christian community who have not personally done so well, nevertheless share in the general sense of well-being. All this I am calling "lift."

When subsidies are provided from abroad, the lift they produce is reproducible only to the limits of mission budget and staff. The whole institutional thrust of many churches on the mission field still depends heavily on Western aid. True, where Christian institutions can get government grants-in-aid, it is possible for a national church to parlay a small amount of aid from abroad into a substantial sum. Given good buildings, a first-class high school in India charges enough fees and gets enough grants-in-aid to maintain itself with very little mission money. Many a mission hospital receives several thousand dollars from abroad, adds to it a hundred thousand from local receipts, and runs a sizable medical work. But all this notwithstanding, the institutional complex and its lift are not indefinitely reproducible.

To the aid received from abroad (from sister churches in other lands and from missionary societies) may be added lift received from the denomination, the institutional complex built up across the decades and the centuries by Christians other than ourselves. The colleges and seminaries and orphanages and retirement homes must be counted as foreign aid. So must publication houses, Bible Societies, and great numbers of para-church organizations. No single Christian and no single congregation could possibly create these. The good life these make possible, the social reform they institute, the more intelligent, sweeter, juster social order they foster, are all foreign aid. All result in lift rather than redemption. The line between these two is, of course, a thin one, and the separation must not be too rigorously interpreted.

CHRISTIANS BECOME SEPARATED

The "redeemed and lifted" become separated from their former associates. Often, especially in mission lands, the blame is not theirs. They are pushed out, ostracized, disinherited, and neglected. They are told never to show their faces in their ancestral homes. They take employment in the church (or mission) because nothing else is available for them.

Often, however, in America and abroad, the process is intensified by the church itself, which insists that Christians must live separate from the world. Sometimes there is no other way for converts to survive. Bitter experience has indicated that those who remain in the midst of their former associates find the pressures too heavy and revert to their former faith. Where resistance and hostility to the Christian religion are high, the lone Christian is terribly exposed. Moreover, most churches and missions stress education and encourage Christians to send their children to school. This furthers the separation process. When Christian youth, educated in Christian schools, marry in the Christian community as churches insist they do, even if the first generation lives out among non-Christians, the second generation comes to think of itself as different from its unsaved relatives.

So, pushed out by their own people and pulled out and transformed by the church, educated and redeemed Christians form a separated community. They begin to move in new circles. They cease to use the dialect and start using the standard language. Crude or obscene talk is repellent to them; they do not want their children to hear it. They no longer like the old life. They are earning more and saving more; they come to have a higher standard of living; among primitive people they are personally cleaner. They imbibe from medical staffs a new attitude toward germs and dirt, flies and disposal of waste. The gulf between them and their old associates grows deeper year by year.

Because of this separation they often cease to be effective communicators among their former intimates and have no kin-contact with non-Christians at their new level. The congregation lives in a refined type of ghetto, as it were. Physical separation may or may not be a factor, but social separation is marked. Christians have a different marriage market. Their web of relationships comes to be radically different. They have little part in civic affairs or tribal business. They worship in churches, not temples. They do not observe the non-Christian festivals. Sometimes social separation is masked, for they work with non-Christian associates, enjoy fellowship with the non-Christian teachers in the school or college, or get elected to the town council and share in its deliberations. Yet underneath the surface unity, separation is there. Non-Christians have a keen awareness that "the Christians are not our people."

How then can the church lift and redeem Christians and yet have them remain in effective contact with receptive sections of society that they can influence? How can we keep goodness and educational advance from creating separation? How can the church maintain solidarity with the world and yet remain church? How can we establish churches that grow among the masses and keep on reproducing themselves without too much aid from the mothering church or mission? In short, how can the church avoid this kind of stoppage? This is the problem.

SOME WRONG METHODS

Nominal conversion of great numbers of the masses might appear to be a solution. It certainly maintains "faithful solidarity with the world." Christians remain little different from non-Christians. Since there is very little redemption and lift in this case, there is very little separation. The non-Christian feels quite at home socially, culturally, and religiously with the Christian. Connections remain excellent. Webs of relationship are preserved intact. The faith can flow over them to the unconverted.

Nevertheless, this method is unacceptable. It creates great hordes of pseudo-Christians. It accepts ignorant, unspiritual multitudes as permanent parts of the church of Christ. In winning men and women into a human organization it destroys the church, the bride of Christ. A religious form holds the people in the church's orbit, but does not lead them on to Christ. Winning the masses but failing to redeem and lift them is the method that the Roman Catholic Church has used in certain stretches of Latin America and the Philippines, where one finds many Christo-pagans. Yet today thoughtful Roman Catholics themselves proclaim that such Christo-pagans are not really Christian. Certain Protestant people movements also have resulted in such very nominal Christians that the label Christo-pagan ought to be attached to them as well.

Another wrong method is the planting of small clusters of nongrowing congregations that strive to be middle-class and form tiny enclaves in huge populations. Far from preventing stoppage, this solution requires it. A ghetto church of four thousand in a population of a half million solves the problem by ignoring it. In making these few Christians, the church has so elevated and separated them from their folk that the salvation of multitudes is effectively prevented. If the first wrong method has been favored by the Roman Catholics, the second has been favored by the Protestants. It also is no solution. It bypasses the masses by going above them and contents itself with carrying on a work instead of bringing nations to faith and obedience. The church may be there as a vaguely Christian presence, but it effectively denies the power of Jesus to multitudes who need him and would become his disciples if they could.

Since this Protestant method absorbs great mission resources and claims the lives of thousands of missionaries, it deserves careful attention. These congregations are not only introverted, but are tied to foreign money and assistance. What they unconsciously proclaim is not the redemption of Christ, but the advantage of cultural lift. When they seek to relate Christianity to all of life, they do so with foreign capital through church finances and staffed institutions.

None of this is in any way to contradict or depreciate the solidly Christian character of little-growing churches that are holding high the banner of Christ in difficult circumstances. They have their fair share of earnest Christians who live holy lives and preach the gospel in street and marketplace. Some of them have borne persecution with courage. Nevertheless, (a) what non-Christians see as they look at these arrested churches is communities that enjoy the rich services of a foreign connection; and (b) these clusters of congregations are growing so slowly that they themselves have no expectation of discipling their peoples. They have no solution to the problem: How can redeemed and lifted churches maintain such solidarity with their segments of humanity that they liberate community after community and multiply cell after cell of the redeemed? Most of them never even see the problem.

It will aid our understanding of church growth if we see this aspect of the whole picture against the stark economic reality posed by the Christianization of the masses. When the masses become Christian, their income does not suddenly quadruple. Christian peasants do not, following baptism, start earning ten times as much as their Buddhist relatives. After becoming Christian, people of the masses will continue to spend 80 percent of their earnings of, let us say, fifty cents a day, for grain to eat. Their margin will continue to be only 20 percent of their daily income, that is, ten cents a day must cover clothes, taxes, education for children, and support of the church! This slim base is all that is available to the church when the masses become Christian. Among the poor of earth it will supply only a very simple kind of Christianity, which affluent churches constantly judge inadequate. They may even say it is no Christianity at all. It certainly is not what they themselves can afford.

The crux of this disturbing situation is this: Which is more pleasing to God—that the receptive masses become Christians according to a pattern possible to *masses who remain masses,* or that the middle-class churches should rule—however unconsciously—that until the masses become wealthy enough to support a middle-class type of Christianity, they shall not become Christians?

THE RIGHT SOLUTION

The right solution to the problem of stoppage due to redemption and lift lies in a combination of the following two emphases.

First, members of the stopped church should see redemption as the supreme blessing of the Christian religion. Redemption is defined as what God makes available to those in unaided churches, simply by virtue of sincere belief in Jesus Christ and unwavering dedication to him. It is the kind of redemption we read about in the New Testament. Its enormous potential should be clearly recognized and constantly stressed. Let us consider several points.

The open Bible should be made available as an essential part of redemption. Since so many of the masses are illiterate—as they were in Europe and America in 1700 and earlier—this involves teaching Christians to read the Bible as a religious duty, an inalienable part of church life. Literacy classes should be in church buildings, closely tied to church programs, and built around a sharply worded doctrine that demands Bible reading as a normal Christian duty.

The presence of the living Christ, the empowering of the Holy Spirit, and the guidance and protecting providence of God should be taught as open to ordinary Christians. For this the New Testament gives abundant illumination, which, however, is hard to realize in the climate of modern thought. The first congregations had neither printed Bibles nor manuscript gospels. Though they had Old Testament scrolls, they depended heavily on oral traditions concerning the teaching of Jesus their Lord, and on the leading of the Holy Spirit. They knew the loving heavenly Father as immediately available to each believer. They taught that the power of Christ drove away evil spirits, the word of God dwelt in the heart, the mighty hand of God averted disaster, and the touch of the Lord cured sickness.

This power is available in congregations made up of the very poorest people. Our Lord does not require literacy, wealth, or a cosmopolitan outlook before he will bring blessing. He requires only burning faith. It is impossible to exaggerate the importance of this first emphasis. The Bible-obeying, Spirit-filled life cannot be stressed too much.

Second, the lift made available through modern education, medicine, and technology should be seen by the stopped church as a derivative part of Christian redemption, particularly valuable when rising out of the unaided efforts of churches. The more abundant material life should be proclaimed also as part of Christ's blessing—a secondary part, to be sure, but still a part.

Missionaries and pastors must believe in the sufficiency of Christ and the Bible—that is, the sufficiency of the unaided church to meet life's deepest needs. At this point, the work of pastors who have given their lives for prayer, revival, and the infilling of the Holy Spirit takes on great significance. A pastor may have spent years working with a congregation, educating it, caring for it, counseling it, preaching the word to it, teaching Bible classes to its youth and adults, and may have seen it full of frailties, sins, tensions, and tears. When revival comes, these ugly manifestations of the old Adam disappear. Men and women, boys and girls, are transformed—some for a week and some for life—but changed as the pastor could not change them.

FIVE PRINCIPLES BEARING ON THE CORRECT SOLUTION

1. Real redemption results in great efforts to grow. This is a rather simple fact. If we really share the mind of Christ, we will be tremendously in earnest about persuading others to become disciples. At the communion table we hear the Savior say, "I went to the cross for the salvation of all.

How far have you gone?" The person who walks with the Savior will devote himself to the spread of the Gospel. It is no accident, as J. Edwin Orr points out, that revivals, where the processes of redemption reach a peak, have initiated advances in the missionary movement.

2. Real growth results in great efforts to lift. Growth is not mere sociological accretion. Church growth, the conversion of unbelievers and multiplication of churches, is God's work. There is no such thing in church growth as mere numerical increase. The increase is always of baptized believers, new members in the household of God, and new churches. New creatures in Christ Jesus will face and journey toward goodness—they may take detours, but in general this is the direction. Indwelt by the Spirit, they will welcome moves toward love, peace, and justice. They are hungry to learn of God's will. In West New Guinea, missionaries found that

> until the people burned their charms, they were not—as a simple matter of fact—interested in the Word of God. They did not care to hear or obey it. After they burned their charms, however, they were eager and hungry to hear and obey the Gospel. Dani believers felt strongly that charm burnings were a necessary step in understanding the Gospel (Sunda 1963:30).

A few months later these new creatures in Christ, striding toward goodness, decided to burn most of their weapons as a sign to all that they were through with fighting and killing.

3. When lift is so rapid that it breaks social contact between Christians and their non-Christian relatives, it ceases to be an unqualified good. Change of language, style of living, clothing, and occupation may appear desirable. These Christians are making great progress, leaders say. But if these same changes tear Christians away from their communities, they are dubious blessings.

Christians must, of course, break contact with all idolatrous ceremonies and those binding them to the non-Christian religion whether that be atheistic Communism, animism, or some other system; but those who guide them would do well to insist that they redouble connections at all other points. Their churches, instead of dwelling on activities they cannot share with unbelievers, should look for those they can share. A rejection of the deep sense of brotherhood must not be a part of their first step into Christianity. Educated Christians' constant emphasis should be, "we are still with you. You are our people, bone of our bone. The differences that have come through education and other factors do not erase our essential oneness with you."

To be sure, the Scriptures command us to come out and be separate. Our Lord called James and John as they were mending their nets, and immediately "they left their father Zebedee in the boat with the hired servants, and followed him" (Mark 1:20). In directions concerning marriage, Christians are told not to be unequally yoked with unbelievers. Nevertheless, it is noteworthy that while the apostles did leave their father and mother and follow Jesus, they did so within the Jewish culture. It was customary for disciples to follow their teachers, while remaining good Jews. In doing so they did not leave the Jewish nation. Together with these words of our Lord must be put those of the apostle Paul, who, when advising Christians in the thorny matter of eating meats sacrificed to idols, said,

> If one of the unbelievers invites you to dinner and you are disposed to go, eat whatever is set before you without raising any question on the ground of conscience. (But if someone says to you, "This has been offered in sacrifice," then . . . do not eat it) (1 Cor. 10:27ff.).

St. Paul was advising Christians as far as possible to maintain solidarity with their non-Christian comrades.

4. It is absolutely necessary, in order to determine the amount of lift, to step resolutely outside one's own cultural heritage or overhang. Much lift has little to do with essential Christianity. It is instituted by Westerners to help people forward into the general culture of the world and thus tends (as we have seen before) toward civilizing rather than evangelizing. Lift wants to break down tribalism rather than to build up the church. It glories in preparing rural Christians to earn good salaries in cities. It cooperates with governments in creating clerks, accountants, policemen, machinists, engineers, nurses, and teachers—all of whom play an important part in the new states that are arising. These are all good activities, and missions and churches should be fostering them. In fact, Christian missions are good for a nation wholly aside from the growth of the church.

Nevertheless, church leaders should discern what part of the total expenditure of effort is devoted to civilizing and what to Christianizing. Good questions to ask oneself are: Did the early Christians in the Judean hills have this amount of lift? Did my own Christian ancestors? Are efforts toward education and other Western advantages keeping a respectful distance behind efforts to multiply congregations?

5. Stoppage is avoided by using a pattern of church growth that is indefinitely reproducible with the resources available to a given church. The following common overseas patterns violate this principle and increase stoppage:

a. Each congregation has its full complement of missionaries, school, hospital, agricultural center, and evangelistic department. This pattern is good for a mission station or church headquarters, but poor for a church that is expected to arise in village after village across a countryside. It is not indefinitely reproducible on the resources available in villages.

b. Each congregation has an ordained minister paid largely with mission funds or the contributions of mission-employed Christians or missionaries. The pastor has full seminary training and is married to a spouse whose gifts and education are comparable. This pattern of ministry, which at first blush seems so desirable, is as a matter of fact undesirable because it cannot be reproduced indefinitely on the resources of the small congregations so typical of the church growing on new ground.

c. Each church building is paid for largely by mission funds. This gives small congregations permanent and fitting places of worship, but since building them requires subsidy, they are not the indefinitely reproducible pattern of church house. They lead Christians and non-Christians to expect church buildings beyond what can be constructed by local congregations.

The following common patterns observe the principle: (i) The congregation normally has no missionary living within its boundaries or mission institution located there. Any educating is done in the church building. (ii) The congregation either depends on unpaid or part-time leaders or has a pastor whom it can support. (iii) The church building is one the congregation can erect and keep in repair by itself. For example, the Pentecostals in Brazil meet in house churches, rented halls, and cheap small chapels in their own neighborhoods. When they grow numerous enough, they pool their resources and erect a large central building. A church ranging from one to five thousand members results and may have two hundred branch congregations. No funds come from the outside. This is a pattern that can be repeated over and over again.

In short, the congregation should be of such structure and pattern that common people can operate it and multiply it indefinitely among the masses.

SUMMARY

Some might object to this whole argument, which subordinates lift to redemption, on the grounds that the church must lift people up. It must not teach them to be content with unjust poverty. Part of the church's task is to create divine discontent with soul-eroding and unnecessary poverty.

The answer to the objection is simple. Nothing in this chapter should be construed as leading Christians to be content with poverty. I thoroughly agree that the church must lift. I want it to lift far more widely than it is now doing. I want a congregation to exist in every section of every city and in every village and hamlet throughout the earth, for only then will the passion of God for righteousness and justice working through people dedicated to his will and feeding on his word be applied to every community.

Existing churches need great growth. They should fear, as a debilitating disease, accepting as a permanent thing the role of little-growing, middle-class churches. They should regard themselves as God's pilot projects, dedicated to liberating the multitudes of their lands. They need to understand church growth. Among the many factors of growth, they should see the one dealt with in this chapter: the difference between the redemption offered by essential Christianity and the lift offered by its middle-class cultural accompaniments. Churches that have been lifted and consequently halted must now break out of their middle-class encirclements, seek receptive peoples in their neighborhoods, and establish constellations of living congregations among the masses. These will be different from themselves yet thoroughly Christian, for they will have the Bible and Christ.

═══ 17 ═══

PEOPLE MOVEMENTS

T HIS AND THE NEXT chapter on people movements apply for the most part to the initial penetration of the gospel into homogeneous units of high people consciousness. As we will see, some cultures know little or nothing of individualized decision-making processes, so common in the West. Important decisions are made only in groups.

However, even those who are called to evangelize more individualistic societies or traditionally Christian, but nominal, areas should pay close attention to people movement theory in general and to what I will later refer to as web movements in particular. Even in an evangelistic target audience such as a rapidly growing U.S. suburb, understanding the dynamics of the web movement is a distinct advantage in leading a church to growth.

As denominations enter new ethnic and social units to propagate the gospel and multiply churches, they will achieve their goal much more readily if they work along people movement lines. The goal should be to start some variation of the people movement to Christ. Any congregation composed of individuals who confess Christ one by one and who come from different social units inevitably becomes a conglomerate organization and tends to be slow growing. It easily becomes a sealed-off enclave.

PEOPLE MOVEMENTS DEFINED

Despite its importance, the concept of people movements is relatively new and needs precise definition. Some objection to the thing itself arises from a misunderstanding of the term that identifies it with undesirable methods. First, then, let us ask, What is a "people"? The word has three meanings. It may mean individuals or persons, as in the sentence, "I met several people today." It may mean the public, the masses, or the common people, as in "The People's Republic" or the phrase "the will of the people." It may also mean a tribe, a caste, or any homogeneous unit where marriage and intimate life take place only within the society. The term "people movement" uses the word exclusively in this third sense. A people is a tribe or caste, a clan or lineage, or a tightly knit segment of any society.

A tribal movement is always a people movement—that is, it is the movement of a single people. The term "tribal movement" is not used here, however, because a tribe is only one of many possible cultural groups that can move together to Christian faith. The society moving may be a caste, a clan, some extended families, or a linguistic group that would resent being called a tribe or caste. The word "people" best describes these various kinds of societies that may move together into the church.

The Jews in the United States are a people. One could have a people movement to Christ from among the Jews. They might then become Christians while maintaining their taboo against pork and their strong desire to marry only within their own community. The first large Japanese movement to Christ (1882-87) was probably a people movement of the warriors of Japan, the Samurai. A small Brahmin people movement to Christianity occurred in Orissa, India. It is not necessary for the people to be primitive, though for understandable reasons most successful people movements have been from among underprivileged masses.

It is helpful to observe what a people movement is *not*. It is not large numbers becoming Christians, although it can be. Many people movements consist of a series of small groups coming to decision. At any one time only one group makes the decision, is instructed, and is baptized. A people movement does not involve careless accessions or hurried baptizing.

> It is a mistake to assume that People Movement Christians, merely because they have come to Christian faith in chains of families, must inevitably be nominal Christians. Such an assumption is usually based on prejudice, not fact. . . . People movements in themselves do not [produce] nominal Christians (McGavran 1955:74).

Neither does a people movement involve neglect of quality and post-baptismal care. Such neglect will, in fact, guarantee the failure of any people movement. Nor are people movements caused by missionaries' hunger for numbers or haste to baptize, so that they can report large accessions to their supporters. Many of them start in the face of doubt on the part of the missionary that they are a good thing.

A people movement is *not* a mass movement. This unfortunate term, which should never be used, gives an entirely erroneous idea that large, undigested masses of human beings are moving instantaneously into the church. On the contrary, what frequently happens in people movements is that relatively small, well-instructed groups—one this month and one several months later—become Christians. Numbers are achieved, to be sure; but usually only with the passage of time.

Bearing these things in mind, a definition of this type of movement can now be given. A people movement results from the joint decision of a number of individuals all from the same people group, which enables them to become Christians without social dislocation, while remaining in full contact with their non-Christian relatives, thus enabling other segments of that people group, across the years, after suitable instruction, to come to similar decisions and form Christian churches made up exclusively of members of that people. Each phrase of this description adds a needed dimension of meaning, and the complete definition helps one to understand the people-movement type of church growth.

Waskom Pickett says that people movements:

constitute for many the most natural way of approach to Christ. The more individualistic way preferred in Western countries is not favored by peoples trained from early childhood to group action. To object to [people] movements is to place obstacles in the path along which an overwhelming proportion of Indian Christians have come to profess faith in Christ Jesus. We see no reason to believe that any considerable proportion of [people] movement converts could have been brought to Christ along any other path. Nor do we see any reason to wish that they had been led by any other way (1933:330).

K. S. Latourette was speaking of people movements when he wrote:

More and more we must dream in terms of winning groups, not merely individuals. Too often, with our Protestant, nineteenth-century individualism, we have torn men and women, one by one, out of the family, village, or clan, with the result that they have been permanently de-racinated and maladjusted. To be sure, in its last analysis, conversion must result in a new relationship between the individual and his Maker, in radiant transformed lives. Experience, however, shows that it is much better if an entire natural group—a family, village, caste, or tribe—can come rapidly over into the faith. That gives reinforcement to the individual Christian and makes easier the Christianization of the entire life of the community (Latourette 1936:159).

The Quantitative Importance of People Movements

At least two-thirds of all converts in Asia, Africa, and Oceania have come to Christian faith through people movements. In many provinces, nine-tenths of all those who first moved out of non-Christian faiths to Christianity came in people movements. Most Christians in Asia and Africa today are descendants of people-movement converts. But for people movements, the churches on those continents would be very different and very much weaker than they are. People-movement growth has accounted for considerable ingathering in Latin America also.

It cannot be forgotten that great movements to Christ were the normal way in which the peoples of Europe, Asia Minor, and North Africa first became Christian. The Reformation faith also spread across Germany, Switzerland, Scotland, England, Scandinavia, and other lands in a special variety of people movements, very different from the growth of congregations today.

But much more than this can be said. The great growth of the future is also likely to be by people movements. It is inconceivable that any other pattern will bring unreached people groups to faith and obedience. The great ingatherings from Islam, for example, will come by people movements to Christ. This has been abundantly illustrated by the tens of thousands of Muslims who have become Christian in Indonesia since 1966. These multitudes did not drip into the church drop by drop; they came in by communities. Whole extended families, minor lineages, and villages moved in together. Indeed, as I have said before, the chief resistance of Islam and other religions is social, not theological. If social resistance can be overcome, the gospel can be heard. The people movement is a God-given way by which social resistance to the gospel can be surmounted.

The Qualitative Importance of People Movements

People movements convey a quality to the Christian church that individual action seldom does. In considering quality, one must not compare people movements in pagan areas with the mode of increase of congregations in Western towns and cities. These are gatherings of persons who are already Christian in some sense. They certainly are not Muslims, Hindus, Buddhists, or animists. Most have grown up in Christian homes and are part of a social web made up of the baptized. Converts join wealthy, adequately housed congregations and are skillfully shepherded by a host of laypersons and a highly trained, paid staff.

People movements must be contrasted with the other main mode of increase from among non-Christians—that is, with the one-by-one-against-the-social-tide pattern of growth so commonly seen among churches advancing on new ground. As soon as this is done, it is clear that people movements bring in qualitatively superior churches.

Communities move in without much social dislocation, without searing wounds between members of the same family, and with their normal relationships intact. The resulting congregations have a social structure complete with leaders and family loyalties. Instead of a conglomerate of converts from many different backgrounds who must learn to get along together, people-movement congregations are comprised of one kind of people accustomed to working and living together. People-movement churches are therefore more stable, less dependent on pastor and missionary, and more likely to bear up well under persecution. Conviction is buttressed by social cohesion. When all my relatives are Christian and renouncing the Christian faith means breaking with my dearest, my love of the Lord is reinforced by my love for my brethren.

Discipline, too, can be more effective and more indigenous. What pastor of a gathered-colony congregation does not know the difficulty of devising discipline that expresses the church's displeasure rather than the foreigner's? The people-movement congregation knows how to keep its members in line. It will enforce whatever it really believes in.

When people come to Christian faith by group decision, community sins and weaknesses can be given up. When the new Christians rule that there must be no more liquor at "our weddings," they have no difficulty in enforcing the ban. When, in New Guinea, clans that had become Christian decided to give up feuds, they ruled that half their weapons should be burned, despite the fact that the non-Christian clans were still fully armed. All the Christians burned half their weapons—not because the missionaries said so, but because the converted villagers thought it a good thing to do.

Seen against the One-By-One Mode

For full understanding, as noted above, the people movement should be seen against the common one-by-one mode of spreading the gospel. The latter can be called Christianization by abstraction and is the second major way in which the church has grown. The people movement is the first.

In the one-by-one mode, leaders *expect* only individual converts. This is how each of them was converted. This is the manner of becoming Christian they have known in their years of experience. It is the way that the few persons they have seen won to Christian decision have come.

As the gospel is preached, the Bible is studied in school, and people are exposed to Christian influences, now and then some individual is attracted to the Christian faith. Maybe the patience of their Christian teacher intrigues them, as in the case of young Rodriguez of the Philippines, who many years later became a bishop of the United Church of Christ. Maybe they healed through prayer or helped through some difficulty. Maybe the straight preaching of the gospel touches them. They attend meetings, read the Bible, and, fearing that their family will object, become secret believers. Gathering courage they declare their faith, and against family opposition and threats accept baptism. They are ostracized and persecuted, but remain firm and thus are added to the Lord.

Pastors, workers, and missionaries often believe that this is the New Testament way. "If a man love father or mother more than me . . ." is often quoted. Many similar passages come to mind. Church leaders conclude that one-by-one-against-the-tide is not only the way conversion usually happens in the U.S.A., but is the right and biblical way for it to happen. Christians must expect to suffer for their Lord.

When leaders preach the gospel and talk with seekers, they unconsciously present this one-by-one pattern. What they expect, inquirers come to regard as the normal pattern and correct way to become Christian. When inquirers become Christian, they in turn expect this pattern and unconsciously proclaim it.

The non-Christian community, too, seeing that some become Christians in the face of family disapproval and community sentiment, conclude that Christians are always rebels against the community. The later educational advance of Christians reinforces that impression. The image gets fixed in the mind of the public that to become Christian is an antisocial act. Once this conviction has seized the minds of church leaders, Christians, and public a people movement is very unlikely, even in circumstances where it might normally occur.

MULTI-INDIVIDUAL, MUTUALLY INTERDEPENDENT
CONVERSION

Some church leaders turn from people movements on theological grounds. They feel that the very idea of group conversion is contrary to the individual faith that leads to salvation. The apostles followed the Lord Jesus one by one. He called them out singly from among the multitude. Mere going along with the crowd, these leaders argue, is not conversion and can never save anyone. This real stumbling block must be squarely faced.

The kind of conversion on which people movements are based is the root of the difficulty. The crucial question is: Do people movements rest on group conversion? The answer is No. There is no such thing as group conversion. A group has no body and no mind. It cannot decide anything whatever. The phrase "group conversion" is simply an inexact description of what really happens.

What really happens is *multi-individual, mutually interdependent conversion,* which is a very different thing. These exact terms are important. One should learn to use them correctly and easily. Just as in nuclear science fusion and fission, or in electrical science direct and alternating current are terms essential to exact thought, so in missiology the words "multi-individual" and "mutually interdependent" are necessary to understanding.

What I am affirming is that conversion does not have to be the decision of a solitary individual taken in the face of family disapproval. On the contrary, it is better conversion when it is the decision of many individuals taken in mutual affection. *Multi-individual* means that many people participate in the act. Each individual makes up his or her mind. They hear about Jesus Christ. They debate with themselves whether it is a good thing to become a Christian. They believe or do not believe. If they believe, they join those who are becoming Christian. If they do not believe, they join those who are not becoming Christian.

Mutually interdependent means that all those taking the decision are intimately known to each other and *take the step in view of what the other is going to do.* This is not only natural; it is moral. Indeed, it is immoral, as a rule, to decide what one is going to do regardless of what others do. Church leaders ought frequently to say to inquirers, "Since Jesus Christ is the Savior, the pearl of great price that you have found, and since you are a loyal member of your family, you do not want to enjoy salvation secretly all by yourself. The first thing you want to do is to share your new-found treasure with your loved ones. The person who loves the Lord most will try most to bring his/her intimates to him. Andrew went and found his brother Simon. You do the same."

In a people movement—whether in Berlin or Bombay—members of the close-knit group seek to persuade their loved ones of the great desirability of believing on Jesus Christ and becoming Christians. Often they will defer their own decision in order to be baptized together. A husband waits six months for an unbelieving wife. A brother labors for two years so that his other three brothers and their wives will all confess Christ together—the conversion made sweeter because it is shared with the people who supremely matter to him. A wise man deciding to become Christian leads many of his fellows to promise that they will accept Christ the same day he does.

Conversion means participation in a genuine decision for Christ, a sincere turning from the old gods and evil spirits, and a determined purpose to live as Christ would have his followers live. The individual decisions within a people movement exhibit all these marks. It is *a series of multi-individual, mutually interdependent conversions.*

Near the city of Raichur in South India, about 120 Madigas were making up their mind to follow Christ. They had considered the step for years. Many of their relatives were Christians. They believed becoming disciples of Christ was a good thing to do. During the year of decision, the question came up as to what they would do with their temple—a small dark room with an idol on a cylindrical stone. After weeks of discussion, all participated in the decision that on the day of baptism they would throw the idol into the village pond, make the cylindrical stone their pulpit, place the Bible on it, and hear what God really had to say. This was a multi-individual, mutually interdependent decision and part of their conversion. Had any of them decided to remain an idol-worshiper, the rest could not have used the temple for Christian worship; but when the group acted as a unit, the change presented no problem.

When the 8,000 Dani in Irian Jaya declared for Christ in a multi-individual fashion, they resolved to burn their fetishes on a certain day. This symbolic act destroyed their former fears and allegiances and opened the way for them to learn biblical truth. When, in another of the Indonesian islands recently, twenty Muslim communities decided to accept Christ and turn their mosques into churches, the very grave decision entailed participation by each person concerned. Each was saved, not by going along with the crowd, but *by participation in the decision.* Multi-individual conversion is not a light matter. It, too, can result in persecution or death. Rejected evil spirits or remaining Muslims might take a terrible revenge. Participating in such a decision requires genuine personal faith.

There is usually room for stay-outers. Most groups are fissured internally. They are full of subgroups. If people have no faith, they simply stay out in company with those who do not wish to become disciples of Christ. This helps guarantee that the decision is meaningful for those who come in.

Multi-individual decisions achieve great power. They enable individuals to do together what they could never do alone. Grains of gunpowder burning one by one have no power, but when they all burn together in a confined space they can blast granite rock to pieces. Similarly, while one woman all by herself finds it difficult to leave father and mother, it is no uncommon sight to see ten women together accept baptism that cuts them off from their twenty parents. The women are parts of multi-individual conversion. Their husbands and children are becoming Christians. They believe that someday their parents, too, will follow. In joint action ten women are granted power to do what would be impossible for one alone.

EDUCATION AND ENLIGHTENMENT IN A PEOPLE MOVEMENT

People movements usually depend on extensive prior education. Now and again one occurs in which there is little antecedent knowledge of the gospel. One thinks at once of the Harris movement in Ivory Coast and Apolonia. Yet the fact of the matter is that plenty of prior education existed even in Ivory Coast and Apolonia. Without prior education it is truly impossible for society to move.

People movements require years—in some cases decades—of enlightenment and gospel impact before they begin. In 1950 a great Methodist missionary, Andrew Mellor of southwest Nigeria, decided that in the last few years of his career he would attempt the conversion of the Egons, a very resistant tribe whose headquarters were at Badagri—a coastal town, and during the eighteenth and early-nineteenth century a noted slaveport. By 1954 this headquarters of fanatical resistance had yielded to the gospel and about two thousand had become Christian. Andrew Mellor set off the decision, but the hundred and ten years of Christian work, the great turnings of the Yorubas to the north, the educated Christian Nigerians who had come to Badagri as government servants, and many other factors had been preparing the Egons.

Much popular education is constantly going on. This is why today is full of promise for the spread of the church. Never in the history of the world have so many non-Christians observed Christian worship and been so powerfully attracted to it. Never has there been as much comment on the new religion as there is today. True, some comment is unfavorable or even hostile; but much of it agrees that the Christian religion is good, Jesus Christ is the Savior, and "we are all going to be Christians someday."

Many popular images are abroad of what it means to be a Christian. Some contain elements that do not bulk large to the Christian leader. Some elements regarded as vital are not there at all. But the images are of what it means to be a Christian and in many populations they are favorable. Christians are humble people, worship God more, do not get drunk, do not fear the same spirits, and do not work on Sunday. They are more dependable and face death with peace of mind. They treat their women better and know God's commands more. In a wayside restaurant near Campinas, Brazil, I asked the waiter what he thought of *crentes* (believers).

"Ah," he replied, "they are good people. My sister is one. They worship God all the time and save their money. I am going to become a *crente* myself one day."

From those hostile to Christianity different views are heard. Christians are traitors to their people, paid to defect, meat-eaters, and no better than we are. If one is an orphan, it is a good thing perhaps to become a Christian, but not for people who are respected in their communities.

Endless debate rages in many populations between those who think it would be well to become Christian and those who do not. The startling conversion of Muslims in Indonesia, mentioned above, was preceded by just that kind of debate, certainly for months, possibly for years. Non-Christians receive much teaching and hear much preaching. Some read the Gospels and tracts. Returned travelers tell of countries where Christians are numerous and being Christian has been good for them. All this is *preparatio evangelica*—education for conversion.

Verbalized theological education, of course, is largely absent. In a population trembling on the edge of a people movement, thousands may believe firmly that Christianity is a good religion without being able to tell a single fact about the life or death of Jesus Christ. We should not scorn this condition. Acts 9 records that after Aeneas, bedridden for eight years, had been cured by Peter, "all the residents of Lydda and Sharon . . . turned to the Lord." While a few Christians lived there before Peter's visit, it would be too much to suppose that all the residents of those two villages had exact theological knowledge of the Lord Jesus. Yet they certainly had much popular education of the kind I have been describing. They turned to the Lord in a multi-individual, mutually interdependent conversion.

Immediately following such conversion, much verbalized theological education should be provided in prebaptismal and postbaptismal courses. The original decision is made more meaningful by conscious instruction in the Bible. This is already common practice among all churches and missions. Hundreds of thousands of converts who come to Christ each year by group decisions are enrolled as catechumens (inquirers, seekers, probationers), and are instructed, baptized, and instructed still further.

GOOD DEEDS AND PEOPLE MOVEMENTS

As churches multiply across the face of a land, Christians find many occasions to do helpful things. Unpremeditated overflow of kindness, just because the messenger is a Christian, is unavoidable. Like their Master, they do good. With the Holy Spirit in their heart, how can they avoid it? At the beginning of the people movement, when numbers are small, nothing but praise to God redounds from this person-to-person service.

When the movement continues, however, and thousands have become Christians in far-flung villages or towns, for a church or mission to do good deeds to all about it in any practical way very soon becomes prohibitively expensive and unnecessary. If well-integrated groups become Christian, the resulting community includes those of substance and responsibility who are accustomed to looking after their own poor. In hard times, the poor are accustomed either to working or to pulling in their belts a few notches and weathering the storm. As soon as relief begins to be handed out, however, a new situation arises in which it is extraordinarily difficult for an outside organization to distribute money, clothing, or food justly. Help given to a few individuals face to face is one thing; given to a whole countryside in the process of becoming Christian, it is something entirely different.

Personal good works soon escalate into organized institutional philanthropy at central stations—schools, hospitals, nurses' and teachers' training institutions, and the like. These are useful adjuncts to any church. Many more people are served. Much greater good is done. Many nationals are employed in the ventures—but, also, many detrimental marginal learnings begin to appear. The large staff employed regard institutionalized philanthropy as their means of livelihood—which it is; and their continued support as the reason for the institution—which it is not. The church appears to be the institutional complex at the big central station rather than the multitude of congregations in the towns of the land. The focus is taken away from discipling the peoples and fixed on maintaining institutions of excellent quality.

As church leaders managing a movement so that the whole people is brought to faith and obedience try to balance institutionalized good works and maximum growth of the churches, what principles should guide them? I suggest three.

1. Those institutionalized good deeds are more valuable to the Christian movement that can be reproduced as far as the fringes of the receptive people. For example, in the Tiv tribe in Nigeria, the CRIs (classes in religious instruction) in 1966 were very simple village schools, run by Christians of little education, who could not demand anything like the salary of qualified teachers in government-recognized and -aided primary schools. The CRIs could be reproduced as far as the Tiv villages ran. Primary schools with their required buildings and scale of pay for teachers could not be. For the expansion of the church, the CRIs had much more immediate value than the central primary schools. This does not in any way diminish the value of primary and secondary schools in the training of an adequate ministry, but it does warn against a disproportionate evaluation of them in the early stages of such an immense task as discipling the million Tiv.

2. The institutions should serve the church adequately. Institutionalized philanthropy, serving chiefly the state, commercial interests, or resistant segments of the non-Christian public, is a luxury Christian mission cannot afford. It diverts Christians from reconciling unbelievers to God. It is a civilizing, not a Christianizing, activity. It is education of resistant oppressors rather than the church growing among the receptive oppressed. Granted that one should not interpret the grace of loving the brethren too narrowly, nevertheless the scriptural injunction is to do good to all people, *especially those of the household of faith.*

3. Institutionalized good works should be oriented to the local situation. Are they such that the churches can soon take them over? Do they meet a felt local need? Will nationals start them if they are not already in operation? Do they meet current need, or has government in fact moved into this field and—so to speak—released the church to attend to other, more pressing matters?

The chief purpose of organized philanthropy should be to help the church disciple receptive peoples—not simply to help the existing church build up showcases at centers of population.

ARE PEOPLE MOVEMENTS SOUNDLY CHRISTIAN?

The student of church growth raises the question as to whether people movements are Christian. Are we not promulgating something that is not biblical? Is there not grave danger that the high standards our denomination has set as it separated itself from nominal Christians will be betrayed in people movements?

These are fair questions. In answer, one should turn directly to the Bible and observe its authority for discipling tribes. At the outset, the whole Old Testament is the story of God's dealing with peoples. God called the Hebrew *people,* the children of Israel, the twelve tribes, out of Egypt. Again and again he disciplined them *as peoples.* Again and again they made group decisions, repented of their sins, and covenanted with God to walk in his ways.

Coming to the New Testament, we note that Matthew 28:19 instructs Christians to disciple the peoples (*ethne*). In Hindi, the national language of India, the words read *sab jatiyan ko chela karo,* that is, "disciple the castes"—a much more accurate rendering of the Greek than the common English version, "make disciples of the nations." What our Lord said was precisely "disciple the tribes," the castes and families of the earth. Just as the Jewish tribes were the people of God, so the multitudinous peoples of the Gentiles should become God's household.

The first ten chapters of Acts make numerous mention of multitudes becoming Christian. In the New Testament we repeatedly come upon the conversion of households—*oikoi* in Greek. The *oikos* pattern, once seen, is a noteworthy feature of New Testament church growth. Christians of the Baptist persuasion have been slow to recognize this, lest it endanger their position that believers only should be immersed. Yet the *oikos* pattern really has nothing to do with who is baptized. Family by family, unbelievers became Christian—this is what is affirmed. At what stage they are baptized is another question. The truer we are to the New Testament, the more we shall welcome *oikos* and other multi-individual conversions.

The Mighty People Movement in the New Testament

Most Westerners, reading their New Testaments through the eyes of highly individualized congregations and interpreters, see a pattern of conversion and Christian decision that closely resembles their own in Chicago or Toronto or Berlin. Yet it is most unlikely that the growth of the church in the highly specialized populations of the Roman Empire would resemble church growth in Europe or North America today. For one thing, those converted then were mostly illiterate, while today most Westerners are high-school graduates. Those then coming to Christian faith previously knew nothing about Christ; most of those who join churches in the West are children of existing Christians. During the writing of the entire New Testament, it is doubtful whether any congregations built meeting houses. Today, ecclesiastical buildings—called churches—are invariably found. In that early period, women had very few rights, and fathers decided matters for their families; today in the West women have equal rights, and children do as they wish. Then, each ethnic unit thought of itself as a special race and had its own language or dialect. Timothy, no doubt, spoke the local Galatian dialect more fluently than he did Koine Greek. It is doubtful that he spoke Aramaic at all. Today everyone in Germany speaks German; in England, English; and in the United States (so the English say), American.

In my earlier volume *The Bridges of God,* Chapter 3 illustrated the people movement from the New Testament. I wrote that chapter not to prove from the Bible that people movements are right, but simply because the New Testament affords a good example of a people movement. The document is open to all and can be studied at leisure. When once the tight social structure of the Jewish community of our Lord's day has been understood, it is impossible to miss the people-movement nature of New Testament church growth. The journeys of St. Paul also, far from being like those of the modern missionary, are typical of the way a movement expanding in a single urban caste or rural tribe follows the line of relations and the natural connections of one family with another.

The fact that the New Testament describes a people movement, however, has weight when we are considering whether people movements are right or not. If it was right for the synagogue community at Berea, for example, to decide for Christ and form itself into a congregation in a very few days, surely community action is one acceptable way into the church. The account of this rapid decision of a considerable number of families to become Christians (Acts 17:10-14), condensed though it is, looks amazingly like a multi-individual, mutually interdependent conversion. Not only did they accept that the Messiah was Jesus but also that Greeks could become Christians without being circumcised. They resolved to form themselves into a congregation despite the hard-core Jews who came down on them from Thessalonica. And all this took place in the few days necessary for word to get from Berea to Thessalonica and for the Jews there to send down their emissaries.

STARVED AND WELL-FED PEOPLE MOVEMENTS

Most objections to people movements come from those who have seen them starved and neglected. Mishandling of these God-given movements is easy—particularly when one comes from highly individualized countries—and results in a caricature of the Christian church.

God sometimes gives the precious beginnings of a people movement to his servants working ahead in the exploratory phase of missions. If they miss the early signals there is a danger that the new churches will be confirmed, not in the faith, but in ignorance and nominalism. This is not the fault of the way non-Christians turn to Christ, but a failure of shepherding. People movements to Christ require special care. The more socially and intellectually removed the missionaries are from the people being served, the more danger there is of their mishandling God's gift.

All this merely underlines the important and cheering fact that a well-shepherded people movement has a soundly Christian character. Let us observe four characteristics of a well-nurtured movement to Christian faith.

FOUR CHARACTERISTICS

First, at the beginning converts corporately renounce loyalty to other gods: their worship, their houses, their priests, and their rituals. Renunciation usually takes the form of destroying the religious objects or symbols. Fetishes are burned. Idols are thrown into the pond. Sacred turtles are killed and eaten. Amulets and charms are taken off and thrown away. Power encounters publicly display that Jesus is Lord of lords. Thus the hold on believers is broken and they become free to follow their conscience.

George Vicedom, in his important book *Church and People in New Guinea,* describes vividly a formal service of renunciation. The following few lines convey the depth of the corporate turning:

> The various clans were represented by their chiefs. . . . Each had small pieces of wood in his hand and said, "The name of this piece of wood is war. We used to fight . . . and kill each other. Since the Word of God has come, peace has arrived. . . . Now what is your choice? Shall we go back to fighting . . . or live in peace?" The people answered, "We choose peace." The chief continued, "See now, as I throw away this piece of wood, we all throw away war." The people responded, "We will not kill any more."

In the same way, sorcery, infanticide, theft, adultery, the worship of ancestors and so on were one by one renounced and thrown away forever (Vicedom 1962:19).

Second, converts corporately accept Christ as Lord and Savior, enroll among his people, and identify themselves with his church. In well-cared-for movements, new Christians build a meeting house and covenant to assemble there, hear and learn the Bible, send their children for regular instruction, commit hymns and Scripture passages to memory, and give to the church.

Third, leaders from among the new converts are trained so that, at the earliest possible moment, the new congregations assemble under their own pastors, deacons, elders, and teachers. J. T. Seamands (1968) credits the healthy expansion of the Methodist Church in South India (from 95,000 to 190,000 in twenty years) to a thorough system of training lay leaders.

Fourth, the regular worship of God, not only on Sunday but during the week as often as possible, is instituted. In India those people movements where the worship of God was a daily occurrence showed much more growth in grace than those where Christians assembled only on Sunday. Congregations that worshiped morning and evening showed more Christian achievement than those which worshiped only in the evenings. Since liturgical worship requires repeated use of Scripture passages, it is especially suited for illiterate congregations. As part of catechetical instruction, all Christians commit the passages to memory. Repeated use inscribes these on the tablets of their hearts. Christian virtues begin to form part of their character. Regular giving also can be taught. It is part of this fourth step.

Since the movement brings eager congregations into existence, these four steps become immediately practical. During the first months after conversion, Christians are highly teachable. They eagerly learn the Christian way. Of course, if neglected for the first few years, they become accustomed to a mere nominal Christianity. It is then more difficult to ingrain these highly desirable habits of attending, learning, worshiping, and giving.

THE FIRST DEDICATION AND MORAL REFORM

Drunkenness, race pride, drug use, infanticide, polygamy, and gambling may be renounced at the very beginning of the Christian life; or they may not. In any case these actions should be regarded as the fruit of the Spirit. They are not legalistic requirements that must be met before unbelievers can become Christians. The gospel is the good news of God's free grace. It is not a legal and moral barrier that must be surmounted before one dare come before the Savior.

One of the mistakes church leaders who desire moral purity in Christians make is to demand that seekers out of paganism, before they receive the Holy Spirit or are baptized, demonstrate conduct that millions of good Christians in the West do not demonstrate after twenty generations in the church. It is no mistake to desire moral purity. There can scarcely be too much of it. And the Holy Spirit will bring purity when he indwells God's people. The mistake is in demanding fruits the Spirit has given as prerequisites to becoming disciples.

However, it should immediately be added that as a Christward movement advances among a receptive people, each new group is more than ready for new standards of conduct. If the new congregations wish, or can be persuaded, to ban liquor, make an advance in brotherhood, give up gambling, free their slaves, outlaw tobacco, provide equality for women, or burn weapons while the movement goes victoriously forward, it would be sinful and foolish not to require these good actions. It would be equally sinful and foolish, however, to refuse baptism to groups who are prepared to carry out all four steps mentioned above, but want to continue drinking beer and smoking tobacco. The general rule should be to load on all the moral reforms possible but, remembering that these are not essential to beginning life with Christ, never to stop a sound movement with legalistic demands. The Holy Spirit must be trusted more than most of us have been willing to trust him.

18

KINDS OF PEOPLE MOVEMENTS
AND THEIR CARE

A COMMON ERROR in understanding people movements is to assume that they are all of one variety and occur only among primitive tribes. The people movement is understood as the way the Pariahs of
South India, the Wallamos of Ethiopia, or the Tseltals of Mexico turned
to Christ. Once this stereotype has seized the imagination, it is easily argued that the movement described in the New Testament was not a people
movement and that, since the number of primitive tribes is limited, the
people movement is of little importance as Christians face winnable
peoples in all six continents.

If we are to understand people movements, however, we must see
that there are many varieties, each fitted to and conditioned by the particular society in which a given church is growing. We have already seen
that people like to become Christians without crossing tribal, racial, class,
or linguistic barriers. Human beings like to become Christian with their
own kind of folk. In receptive populations, people movements result when
adequate account is taken of this principle and provision is made for multi-
individual accessions. Men and women of any society, advanced or primitive, urban or rural, literate or illiterate, can come to Christian decision by
the people-movement route, though the pattern of movement in each
society will differ from that in any other.

A people movement in a strong, proud people group will be unlike that in a weak, submissive people group. A people group in contact with the modern world in a thousand places will not turn to Christian faith in the same way as the tribes of Papua New Guinea. It would be quite conceivable for the Jews of America—surely a most advanced and cultured race—to decide that they would become Christians while maintaining their identity as Jews. But in order to do so, Jews would have to adopt a non-Gentile form of Christianity in a people movement. Such a movement would be very different from that of the Malas and Madigas of Andhra Pradesh, but it would nevertheless be a people movement to Christ.

OPPOSITION IS LARGELY SOCIAL

At this point I will repeat that most opposition to the Christian religion arises not from theological but from sociological causes. Individuals resist separating themselves from their own people to join another. This rouses their emotions. They then look around for reasons to back up their feelings of fear and disgust and announce that they reject Christianity because of some theological weakness in it. For example, Muslims say it is blasphemous to affirm that God has a Son; but for tens of thousands of Indonesian Muslims this theological objection vanished like the morning mist as soon as they found they could become Christians without abandoning their people. One should not affirm that theological objections are mere rationalizations, but it can scarcely be doubted that they have been greatly overrated. If Jews could come to Christ without losing their identity as Jews, many of their theological difficulties would—to say the least—be greatly reduced, as Peter, James, and John well know.

The degree of dissatisfaction, disintegration, oppression, and tension in any society also affects the kind of movement possible to it. A society in the last stages of disintegration, for example, could not move as the Icelanders did whose trek to Christ is recounted in the first chapter of this book. Members of an oppressed people, such as the Chamars of India, are powerfully impelled toward Christianity, but extreme economic and social dependence on the higher castes handicaps their ability to act. Chamar movements of North India have manifested a different pattern from those of independent animistic tribes of Assam. A people that forms but 5 per cent of the total population cannot move in the same way as one that form 95 percent.

When a receptive caste lives in large settlements (40 to 100 houses per village), its members move to Christian faith more easily and can be formed into better churches than when the caste lives in small settlements. The people are less afraid of their overlords and, once Christian, form larger congregations that can be instructed more easily and support an indigenous ministry better than small scattered churchlets of three or four families to a village.

In North America the many strata of society are satisfied or dissatisfied with themselves in different degrees. Each has a different degree of winnability. First-generation immigrants as a rule are much more winnable than third- or fourth-generation. Each segment of society (including the many segments of the old white population) poses its own problems and offers its own opportunities to multi-individual conversion. Web movements in different homogeneous units are quite dissimilar.

The significant turnings to Christian faith yet to occur among the great populations of Asia, Africa, and Latin America will come by people movements. It is inconceivable that any extension of the one-by-one-against-the-social-tide pattern could be great enough to bring to the castes of India and the city masses of China and Japan the blessings of reconciliation with God in Christ. In years to come, whole families and groups of families, without social dislocation, within their culture, and carrying on their accustomed means of livelihood, are going to become Christian. They will be well instructed and will commend the Christian faith to others. That is, they will come to faith and obedience by the people-movement route. This is what people movements are. Future movements of great peoples, however, will be different from those among the Uraons and Mundas near Calcutta or the Maasai movements starting in Kenya in 1980.

One of the great advances in evangelism urgently awaited is the working out of patterns by which it is possible for advanced peoples—West as well as East—to become disciples of Christ. Canjanam Gamaliel, a third-generation Lutheran minister in Kerala, maintains that in India caste should be recognized as one of "God's orders of preservation." He insists that breaking this social structure, this order of preservation, is no necessary part of becoming Christian and proposes that churches and missions boldly plant churches in all castes, which for some time would remain one-caste denominations or sections of the universal church (Gamaliel 1967).

His proposal is in line with missionary practice in India between 1705 and 1820, but contrary to practice from that time to the present. The proposal would make possible caste-wise movements to Christ in the great Indian social structures. He is confident that becoming Christian and accepting the Bible as the only Scripture will destroy the religious sanctions that reinforce the Hindu caste system; and that with religious sanctions gone, the sense of separateness and class distinction will gradually disappear while conserving the riches of Indian culture. Gamaliel's proposal, if put into practice, would give rise to new and interesting forms of people movements. Whether existing churches and missions follow his proposal or not, it is very likely that truly indigenous churches of this pattern will arise of themselves in Indian castes, much as the Independent African churches have arisen in Africa.

SOME TYPES OF PEOPLE MOVEMENTS

Classification of people movements is yet in its infancy. The scores, and possibly hundreds, of varieties of movements need to be clearly seen. Merely naming the different kinds of movements would help us to understand our task and reveal both its complexity and its promise. Classification should help discipling in a major way. As a beginning, I would suggest four kinds of people movements, based on the kind of church that results. Then I discuss a fifth, web movements. I do this with the understanding that this list is not exhaustive. How many types of people movements exist, I do not know. Instead of five there may be fifty or one hundred and five.

1. Lyddic Movements

And all who dwelt at Lydda and Sharon saw him and turned to the Lord (Acts 9:35).

In a Lyddic movement, the entire community becomes Christian. The United Presbyterians in the Punjab experienced a Lyddic movement among the Chuhras. Within half a century hundreds of Chuhra communities became Christian and the communities remained intact.

On the other side of the world in Irian Jaya, James Sunda calls this kind of movement the "clean sweep," and under that heading describes a Uhunduni movement thus: "One thousand four hundred Uhundunis live in the Ilaga and three thousand one hundred live in the Beoga Valley. Nearly all adults in both valleys have been baptized" (1963:18).

2. Lystran Movements

And Jews from Antioch and Iconium came [to Lystra] and persuaded the multitudes; and having stoned Paul, they dragged him out of the city, supposing him to be dead. However, when the disciples gathered around him, he rose up and went into the city. And the next day he departed with Barnabas to Derbe (Acts 14:19-20).

In a Lystran movement, a part of the people become Christian and the balance become hostile to the Christian religion. The people movement, by virtue of resistance, opposition, or even mishandling by the evangelists, splits the existing people group. Lystran movements are much more common than Lyddic movements, although a Lystran movement if properly nurtured can often become a Lyddic movement.

3. Laodicean Movements

And to the angel of the church of the Laodiceans write . . . I know your works, that you are neither cold nor hot. I wish you were cold or hot. So then, because you are lukewarm, and neither cold nor hot, I will spew you out of My mouth (Rev. 3:14-16).

A Laodicean movement slows down and stagnates. It becomes full of nominal Christians. It loses its first love and is a caricature of what a Christian church should be. This is usually the outcome of a failure to shepherd or to help the new believers progress in their discipleship. More than anything else, the key to strengthening a people movement is post-baptismal care. Without it the movement can starve and stagnate and become Laodicean.

4. Ephesian Movements

. . . Paul . . . came to Ephesus, and finding some disciples he said to them, "Did you receive the Holy Spirit when you believed?" And they said to him, "We have not so much as heard whether there is a Holy Spirit." And he said to them, "Into what then were you baptized?" So they said, "Into John's baptism." . . . When they heard this they were baptized in the name of the Lord Jesus (Acts 19:1-7).

An Ephesian movement is an irregular form of the church that emerges among those who are truly drawn by the Holy Spirit to follow

Jesus, but begin to do so on the basis of incomplete or even at times somewhat twisted information about Christianity. These irregular forms of the church are often established in advance of the arrival of traditional churches. Autonomous churches arise that to the traditional churches may seem to have grave deficiencies. We may confidently expect many more of these in the future. The eight thousand independent African denominations, the Congregacao Crista and other indigenous churches in Brazil, the Spirit of Jesus Church in Japan, and many others come to mind. All are forms of people movements—some quite orthodox and some heretical—and present Christian mission with both a challenge and a problem.

WEB MOVEMENTS

A fifth and highly important type of people movement is the web movement. Notable web movements have occurred all across the United States and Canada as the faith spread among relatives of existing Christians. The spread was seldom confined to relatives, but the Scottish, Irish, Swedish, German, and Welsh communities were the seedbeds of certain whole denominations. A valuable, practical application of web movement theory has been written by Win Arn and his son Charles: *The Master's Plan for Making Disciples* (1982). It should be read in conjunction with this section.

In Latin America among the Portuguese- and Spanish-speaking populations there are no castes or tribes, but tightly knit webs of relationship and many extended families are the rule. As tribal society breaks down all around the world, its place is taken not by highly individualized persons, but by communities with a strong family life. A close blood and marriage web is clearly discernible long after tribe and caste have ceased to exist.

Some Western families value their relationships very highly; but for the most part Westerners do not know their own second and third cousins. They may see their nieces and nephews and immediate in-laws now and then, but what they do is of little moment to them. In individualistic, mobile societies one's intimates are not likely to be those of his own household. The web often does not count for much.

In most parts of the world, however, the web counts tremendously. All know, and are intimate with not merely brothers, sisters, parents, and grandparents, but also with cousins, uncles, aunts, great-uncles, sisters-in-law, mothers-in-law, godfathers and godmothers, grandnieces and grandnephews, and many others. In their world, these are the people who count. They can expect a night's hospitality in any of these houses. They belong. Relatives will shield them from the law, try to get them a job, or help them select a wife or an ox in case they should need either. News of deaths and marriages within the web passes through the family like lightning, and relatives drop all other duties to go to the funerals or weddings. Members of other clans or families can become Christian and they remain unmoved; but let "one of us" become Christian and they are deeply stirred.

One-by-one-against-the-tide is a mode of conversion that pries a single person out of this social matrix and leads him or her to become a Christian. It encourages that individual to renounce his or her people. It assumes—often with good reason—that the tribe or the family will be hard against the Christian religion. The family gathers on the tenth day to eat the funeral feast and feed the ancestors. Since this is forbidden to Christians they are conspicuous by their absence. Frequently the very people who will not hear their testimony are those of their own household. They regard the new convert as a traitor and the evangelist as one who goes about snatching individuals out of families. Once this image has been firmly planted in any population, the church grows very slowly. Against this one-by-one mode we must see the web movement to Christian faith, which may be thought of as a somewhat disconnected and long-drawn-out people movement. A diagram will illustrate the point. Despite its over-simplification the diagram will help us to see the real situation in community after community in most countries.

In every *rancho* in Mexico, *barrio* in the Philippines, *gaon* in India, or compound in Africa, the ambassador of Christ should see not simply Mexicans, Filipinos, Indians, or Africans, but webs of relationship—that is, organisms composed of individuals closely and permanently linked together. Evangelists should memorize the two or three dozen technical words that describe the common relationships. They can then learn the names of the yet-to-be-won relations in each group of new Christians. They will thus become aware of the extensive nature of the web and see the true dimensions of the task. They soon come to see that faith can flow through the lines of relationship that comprise the web—or, not using these, can be effectively halted.

In the figure, the numerals indicate the order in which these individuals became Christian. The circular lines include all the individuals who acted together at one time to become Christian.

THE WEB MOVEMENT

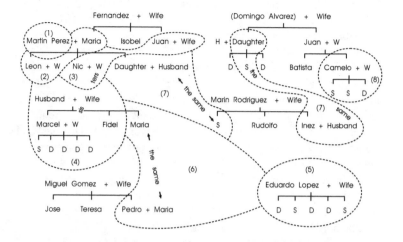

The first to become an evangelical was Martin Perez (1). His action was shocking to everyone else in the rancho. His wife and children drew back in fear and disgust. His father-in-law, old man Fernandez, was incensed at his son-in-law's infidelity to the Virgin Mary. After some months, however, his wife Maria and his son Leon with his own young wife (2), observing what it meant to be an evangelical, hearing the Bible, and impressed by Martin's witness, decided to become evangelicals and were instructed and baptized. The four assembled together for Bible study and prayer, walked to a nearby evangelical churchlet for worship, and behaved like good Christians. Leon's brother Nic and his wife and Maria's younger brother Juan and his wife (3) used to attend these meetings, and within the year became believers themselves.

All this had not been going on in a corner. Everyone else in the rancho was deeply stirred. Some would curse the evangelicals. Others would drop in to see them worship or pray. Nic's wife had a sister whose husband Marcel was a good friend of both Leon and Nic. They often worked together. Marcel said to his wife, "Why not let us become evangelicals? My father and mother are willing and so is Fidel (4). The evangelicals are good people. They do what the Bible says to do. I like their worship." All these decisions, however, hardened Isobel, who withdrew from association with her brothers and lived more and more with her old parents.

Eduardo Lopez and wife (5), newcomers to the rancho, had no close relatives, though both were distantly related to almost everyone there.

After attending an occasional meeting for two years, they decided to accept the Lord. And very shortly afterward Maria (sister of Fidel and Marcel) persuaded her husband to become a believer (6). She liked to sing and invariably attended the worship services.

The only daughter of Martin and Maria, with her husband (7), followed suit—persuaded by the visiting pastor on the one hand and Maria and Martin on the other. At the same time Marin Rodriguez's daughter Inez and her husband joined her big brother in baptism (7). Marin was not hostile to the act. He was, in fact, a frequent attendant at the meetings of the church, but was by no means a believer. Inez and her husband cared for his widowed grandmother (daughter of Domingo Alvarez, a famed character in the rancho, long since dead). Carmelo, a cousin-in-law of Inez, had been a chief opponent of the evangelicals and at first laughed loudly when he was told that his cousin and Inez were praying for him. But when he fell ill, and they prayed at his bedside and he got well, he bought a New Testament and read it carefully. When he found no prayers to the Virgin Mary in the New Testament and no mention of purgatory, he concluded that the evangelical religion was the true faith and confessed Christ with his wife and three children (8).

This highly simplified account merely suggests the part the web of relationships can play in the spread of the church. It is instructive to consider each of the eight accessions and to name the relatives who preceded them into the Baptist church. Thus Leon could have said, as he was being baptized, "I am joining my father in the true faith." Juan could have said, "I am joining my sister Maria and my brother-in-law and my nephew Leon." But by the time Inez was baptized, the rest of this page would scarcely suffice to name the relatives whom she was joining in baptism.

The diagram also indicates those members of the web who would most likely have the prayers of many loved ones focused on them. After the eighth group was baptized, Marin Rodriguez and Isobel would be particularly moved by the prayers of all their relatives—so might old man Fernandez and wife, particularly if his evangelical children and grandchildren were affectionate and helpful.

No one should conclude that web ingathering is a method of evangelism that will invariably sweep in whole communities. People do not "sweep in." They become suspicious if made the special objects of a sales campaign. Instead, the evangelist should say: I must remember that whole families make stronger, better Christians than lone rebels, and congregations built of interrelated persons have more endurance and communicative ability than those built of disparate individuals. Hence I shall seek to rebuild the web inside the church. To be sure, since "it is better to enter life lame than with two feet to be thrown into hell" (Mark 9:45), I shall accept single individuals when they cannot persuade their relatives; and single families when, after effort, their relatives refuse to come with them. I shall press on steadily, seeking lost men and women. I shall learn the web in each community so that I know who belongs to whom. I shall carry good news from one section of the web to others and constantly teach that in Christ family webs are stronger and family joys are greater than in the world. Evangelists who say this open themselves to the leading of the Holy Spirit as he inclines natural groupings—families, minor lineages, major lineages, and clans—to accept the Savior.

A further consideration is now possible. The foregoing sequence of baptisms took place in a denomination and a country dominated by the North American individualistic pattern. It took more than four years for eight small groups to decide to become evangelicals. Each made a decision against the total group that surrounded them—though as the number of evangelicals increased, each decision more and more meant "joining my people who are now evangelicals."

Suppose a multi-individual decision-making pattern had instead been dominant. Suppose Martin's baptism had been deliberately delayed so that he could, while still entirely solid with his relatives, communicate his new-found convictions to them. Suppose he had proposed to all his relatives—both those who later gradually believed and those who later turned stiffly away—that they become biblical Christians as a whole, build a meeting house, and continue on in the new faith with relationships intact. Instead of a series of decisions against the group, might not the unity of the group have been preserved and enhanced? Within that unity, a prolonged vote-taking could have occurred and common sins would have been renounced. Much teaching would have been received and much Bible study done. A multi-individual, mutually interdependent decision might have been made. Had this been the pattern of church growth in that land, the outcome might have been a larger and better church than the one that was established.

POSTBAPTISMAL CARE

The quality of people-movement churches is uniquely dependent on post-baptismal care. In these movements relatively large numbers of converts form new churches quickly. If they are neglected, or if it is assumed that the same amount and kind of care that new Christians received back in California will be sufficient for them here, a starved and nominal membership can be confidently expected. If, on the contrary, new congregations are nurtured with imagination and faithfulness, in ways that lead their members to a genuine advance in Christian living, solid congregations of sound Christians will result. Much of the failure in people movements is wrongly ascribed to the multi-individual way they decide for Christ. It should be ascribed rather to the poor shepherding they receive, both before and after baptism.

Pickett's studies published in 1933 show conclusively that the motives from which unbelievers turn to Christian faith play a smaller part in developing Christian character than good postbaptismal care. Converts who came for rather secular or social motives became good Christians when they became parts of congregations that faithfully worshiped God. Converts who came for spiritual motives and became parts of poorly led and scandalously neglected congregations became weak Christians.

Postbaptismal care involves a whole complex of activities. Prominent among these are instituting regular worship and securing a place of meeting. For congregations to continue for long with no place to meet is to court disaster. House churches, rented halls, or other provision if the congregations arise in towns and cities, or buildings of light materials easily erected if they arise in the country, are an early necessity. Together with this, the systematic worship of God is essential. For literate Christians, regular study of the Bible at home and regular teaching on Sundays are valuable. For illiterates living in barrios or villages, daily worship after the evening meal is highly beneficial. At no place does the Western pattern damage new movements more than in the assumption that because good Christians in Edinburgh or Nashville meet only Sunday morning at eleven, it would therefore be unadvisable for new Christians in Peru or Pakistan to assemble each evening. On the contrary, regular evening worship for the whole new Christian community is not only feasible, but soon comes to be a cherished experience and is influential in developing a truly Christian character.

For illiterates and semiliterates liturgical worship using memorized passages such as the Lord's Prayer, the Ten Commandments, the Twenty-third Psalm, Romans 12:9-16, the Apostles' Creed, and a few hymns or praise choruses is especially valuable. If a passage from the Bible is worth committing to memory at all, it should be repeatedly used in worship. To commit a passage to memory and then not use it regularly is to waste the time spent in learning it, for it is soon forgotten. What is used a hundred times a year, on the contrary, becomes part of the spiritual equipment of the Christian. They can quote it at any time, night or day. They lean on it in hours of stress and teach it to new converts. Liturgical worship, contrary to the expectation of missionaries from the nonliturgical traditions, does not get tiresome to village Christians. They rejoice in its familiarity, comfort, and certainty.

Lay training is essential in postbaptismal care. Younger folk welcome such training. Unpaid leaders are needed in every congregation. *As soon as they learn anything they should teach it to new converts and others.* This provision of a body of essential Christian knowledge, the same for all in that denomination or cluster of congregations, helps insure that learning is meaningful and ties the new church together. In young churches much emphasis should be laid on teaching laymen and laywomen the way of salvation—the kind of knowledge they need to meet common objections to Christian truth and to persuade others of the value of the Christian religion.

PART VI

ADMINISTERING FOR CHURCH GROWTH

19

STREAM ACROSS THE BRIDGES

EVERY HUMAN SOCIETY is like a town on one side of a river over which at convenient places bridges have been built. Citizens can cross the river at other places, but it is much easier to go across the bridges. People near the bridges are better connected than those far from them. Ideas, foodstuffs, processions, and convictions flow to and fro across the bridges.

As those involved in world evangelization administer for church growth, they ought to discover and use these bridges to the unreached. Good stewards of the grace of God should remember the bridges and stream across them. "Find the bridges and use them" is excellent strategy for all who are impelled by the Holy Spirit to share the good news.

During the years of research that led to writing *The Bridges of God* I was constantly impressed by the crucial role played in the expansion of the Christian faith by the relatives of Christians. Again and again I observed that though Christians are surrounded by thousands of fellow citizens, the Christian faith flows best from relative to relative or close friend to close friend. This was true whatever the nationality or language. It was as true in the heartland of America as in Uganda or the High Andes.

In 1955, in *The Bridges of God* I wrote:

Every nation is made up of various layers or strata of society. In many nations each stratum is clearly separated from every other. The individuals in each stratum marry chiefly, if not solely, with each other. Their intimate life is therefore limited to their own society, that is, to their own people. They may work with others, buy from and sell to individuals of other societies; but their intimate life is wrapped up with the individuals of their own people. . . . When (these) start becoming Christian, this touches their very lives (1955:1).

In 1979 George Hunter wrote:

A strategic American church will continually work to locate and reach out to kinsmen, and especially to the friends of active Christians and new converts. The church will also encourage its members to make new friends in the community continually. People are more receptive when they are approached by authentic Christians from within their own social network (1979:126).

BRIDGES HAVE ALWAYS BEEN IMPORTANT

The early church used its bridges to good effect. It started among the common people of Jerusalem. Their bridges were to the common people— their relatives and intimates. While a few of the scribes and Pharisees did become Christian (Nicodemus, Joseph of Arimathea, and Saul come immediately to mind), most Christians were not of that high stratum of society. When persecution drove Christians from the city, they went of necessity to their relatives in the villages of Judea for shelter. There they preached the gospel, that is, they told their intimates about the Lord Jesus and the way of salvation opened for all who believe. The church grew greatly among the peasants of Judea.

Barnabas was a Levite of Cyprus. How natural that the first missionary journey was to Cyprus, where his family lived. How natural also that on his first missionary journey Paul visited Derbe, Iconium, and Antioch. These towns were only 125, 150, and 200 miles west of Tarsus on the main Roman road. It is highly likely that Saul's father had commercial dealings with many of the Jews in those towns. Saul was probably known by them as a brilliant young rabbi of Tarsus, who had studied under Gamaliel in Jerusalem. He was always invited to speak in the synagogues.

The last chapter of the Epistle to the Romans gives vivid evidence of the bridges Paul habitually used. He mentions twenty-six Christians in Rome by name, and knew of several others—though he had never been in Rome. Some of these were his own relatives. One—Rufus's mother—may have been his own mother, though it seems more likely that Paul meant "she has been like a mother to me." All of the twenty-six had relatives and intimates in the Jewish community in Rome. So while Paul considered himself a special messenger of Christ to the Gentiles, he streamed out to them across his bridges in the Jewish community and their bridges to others. One can rejoice in the bridge that Roman Christians had to Caesar's household (Phil. 4:22). It may have been built after Paul arrived.

Down through the centuries the great expansions of the faith have commonly been along lines of relationship. Latourette tells us that the conversion of the Anglo-Saxons in England around the year A.D. 600 began and continued along lines of relationship. Gregory the Great in Rome had sent Augustine the missionary to England. His party landed on the island of Thanet at the mouth of the Thames River, and proceeded to contact Ethelbert, King of Kent—the southeasternmost kingdom of England, which had:

> already been . . . touched by influences from the mainland. Its ruler, Ethelbert, had for wife a Christian Frankish princess, Bertha. As a condition of the marriage, Ethelbert had promised that she would be allowed to observe her religion, and a bishop Luidhard had accompanied her. She worshipped at Canterbury, the capital of Kent (45 miles southeast of modern London), in a church dedicated to St. Martin which is said to have been built in Roman times. . . . Augustine and his party were established in Canterbury. . . . Presently Ethelbert himself was baptized . . . accessions rapidly increased. . . . A letter of Gregory, undated, speaks of ten thousand having been baptized by Augustine on one Christmas (Latourette 1938:66).

In the nineteenth century the great turnings in Burma took place along lines of relationship. An early convert of Adoniram Judson was a Karen, Ko Tha Byu. Judson considered his main work to lie with the Buddhist Burmese, but Ko Tha Byu went to his relatives among the Karens and from these, groups became Christian. The Karen people movement had begun. It spread almost exclusively from contact to contact, relative to relative until today more than half a million Karens are Christians and the Karen church is one of the strongest in all Asia.

In the United States in the late seventies, the research of Lyle Schaller and Win Arn showed that most accessions to churches came through the efforts of friends and relatives. Many congregations then resolved to discover and befriend the relatives and close friends of families from which one person was an active member. Sometimes this was a husband or wife, sometimes a son or daughter, and sometimes a brother or sister. In every case from one to ten other people immediately came within the circle of congregational concern. Befriending meant much more than inviting them to church. On occasion it meant having them over for a meal or to a neighborhood party. On occasion it meant loaning them a lawn mower or joining their car pool. Several times it led to playing golf together.

One congregation had in it several ardent professional football fans. These bought season tickets to the series and invited an equal number of unbelieving husbands (whose wives were already active Christians) to go with them to the games. Going there, coming back, and the intermissions offered many opportunities for natural conversation about the church and Christ. The unchurched husbands soon came to think of Christian men as normal human beings who rooted for the right teams and knew the right players by name. They went with their new-found friends (and their own long-time wives) to church and became active Christians themselves.

Streaming Across

"Streaming across the bridges" works equally well among unreached tribes. James Sunda tells of the beginning of the remarkable ingathering among the Danis in the Baliem Valley in Irian Jaya. I have mentioned this great ingathering previously, but the important part played by relatives in beginning the movement is well worth recounting. Until 1954, the West Danis were a Stone Age tribe with very few contacts with the outside world. In April 1954 missionaries flew into the high valley (5,000 feet), landing on the Baliem River. Perhaps a dozen mission stations were established, the language was learned, medical relief was given, and evangelism was carried on. But no one became Christian. The Danis whose villages dotted the valley were indifferent and even resistant. It looked as if decades of seed sowing lay ahead.

Then, from November 1958 to February 1959 in the Ilaga Valley, four days' march to the west across a high, cold, 11,000-foot plateau, 2,000 Danis burned their fetishes and became Christian. They were well instructed by missionary Donald Gibbons at a witness school to which especially intelligent married couples were sent. These remembered the main tribe four days' march away, who knew nothing of Christ, though many missionaries worked in their midst. The Ilaga Valley Dani resolved to send their best Christians to the Baliem Valley. Since they had to travel through enemy territory, they took their white missionary along with them. His presence guaranteed them safe passage on that historic journey of February 1960.

Arriving among their relatives they told them, "Become Christians like we did. Hold village meetings and as a group resolve to burn your fetishes. Get all your fetishes, carry in wood and make a long funeral pyre, put your fetishes on it, and burn them all. Declare for Christ. Appoint the men you desire to be your teachers and pastors. The missionaries will instruct them. You will give them food so they will have time to teach you. God will bless you. That is the way you become Christians."

Within a very short time 8,000 Danis in the Baliem Valley had come to group decisions and marched in to the mission stations. Faced with this novel way of becoming Christian, the missionaries scarcely knew what to do. Some opposed any such decision for Christ; but most accepted it as a first step. By 1967 most of the 8,000 had been baptized.

By 1980 more than 30,000 Danis and thousands of men and women of other tribes had been baptized. The highlands of Irian Jaya have become substantially Christian, though outlying tribes are still being evangelized, baptized, and incorporated into Christian churches.

Until approached by their own people, relatives and friends, the Danis were indifferent or hostile. When they heard the word from those from within their own social network they proved exceedingly responsive.

The remarkable multiplication of Chinese Alliance churches across Canada in the late 1970s beautifully illustrates the point I am making. When to become a Christian meant to leave the community and join a Caucasian congregation, then very few Chinese became Christians; but when Chinese from Hong Kong, who had become Christians there in Alliance congregations, immigrated to Canada, and settlements of Cantonese-speaking Chinese were evangelized by Chinese Alliance pastors from Hong Kong, new Chinese congregations sprang up in many cities.

In North America the large ethnic minorities, some of which have been solidly resistant to earnest Protestant denominations, are like the West Danis and the Chinese in Canada. Each awaits the creation of apostolic teams of their own relatives and close friends.

Bridges Are Not Always Relatives

The bridges of God are not always relatives. Often good friends serve Christians as natural avenues of communication. Campus Crusade for

Christ built its vast organization on the fact that college students can speak normally and effectively to other collegians.

In this connection it is interesting to remember that Patrick, who is credited with the conversion of the Irish tribes, was not an Irishman. He had no relatives in that land. He, an English youth, was captured by a band of Irish raiders and carried off to many years of servitude in Ireland. He fled Ireland and went to France. As his Christian conviction grew, he believed God was calling him to go back to Ireland and tell the good news to his captors and multitudes of other Irish. Most missionaries, by definition, are not of the people they evangelize. Missionaries find bridges (or make them) and carry on cross-cultural evangelism across them.

A very nice example of making bridges occurred in England in the years 1975 and 1976. A dying congregation, which had once filled its sanctuary with 300 worshipers, was reduced to 27 persons, all fifty years of age and above. A couple of young American missionaries threw in their lot with this congregation. They made it their special purpose to dress as young people of the factory town dressed, to frequent the places they frequented, and to be interested in the sports and entertainments that drew their attention. Thus they manufactured a bridge. In the course of the next two years, the attendance at that church mounted to 230 and its baptized membership to 119. To be sure, the style of the service was fitted to the newcomers' needs and many other steps were taken; but without building that bridge none of the later steps would have led to church growth—or indeed, to have been possible at all.

BRIDGES IN TIGHTLY STRUCTURED SOCIETIES

In tightly knit societies, where people consciousness is high, and all marriages take place within the segment of society concerned, the chain of relationship is particularly strong. Once Christianity has been established, once a couple of thousand have become Christian, tens of thousands of bridges become available. The potential for explosive growth is high, because across all such bridges the faith may flow. In times of revival when large numbers of Christians are acutely conscious of the power of God in their lives, they stream out across many bridges.

In loosely knit societies, however, where individuals from many segments of society are living together, bridges exist but they are not so influential. More exactly, there the weak, narrow bridges of casual contact are numerous. They do not carry Christian conviction so well. When the gospel flows across such bridges it does not carry as much power. Individuals are won, but not groups. And, those won are not so likely to go on and win others.

Nevertheless, since more and more people live in loosely knit societies, Christians should stream across the numerous bridges there—narrow and weak though they may be. They are God's bridges. He wants us to use them.

Bridges Are Frequently Neglected

In pluralistic societies, the feeling grows that what individuals believe is their own business. Others should not interfere. We should simply accept persons as they are, recognizing that within the nation are many different life-styles and many different scales of values. All are equally citizens of the state. Provided that citizens do not hurt other people, they ought to be free to believe and do whatever they wish. I am not commending this point of view, but merely noting that it is prevalent.

In such a climate of belief, many congregations perhaps unconsciously act as if their main duty were to live as Christians, worship God, feed on his word, and be friendly toward those who seek them out. "Our door is always open to those who come to worship with us. We are very warm and cordial. But quite frankly, we do not think it our duty to speak about our faith to others—perhaps especially not to those near and dear to us. They may believe something quite different and we might find their religious beliefs separate us." Thus spoke an elder of an influential church—which had been static for many years. It was not only neglecting its bridges, but had formed a philosophy of life that denied their importance.

Many congregations never consciously seek bridges or instruct their members in how to find and use them. Their evangelistic opportunities are limited to making their church attractive, locating it on a much traveled street, and providing facilities such that visitors who have already decided to choose a church home will conclude that this is the church of which they would like to become members.

Using bridges before they disappear should be ordinary procedure for congregations and Christians everywhere. In the January 1977 issue of *Church Growth Bulletin,* in discussing reasons why Pentecostal churches grow, I wrote the following paragraph:

Common Christians—soon after they become disciples of the Lord—have multitudinous good connections with friends and rela-

tives among secularists, Buddhists, Hindus, Jews, materialists, ag-
nostics, and other worldly people. It is along these connections, these
bridges of God, that the gospel flows. Those who have been Christian for many years, or who grew up in Christian homes and have
married Christians and thus have few intimates among the worldly,
do not have such bridges. They have few intimates among the worldly
and so are not evangelistically as potent. Old Pentecostal congregations find the same thing operative among them. It is the new congregations which are potent. Pentecostals have more new congregations than most denominations—and trust them more.

Danger of Segregation?

Does streaming across bridges produce segregated congregations? Are
such congregations likely to be racist or at least introverted and concerned chiefly about themselves? Is going to one's own relatives and
intimates dangerous advice to give to churches as they become concerned about effective evangelization? These questions deserve careful
answers.

As a result of such evangelism, one-segment congregations do arise.
This is beyond question. When university professors evangelize people
of their own kind, with whom they have normal intimate fellowship, the
resulting church is likely to be largely composed of members of the university community. When Rev. Argos Zodiates evangelizes Greek Americans in Boston, he builds up a 300-member evangelical church made up
almost exclusively of Greeks living in New England.

Overseas monoethnic congregations and clusters of congregations
certainly do arise. In northeast India, when the first Mizo converts in the
Lushai Hills streamed out across their bridges, they had to go to their own
people. As a result, of the 400,000 Christians in the new Indian state of
Mizoram in 1980, more than 90 percent are Mizos. The mature denomination is sending Mizo missionaries to other peoples in Tripura, Korku-
land, and Arunachal.

When in the first decade of the twentieth century the Mono tribes
living in Equatorial Province of Zaire started turning to Christ, they went
exclusively to their own fellows. They had been at work with surround-
ing tribes for hundreds of years. Their obvious first duty was to Christianize their own relatives. By 1969, the official statistics recorded 229,856
baptized believers. Practically all of these belonged to Mono tribes
(McGavran and Riddle 1979:113). If this church is to evangelize other

peoples it will have to send Mono missionaries and keep them at work in cross-cultural evangelism.

Must we, therefore, conclude that multiplying congregations largely of one kind of people in Boston, university campuses, or Burma is a step backward? Must we resist it and declare that we want real Christians, who feel brotherly to all peoples, and who in their congregational structure and worship demonstrate that the two peoples concerned have actually become one in Christ Jesus? The answers to these questions must be a firm, though qualified, No. Multiplying churches largely of one kind of people is not a step backward. It is an essential step forward. There is no other way in which the multitudinous pieces of the human mosaic can become Christian. Such churches are Christ's way to the hearts of those peoples. Requiring converts to join conglomerate congregations will hinder the church from rapidly spreading to *panta ta ethne*.

The options then are: (A) building conglomerate congregations that from the beginning bring men and women of many different ethnic, linguistic, and educational backgrounds into one new family of God; and (B) rapidly building up congregations of one kind of people. In many populations (A) is a weak option. Only in true social melting pots is it a significant option. There old segments of society are in fact breaking down. Many mixed marriages are taking place. Children growing up together in school regard each other as essentially one people. There conglomerate congregations are both possible and desirable. There the best opportunity for growth may truly be that of bringing into one congregation converts of the new people being formed. Elsewhere the church of God should press ahead making sure that congregations arise within each segment of society. These will be led by elders and deacons of that segment and will ordain pastors of that segment, too.

Four Qualifications

I said that the answers to these questions must be a firm but qualified No. Let us consider four qualifications. Qualification one is that most segments of humanity are themselves mosaics. Each segment includes individuals who belong to other segments. The university community includes some who live in the country and are gardeners or small farmers as well as teachers. Many white congregations have black members whose place of residence, education, and income make them feel at home in such churches. Hispanic Americans include fourth-generation citizens who may speak no Spanish at all, immigrants from Argentina who arrived six months ago, and every shade in between. Every congregation, therefore, is likely to have a wide spread of members. Going to relatives and friends does not mean going to an increasingly narrow segment of society. Friends often come from other sections of society, and increasingly relatives do too. A Thorwaldson marries a Rodriguez, a Chen marries a McDonald, a Kowalski marries a Vanderveld. Consequently each congregation as it follows its relatives and friends disciples many kinds of peoples.

Qualification two is that every large congregation has many small groups meeting around different interests. The choir draws in those of musical ability and obviously will welcome a rich tenor and a lyric soprano, whatever classes or ethnic backgrounds they come from. The leaders of the scout troop and the sewing circle eagerly look for those who want to engage in these activities. Streaming across the bridges must not be distorted to mean limiting a congregation to the relatives of its dominant group. All the data indicate that in urban society using the bridges leads to the inclusion in many small groups of many different kinds of people.

Qualification three is that many congregations already have won most of their own narrowly conceived connections. Thus an Episcopal congregation in a typical town already has those who are Episcopalian by upbringing or inclination. A Mennonite congregation already includes in its oversight all Mennonites in its parish area. Streaming across the bridges certainly does not mean limiting oneself to such little enclaves.

Common sense is assumed. Christians—just because they are one in Christ—in an open-ended society welcome every opportunity to expand the fellowship. They make strangers welcome in the church. They demonstrate inclusiveness. At the same time, Christians should start new congregations in largely unchurched populations. Anglicans in England will find that new congregations of working-class men and women, in which leaders of labor unions are the elders or influential members, will evangelize this important segment of British society more effectively than bringing a few working-class people into existing middle- and upper-class congregations. The latter, of course, is being and should be done; but it would not be wise to depend exclusively on it.

Streaming across the bridges of friendship and relationship will not normally lead to segregation. If any tendency in that direction is discerned, the principle is being misused.

Qualification four is that congregations and denominations of similar people should recognize that they are tempted to become exclusive and sub-Christian. The very fact that most of their members are of one cut of society makes it easy for them to object to apartheid in far-off lands and to talk about brotherhood while they themselves are not practicing it. It is easy to overlook the Gentiles and Samaritans in their neighborhood. Each one-class congregation and denomination, therefore, should lay great stress on the unity of all Christians. All are one people in Christ. The missionary obligation of each segmental church to evangelize across the linguistic, class, and race gulfs that surround it should be heartily empha-sized. Black congregations and denominations in the United States, for example, should send out large numbers of missionaries to unevangelized hidden peoples in Asia, Africa, Europe, and other lands. The Mizo Church does well to send out scores of missionaries to other castes and tribes in India. Every Christian is saved to serve.

DEFINITE PLANNING TO USE THE BRIDGES

The tendency of churches to devote themselves to maintenance rather than evangelism is strong. Water runs downhill. Intellectual assent to the prin-ciple that we should use our bridges will help, but of itself seldom pro-duces ongoing expansion. For that to happen, leaders will have to plan continuous use of the bridges. In a letter to me, Met Castillo of the Phil-ippine Alliance Church declares,

> Adequate plans intended to multiply churches in rural and urban cen-ters of population are urgently needed if we are to fulfil the mandate of the Lord of the Church. . . . Good planning minimizes waste of time, resources and personnel. It insures continuous growth.

His statement is particularly impressive in view of the fact that in the five years after 1975, his denomination planted 339 new churches and in-creased the membership from 26,830 to 51,629, a 270 percent DGR.

One of the most effective plans to come to my attention, and one that could be used in congregations in the United States and every other na-tion, was the focusing of prayer by every member of the congregation on carefully chosen individuals. The story is this. In twenty-three small-town congregations of one denomination all but one were static. They had stopped growing at about forty members. They believed that in their cir-cumstances, they could not grow more. One, however, had grown from the typical forty members to two hundred and twenty! What had caused this phenomenal increase? The town had grown no more than the other twenty-two. Of the several factors that influenced growth, one was, by the people themselves, called the chief factor.

Each year in January that growing congregation had led every member to select from among his or her relatives and intimates that one person who appeared most winnable. "I like him very much." "We spend much time together." "She thinks a great deal of me." Each member then covenanted to pray daily by name for the salvation of that person. The pastor in the course of the weeks often prayed publicly for "our friends for whom each of us is praying." The whole congregation had a keen consciousness of being God's instrument in the salvation of scores of their own best friends and loved ones. The outcome was summarized by one of the leading women, "We pray and every year God gives us those we pray for—some years ten, and some years twenty, and one year sixty new members." The empirical relationship of prayer to the growth of churches is a field begging fresh research and understanding.

CONCLUSION

Of all the factors that influence church growth, none is more immediately available to all Christians than to evangelize the natural fringes of the existing church. This is where most growth occurs. These are the nearest of the fields white to harvest. These are the people who already have some knowledge of Christ and the Christian life. Evangelizing each network of social connection out to its fringes is always sound procedure. True, it must always be supplemented by deliberate attempts to go to the Samaritans among whom Jews have no relatives and few friends. The huge numbers of unreached peoples of the world warn us not to limit evangelism to networks of friends. New congregations in every *ethnos* on earth are essential strategy if Christians are to obey the Great Commission. Nevertheless, once the new start has been made, its network of relatives and intimates is very likely to be its best avenue for expansion. Use the bridges.

20

SET GOALS

NOTHING FOCUSES effort like setting a goal. As Christians seek to do effective evangelism, they need to set membership goals. This focuses their efforts on the main task.

Goal setting requires securing needed facts. It reminds pastors and missionaries of their basic responsibilities and available resources. It forces them to arrange their priorities aright. It locks them onto their polestar.

It is essential that Christian leaders align their basic purposes with the eternal purpose of God to save unbelievers through faith in Jesus Christ. This is the first step in the consequent growth and development of the church. Goal setting helps implement such alignment.

World evangelization is a very wide enterprise. It runs from pre-evangelism through proclamation, persuasion, baptism or incorporation, growth in grace and knowledge of the Lord, to men and women mature in Christ. It inevitably includes corporate aspects of life. Social structures must be Christianized more and more thoroughly. In the academic field, both evangelism in one's own culture and mission to other cultures are concerned. Both must harness many disciplines and sciences to the one goal of discipling *panta ta ethne*. Sociology, communications, religions, anthropology, theory and practice of education, ecumenical relationships, history of evangelism and mission, biblical studies—all have substantial contributions to make.

This very wide enterprise, however, must always remember its center—God's unswerving purpose that every knee shall bow. Goal setting helps it to do so. Missiology is not a mishmash of many different ingredients. Rather it is that science whose steady aim is world evangelization in all six continents, Europe as well as Asia, America as well as Africa. The Savior is its center and drive shaft. Evangelization and mission are not a hundred good enterprises all of equal value, it making no difference which gets done and which is omitted. World evangelization must be carried out to the specific end that in accordance with the Master's express command all peoples shall be discipled. The thousands of unreached peoples, the over three billion who have yet to believe, stand as both rebuke and challenge to all teachers of evangelism and missiology.

WALKING PAST THE LIONS

Setting membership goals has only recently become popular. Lions have stood in the way. The present situation and the notable service that C. Peter Wagner, Paul Yonggi Cho, and others have rendered in applying this principle to evangelism and church growth must be seen against the long years when growth goals were neither set nor considered proper.

Churches in North America

Churches in Canada and the United States have seldom set membership goals. Indeed, most of them have never seen a line graph of their past growth or made a projection of what future growth might be. Were one to ask what the rate of growth of the church was, the average pastor would not know.

American congregations have set goals neither for their total membership nor for its various parts, such as young adults, seniors, middle-aged, and the college contingent. The question, "Is the number of your communicant members who are permanent residents of this community likely to increase in the next five years?" would not usually get a firm answer.

Setting goals for membership increase is beyond the thinking of most Christians. They set goals for their business activities, the number of cars they will sell, the amount of steel they will produce, or the number of new buildings they will erect; but not for the number of converts their church will win.

To be sure, evangelistic campaigns are mounted and pastors call on prospects who visit the church or move into the neighborhood, but before 1972 it was a rare congregation or denomination that had studied its past growth and made faith projections as to future growth.

Missions Overseas

Missions overseas also traditionally have not set membership goals. As missionaries arrived in some new land, they faced years of exploratory activities—learning the language, finding a place to stay, overcoming indifference or hostility, maintaining health under difficult conditions, and on and on. Often it was many years before the first converts were won. Sometimes famines, epidemics, revolutions, and the like prevented systematic work. The population had never heard of Christianity or of Christ. In that language the Bible was not available. Under such circumstances, to set a membership goal would have been foolish. Such missionaries did well simply to hang on.

Even after a settled mode of work and a firm base of operations had been established, converts were so slow in appearing that the goal rightly was considered to be "mission work" rather than membership increase. Much opposition to church growth arises precisely because even today missions under such circumstances, feeling that membership increase is chancy and the real task is proclamation of Christ and service of the people, reject the very idea that membership increase should be a criterion. Setting a goal, such as doubling membership in the next ten years, would be considered unwise.

During the early stages of mission in most populations of planet earth the task is commending the gospel by good works, learning the language, translating the Scriptures, producing and distributing Christian literature, and serving the people with medicine, agriculture, education, development, or other tools.

Missionaries tend to say, "As far as members are concerned, let us take what God brings to us, love them and rear them as good Christians. Let us teach them the Bible, habituate them to weekly worship, and train indigenous leaders for them. The tithe must be taught, congregations organized, problems of the new churches solved, and Christians made into good Christians. We must establish a form of Christianity that fits the existing economic level, and the dominant culture. While some noxious elements of the culture (such as idol worship) must be purged, most elements can be brought into the church, which will increasingly take on a thoroughly indigenous hue. The task is not setting membership goals but laboriously and lovingly forming the kind of Christian community that is thoroughly Christian and that feels thoroughly at home in its culture."

Furthermore, promotional concerns weigh heavily in the minds of missionaries and executive secretaries of supporting boards. Where the growth of the church looks difficult, what will happen if great goals are set and then few are baptized? Will this not discourage supporters? A mission executive once said to me, "The most dangerous thing I could do, would be to allow the supporters of our mission in Pakistan to think that the church there could and ought to grow. When they learned that it had not been growing, their giving would drastically decline."

These lions have stood in the way of setting membership goals in America and overseas.

Even more threatening are the theological lions. Because slow growth or no growth has been common, the task has seemed to be that of caring for existing members and their children. A maintenance mentality has characterized most congregations and denominations and defended on biblical grounds. Caring for those in the fold has been deified, and searching for lost sheep has been denigrated. Some have gone so far as to suggest that evangelism is an imperialistic imposing of one's own beliefs on others. Some have called all evangelism "self-aggrandizement." Goal setting has been viewed as abhorrent to God and contrary to the spirit of Christian kindliness.

It is surprising to what degree the Bible has been read in this light. To sealed-off and declining denominations, the Bible appeared to be speaking exclusively to Christians. For example, in Ephesians, Paul, kneeling in prayer, asks God to grant the Ephesian Christians strength to comprehend "what is the width and length and depth and height—to know the love of Christ. . . ." In view of the fact that Paul's prayer begins reminding his readers that every family on earth takes its name from the Father, and concludes "throughout all ages, world without end," it is clear that the inspired word is here referring to a love that extends to all throughout all generations. The prayer is that Christ may so dwell in the hearts of Christians that, overcoming their provincialism and tendency to think only of themselves, they will be strong to grasp Christ's purpose that the gospel be preached to all peoples. Of Christ's love, they are to know its *length* (to earth's remotest bounds), *breadth* (to the myriad societies of mankind), *height* (up through all principalities and powers), and *depth* to the most desperate needs of the unsaved). Instead of this missionary interpretation of the passage, Christians in static churches take the four words to mean exclusively qualities of Christ's love for Christians and the church.

The correct interpretation includes both emphases. It is wrong to hold that this Scripture refers exclusively to the unsaved in faraway lands or exclusively to existing Christians. Not only must both emphases be seen in the words, but their outward thrust must be seen to be as fully potent as their inward. Congregations and denominations dominated by a maintenance mentality seldom see this.

With such a defective ethnocentric view of Scripture, it is not surprising that theological lions such as the following should stand, growling at goal setting.

We do not convert. The Holy Spirit does. Consequently it would be presumptuous for us to set goals or to assume that we shall win such-and-such numbers to Christian faith.

We are commanded to preach the gospel to the whole creation (Mark 16; Acts 1). We are to let the earth hear his voice. But we are not commanded to church the nations. God gives the increase as he sees fit.

We are to expect few Christians. The gate is narrow. Many are not going to be saved (Matt. 22:14; Luke 18:8).

The task is to make real Christians. To be avoided at all costs is cheap grace. We ought not to rush out and increase our membership. A large number of baptized heathen is not the goal. Care for the flock has abundant biblical support, but we find no impassioned pleas for Christians to surge out in evangelistic efforts. In the July 1979 *International Review of Mission* Lesslie Newbigin wrote:

> You cannot find in Paul's letters a single passage where he urges his readers to be more active in evangelism. There is absolutely nothing in the New Testament corresponding to the almost frantic appeals for missionary activity which has been common in Protestant missionary practice (1979:308).

The Lions Are Chained

As Bunyan noted in *Pilgrim's Progress,* lions deter only the fainthearted. As courageous Christians carry out God's will, they find the lions just described securely chained.

The Scriptures must be used intelligently. When the whole inspired word is read, we find that while the Holy Spirit converts, he operates in most instances through Christians. The Holy Spirit said, "Set apart for me Barnabas and Saul." The Lord said, "Go, disciple *panta ta ethne.*" Paul said, "Imitate me in this tremendous concern I have by all means to win some."

When the Lord said to his disciples, "Whatever you bind on earth will be bound in heaven, and whatever you loose on earth will be loosed in heaven," it is difficult to hold that evangelism is mere proclamation. The Lord committed to his followers the duty of persuading unbelievers to believe and then purposefully completing the complex tasks of incorporating believers into visible, countable congregations and denominations. The Holy Spirit was certainly at work in all this, through men and women filled with the Holy Spirit.

In Acts we read,

> Paul . . . reasoned in the synagogue every Sabbath and persuaded both Jews and Greeks. When Silas and Timothy had come from Macedonia, Paul was constrained by the Spirit, and testified to the Jews that Jesus is the Christ. . . . The Lord said to Paul in the night by a vision, "Do not be afraid, but speak and do not keep silent" (Acts 18:4-5, 9).

When the Jews dragged Paul before Gallio, the proconsul, they charged him with "persuading men." In view of these passages it is difficult to hold that deliberate plans for persuading men and women to become followers of Jesus and for incorporating them in churches are in any sense presumptuous. Setting membership goals is in accordance with God's eternal purpose. Goal setting in the service of the Great Commission is pleasing to God. The lions may growl, but they are chained. Scripture is solidly on the side of careful planning for church growth.

THE HISTORY OF GOAL SETTING

Against this background we briefly consider the three thrusts that in the past few years have made the setting of church growth goals such a helpful part of the Christian movement.

Laying the Foundations for Goal Setting

The Bridges of God (1955), in a time of missionary retreat, maintained that great growth of the church was what God desired. The book compared growth by the mission-station approach to that by the people movement and maintained that God granted both. Sentences such as the following sum up the book.

In this day the Christian churches can win their most notable victories. Out of imminent disaster . . . they can contribute the only enduring bases of national well-being—great numbers of living churches which fear and love and worship the true and ever-living God (McGavran 1955:155).

The peoples who can today be discipled consist of millions of individuals whose salvation God wills (McGavran 1955:156).

George Fox, at the beginning of that great People Movement which soon brought one in a hundred of the population of England into the Society of Friends, had a vision in which he saw "an innumerable company, as many as motes in the sun which shall come to the One Shepherd and the One Fold." It is given to all of us to see that same vision (McGavran 1955:157).

The first edition of *Understanding Church Growth* (1970) printed what had formed the substance of church growth seminars, classes, lectures, and articles in the preceding fifteen years. From beginning to end it assumed that quantitative growth of the church was God's will and ought to be measured, depicted, discussed, and made the basis for evangelistic and missionary labors.

Between 1955 and 1965 these and other church growth concepts burst on the scene. Some churches and missions welcomed them and found in them new courage and new direction. Some resisted them. In both cases, the growth concepts prepared the ground for goal setting. Had these concepts not plowed the soil for more than a decade, goal setting anywhere would have been difficult, if not impossible.

At the Institute of Church Growth in Oregon (1961-65) and the School of World Mission in California (1965-on) scores of career missionaries studied a missiology of which the Great Commission was the dynamic center. Missiology included more than Christ's command to disciple all nations. It included religions, sociology and anthropology, missionary methods, biblical studies, theologies of mission, history, leadership theory, and ecumenical endeavors, but no one of these was its center. None could have created the world mission of the church. That is uniquely dependent on God's eternal purpose to save people through belief in Jesus Christ, the Savior. God's purpose being to save countable persons, the vast mission enterprise and the foundational concepts of church growth necessarily follow.

Those who studied at Fuller went back to their countries resolved to do theology and mission in the light of the clear biblical directives to advance the gospel and spread the faith.

In 1963 as director of the Institute of Church Growth in Eugene, Oregon, I applied to many foundations for a substantial grant for a continent-wide survey of church growth in Latin America. In January 1965, I received a grant from Lilly Endowment of $54,000, and by May had secured William R. Read, Victor Monterroso, and Harmon A. Johnson as researchers. For the next three years these men (operating out of Pasadena, California, where by then I had gone as founding dean of the School of World Mission) carried on the study of church growth in 17 nations. Carrying out such a survey furnishes innumerable opportunities for impressing on denominations, congregations, mission boards, and missionaries the fact that they are working at an enterprise that can be and ought to be measured and charted.

When *Latin American Church Growth* was published in 1969, its findings fell like a bombshell on the missionary societies at work in Latin America—particularly on the conservative evangelical boards, grouped under the EFMA/IFMA standards, whose labors were resulting in relatively little church growth. They believed themselves to be theologically sound, and knew they were working hard; yet they were experiencing less growth than the mainline missionary societies and the Pentecostal churches. They were troubled.

Consequently, they called a consultation in Elburn, Illinois, in September 1970. The co-chairpersons were C. Peter Wagner of Bolivia, who the following year joined our faculty at Fuller, and Vergil Gerber, director of Evangelical Missions Information Service in Wheaton, Illinois. More than 50 executives of mission appeared and spent two days discussing ways and means of getting on with their main task. They had never seen an authoritative, quantitative analysis of their labors before. They had been carrying on splendid mission and drinking satisfying drafts of promotional presentations. The landmark book *Latin American Church Growth*, with its 174 pages of pictorial representations of growth and 209 pages of convincing analysis of the factors governing growth, drove them to devise a new vehicle for spreading the eminently useful church growth way of thinking. They asked, "How can we get our missionaries and the pastors of churches in Latin America to see that their basic task is communicating the gospel to more and more people?" Church growth dynamics were leavening the whole lump.

As other researches in church growth were published, they too awakened leaders in many lands. William R. Read's *New Patterns of Church Growth in Brazil* (1965) and Roy E. Shearer's *Wildfire: Church Growth in Korea* (1966) had profound influence. John B. Grimley and

Gordon E. Robinson's *Church Growth in Central and Southern Nigeria* (1966), J. C. Wold's *God's Impatience in Liberia* (1968), Jim Montgomery's *Fire in the Philippines* (1971), my *Church Growth in Jamaica* (1962), and Keith E. Hamilton's *Church Growth in the High Andes* (1963) roused mission leaders in many nations to the actual state of the church. Granting that it is important to know whether the church is soundly Christian or nominal, it is also important to know whether it is one-tenth of one percent of the population or half of it; and whether it is growing vigorously or declining.

In 1970 Alan Tippett decided that the constant attack on church growth was subbiblical and must be ended. He consequently wrote a most influential book, *Church Growth and the Word of God.* The biblical base proved in that and other books freed pastors and leaders from the burden of guilt—that growth was somehow sinful. It argued convincingly that the word of God authorizes church growth.

By 1970 the stage had been set for systematic goal setting as essential missionary strategy. The ground had been plowed and sown. The foundation for the edifice had been laid.

An important step in laying the foundation was taken by Leonard Tuggy. The story is worth telling. He had studied in Fuller in 1967-68 and was appointed by the Conservative Baptist Foreign Mission Society to the all-Philippine survey team. With Ralph Tolliver, he put in more than two years charting the growth of the many denominations that make up the evangelical church in the Philippines. The Tuggy-Tolliver research was published in 1971 under the title *Seeing the Church in the Philippines.* Believing ardently in church growth and seeing the great growth possible, in 1971 Tuggy proposed to his Baptist colleagues that they (who at the time had about thirty congregations and 2,000 members) set a 1981 goal of 200 congregations and 10,000 baptized believers. Thus "Operation 200" was born.

While many graduates of the Fuller School of World Mission were working for church growth, and while researches, charts, and revolutionary concepts were stimulating large numbers of pastors and missionaries to communicate the gospel more effectively, Tuggy's was the first deliberately to set goals. Furthermore, he followed up his goal with a well-thought plan, revised annually. In the light of what growth had been granted, resources were allocated. The goal became the guiding star of the Conservative Baptist Church and its assisting mission, and it was fulfilled. The foundation was now complete. Goal setting was about to become popular. The strategy of mission would be strengthened by a most effective tool.

Building Walls or Setting Goals Overseas

New walls were about to be built on the theoretical and theological foundations that required open acknowledgment of countable Christians as a legitimate indication of faithfulness in Christian mission. C. Peter Wagner and Vergil Gerber played the key role in building those walls—seeing goal setting as a necessary strategy of evangelization and demonstrating how to carry it out.

Wagner had pointed out the urgency of strategy in his influential book *Frontiers of Missionary Strategy* and had trumpeted: "Strategy cannot be accurately planned or effectively evaluated without measurable goals" (1971:132). He further declared that the ultimate objective of all evangelistic goals must be increase in the numbers of faithful followers of Jesus Christ. "The inexorable goals of any evangelistic program should be the making of disciples" (1971:145).

In late 1971 the Evangelical Committee on Latin America (ECLA) named Wagner, ably assisted by Vergil Gerber and Edward Murphy, to conduct a series of three pilot workshops in Venezuela. The purpose was to lay heavily on the hearts of the participating pastors that making disciples was a necessary and measurable objective of their labors. The first workshop was held in June 1972 and 47 pastors attended. In the July 1972 issue of *Church Growth Bulletin,* Wagner tells the story of that historic venture.

In November 1973 *Church Growth Bulletin* published the following summary of the Venezuela workshop program, which by that time had become standard for workshops in many other countries.

Spanish-speaking pastors of ordinary churches brought records (some woefully inadequate) of their membership during the past ten years. Workshop leaders taught them how to analyze, chart, and understand the growth which had taken place and was taking place. That provided a background of reality. The pastors were talking about their own problems, tasks and opportunities. They were not reacting against new North American schemes! In that setting it became fruitful to set forth church growth principles—they could then be seen as "something *we* need." The third step was to ask the participants, on the basis of their past experience (in faith and after prayer), to project the growth they believed God was calling on them to attempt. The fourth step was to calculate what the average rates of growth during the last ten years had been, and during the coming five years would be. The last step was to plan for another workshop a year later, attended by these same men, to see what in fact had happened.

The Venezuelan experience furnished a base for a significant advance in church multiplying evangelism. Dr. Gerber prepared a small book, *A Manual For Evangelism/Church Growth,* which told how any group of pastors and/or missionaries could hold a church growth workshop (McGavran 1973:368).

All around the world Christian leaders, who had been imbibing church growth ideas and who believed that the first business of the church was to lead men and women to Christ, were looking for a tool they could use to get pastors thinking about the vast opportunities for the spread of the Christian religion. The Gerber manual *God's Way to Keep A Church Going and Growing* (1973) was that tool. As soon as leaders discovered it, they held similar workshops and planned for others. Vergil Gerber was flooded with invitations from many nations to hold demonstration workshops there. In August 1973 he took a team with him to Kenya, Nigeria, and Ivory Coast and, similarly, year after year to many other lands. By 1978 he had been in 48 different countries. *God's Way* had been published in 32 languages and translated into several more. By the end of the decade, poor health forced him to retire. As he did, God raised up Jim Montgomery to pioneer the DAWN (Discipling a Whole Nation) movement to catalyze effective evangelism in country after country.

One of the basic emphases of the Church Growth Movement is that methods should be evaluated in the light of whether they actually produce growth. Methods that have worked somewhere else or ought to work, but which add few if any to Christ's body are, alas, all too common. One of the gratifying features of the Wagner-Gerber thrust around the world is that in many regions, after goal setting in seminars and workshops, congregations and denominations have shown marked growth. In the Philippines, for example, from 1964-74 the organized churches of four denominations (Conservative Baptist, Christian and Missionary Alliance, Southern Baptist, and Foursquare) increased from 1,148 to 1,331—a new increase of 183 congregations. Then after the 1974 church growth workshop, called and sponsored by James Montgomery and led by Vergil Gerber and me, the same denominations in only four years planted 879 new churches. The decadal growth rate (DGR) for the previous ten-year period was 16 percent, and for the subsequent four-year period 255 percent. Membership naturally increased significantly as well.

It must not be supposed that explosive growth everywhere follows goal setting. Where there has been no prior laying of the foundations and little follow-up, goal setting often results only in a short spurt of growth. In a highly resistant population, or by using ineffective methods, it may result in no growth at all.

Nevertheless, across the world, the outcome of goal setting has been gratifying. The evidence is in. Where goals have been set, most churches have grown. Goal setting is a most rewarding step in carrying out the Great Commission.

Setting Goals in America

In 1971, the need for church growth thinking in Canada and the United States was enormous. Out of a combined population of about 221,000,000 only 65 million, at a generous estimate, were committed Christians. About 90 million were nominal Christians, and about 66 million were either lapsed Christians or purposefully non-Christian men and women. Most denominations (Protestant and Roman Catholic alike) were either plateaued or declining, and most Christian leaders were saying that they wanted quality, not quantity. The church apparently would soon follow Europe's lead and enter a post-Christian era. The attention of the church was on other things. Indeed, the stage was set against acknowledging church growth as a desirable goal. While the Church Growth Movement had achieved considerable acceptance overseas, in 1971 it still elicited patronizing smiles when mentioned in America.

The awaking of America to church growth owes a great deal to two leaders, C. Peter Wagner and Win Arn. In 1972 Wagner, convinced that America needed church growth, enrolled prominent pastors and lay leaders living in and around Pasadena in a regular seminary course in church growth. He asked me to team teach it with him. We met in the Lake Avenue Congregational Church every Tuesday morning from seven to ten. Tuition was charged and seminary credit given.

After the various rationalizations of defeat that were common coin in ministerial circles had been examined, held up to the light, gently laughed at, and laid to rest, the pastors ate up church growth. It was thoroughly germane to their deepest convictions. They began to chart the past growth of their congregations and to envisage future growth. Of course, they were interested in more Christians! In this they were unconsciously demonstrating the way thousands of other gatherings of pastors and people in the seventies and eighties would feel.

Win Arn was a member of that famous class. At the time he was Director of Christian Education for the Pacific Southwest Conference of the Evangelical Covenant Church in America. As he saw the critical need for growth and the potential of the Church Growth Movement, he determined to resign as director and start the Institute for American Church

Growth. He would gather ministers into seminars, give them two or three days of concentrated study of church growth, have them set goals, and send them back to turn their churches around. He would publish a magazine called *Church Growth: America.* He would make color films preaching church growth. His only source of income would be the registration fees that those attending the seminars would pay and proceeds from the sale of resources. His program, starting from zero in 1972, by the end of the 1980s was training twenty thousand pastors and key lay leaders each year, and spending over $300,000 a year doing it. His films "How to Grow a Church," "Reach Out and Grow," "They Said it Couldn't Be Done," "Planned Parenthood" and many others have been seen in tens of thousands of churches. In all of these, recognizing the biblical imperative to make disciples, charting past growth, and setting realistic and devout goals for future membership increase became acceptable procedure.

C. Peter Wagner, in addition to his duties on the faculty of the Fuller School of World Mission, was the chief executive officer of the Fuller Evangelistic Association through the 1970s. There he founded the Charles E. Fuller Institute for Evangelism and Church Growth, directed by John Wimber from 1975 to 1977 and by Carl F. George since 1978. By 1989 over 12,000 pastors and denominational executives had been trained in church growth principles through seminars such as "How to Plant a Church," or "How to Lead and Manage the Local Church," or "How to Break the 200 Barrier." Naturally Wagner, whose main thrust was strategies of evangelism, emphasized setting goals. His mature thinking on the subject is found in his *Strategies for Church Growth* (1987).

The denominations started catching fire. For example, in two decades from 1965 to 1985, the United Methodist Church had lost two million members. Its main emphasis was social action, brotherhood, peace, and other such causes. Evangelism and church planting were at a low ebb. It became obvious that unless the decline was reversed, the denomination would grow less and less influential. The Methodists appointed George G. Hunter III, professor of evangelism at Perkins School of Theology in Texas, as executive for evangelism of the United Methodist Board of Discipleship, and gave him a quarter million dollars a year budget with a mandate to reverse the downward trend. He studied every aspect of Methodist increase and decline. Under his guidance Methodists started to see the quantitative dimensions of their denomination. They, too, began to set goals.

The Church of the Nazarene, which began in 1906, had grown very vigorously in the early years but started slowing down in the fifties. By

1970, with a membership of 600,000, it showed signs of plateauing. In 1974, it threw itself into the recovery of growth. Its national leaders called meetings of all pastors. Raymond Hurn, then head of the Home Mission Board and now a general superintendent, committed his board to planting many new churches and allocated personnel and money to that goal. It created a Department of Church Growth and appointed Bill Sullivan as director.

Many other denominations and thousands of individual congregations to varying degrees began to think quantitatively about church growth.

None of the denominations turned away from qualitative to quantitative growth. Rather they saw that any true qualitative growth would of necessity be concerned that the lost be found and brought to the fold. They recognized that a quality unconcerned with the salvation of multitudes would be doubtfully Christian.

All these activities of congregations, denominations, and church leaders threw the spotlight of truth on the growth and decline of churches. All necessitated counting Christians and setting goals for increase of members. By 1980 it had become commonplace in thousands of congregations to see the complex subject of church growth in scientific detail. Various strands of growth had been charted, analyzed, graphed, discussed, and viewed in time perspective. Goal setting had become thoroughly at home in the American church.

However, much remained to be done. Of the more than 300,000 American congregations, only a fraction had been aroused to church growth. Great segments of the church slept on. Even some of those who had drawn up church growth goals, failing to allocate resources to growth, had sadly concluded that this latest fad had not worked. As the eighties progressed, the turnaround of mainline U.S. and Canadian denominations was still not assured. But goal setting was helping churches evaluate what they had done and set forth clearly what they intended to do.

SETTING GOALS

Three Essential Steps in Goal Setting

The first step in setting goals is to emphasize that evangelism is a thoroughly biblical activity. In the midst of hundreds of good things to do, Christians should be clear that the chief and irreplaceable task of Christian mission is always that of bringing unbelievers to saving faith in Christ and into responsible membership in his church. Finding the lost, bringing them back to the fold, teaching them all things, and sending them out to find others is a main thrust, perhaps the main thrust of the New Testament. Goal setting should start by teaching that measurable church growth is biblically required.

The second step is to chart past growth. Occasionally the chart will go back fifty years; but more often ten years is sufficient—and much easier to do.

Total membership of the congregation or the cluster of congregations concerned for each year should be ascertained and a simple line graph constructed that will show the rises, plateaus, and declines.

As previously indicated it is desirable to know where the members come from. Are they children of existing members? Or Christians transferring in as they move to this locality? Or converts from the world? Realistic goals must be set in the light of biological, transfer, or conversion growth.

Charting past growth involves calculating the rates of growth. If a church has been growing at 15 percent DGR (decadal growth rate) without any specific attention to evangelism, it is reasonable to judge that as the congregation emphasizes evangelism a much higher rate will be possible.

The third step is to make faith projections. These are considered estimates as to what growth God desires to grant this congregation, or denomination, facing these circumstances and made up of these strands of members. Might we grow more from the Appalachian factory workers or the business community? Would membership increase more from university students or people who buy houses in this suburb? In Madras City, would certain churches increase more from Mala or Madiga background converts? In Mindanao, might our denomination increase more rapidly from the Christian immigrants or the tribal populations? In Guatemala—on the basis of the charts of past growth and other pertinent facts—should we anticipate more growth from the Quiches or the Mams?

In making projections we are confident that the present rate of biological growth will continue. It requires little faith to assume that. So the faith projection should be on top of an assured biological growth. Similarly, if in the past ten years three-fourths of all growth has come from country Christians pouring into our factory town, faith projections should be calculated on top of a large transfer growth. If a people movement is in full swing, the faith projection will be much larger than if the congregation faces continuation of the one-by-one-against-the-current pattern of growth.

Faith projections are made in prayer and with a confident assumption of the continued presence of the Holy Spirit. Faith projections are what we feel God wants to do through us. As responsible stewards of his grace we ask what we believe is in accordance with his will.

Adjusting to Specific Situations

The discipling of *panta ta ethne* goes forward in the midst of rapid social change. Huge urbanizations are changing the nature of whole populations. Printing, universal literacy, radio, and television give wings to radically new ideas. Expectations rise. Demands increase. Marxists teach that capitalistic nations are sucking the blood of the developing world. Cuban troops liberate African countries. Half the population of Kampuchea is wiped out. Two million Chinese are hounded out of Vietnam. An amoral society develops in great areas of the inner cities of America. Secularism and materialism become the religions of hundreds of millions. One land opens and another closes to missionaries.

World evangelization proceeds in this kind of world. It is in this milieu that congregations and denominations grow and decline. Each one, therefore, must set its growth goals in the light of its own specific situation. All these factors and many more have influenced the past growth and will influence future growth.

Calculating Growth Rates

While graphs of growth reveal a great deal about the growth dynamics of a church or denomination, the rates of growth reveal more. For example, if a church of 100 grows to 200 in five years and another church grows from 600 to 700 in the same five years, they have both added the same number of members, but the first church has grown at a much higher rate. The DGR (decadal growth rate) of the first church is 300 percent, almost ten times the 36 percent DGR of the larger church.

Ralph Winter, drawing on his background as a civil engineer, devised the formula for calculating growth rates. The process is similar to computing interest compounded annually. Just as the interest in a savings account is reinvested to draw further interest, so in churches new converts can be led to effective evangelism by which new members are added to the church. Churches that are maintaining high annual or decadal growth rates are seen to be obeying the Great Commission more effectively than others.

Special calculations are not required to figure growth rates for periods such as one year or ten years if the membership at the beginning and at the end of each period is known. Most junior high level students could figure it. But when the periods over which the rates are calculated are longer than one year or different from ten years exactly, the special formula is needed. Suppose we are studying a seven-year period of growth. The standard church growth methodology is either to reduce it to AAGR (average annual growth rate) or expand it to DGR (decadal growth rate). The resulting figures are equally accurate. Some church growth researchers prefer one, some the other. The DGR figure for many is an easier one to handle, and some mission agencies are now reporting the growth of churches on their fields with DGR figures.

Bob Waymire, another engineer/missiologist, teamed up with C. Peter Wagner to produce *The Church Growth Survey Handbook* (1984). This is a very practical, simplified, instructional workbook on calculating, graphing, and analyzing church growth. It is an inexpensive tool for any researcher. All are at liberty to reproduce or copy the graph paper or any other part of the book. The authors receive no royalties. It can be ordered from The Charles E. Fuller Institute, Box 90910, Pasadena, CA 91109-0910. It is highly recommended that anyone who is embarking on a study of a local church, a denomination, or an entire geographical area secure this manual and utilize the research methodology it outlines. Not only will the outcome prove to be valuable research, but it will also be comparable to that of hundreds of other Christian leaders who are using the same methodology.

Waymire and Wagner call their goal-setting section "Faith Projections." In it they say:

"Without faith it is impossible to please Him," says Hebrews 11:6. Your faith projection is a God-pleasing exercise. It will release a growth dynamic that otherwise will remain stopped up (1984:31).

21

MAKE HARD, BOLD PLANS

IN MANY EFFORTS at world evangelization, it is common to assume that church growth will take place without planning, that is, that church planting is an inevitable outcome. Evangelism, it is frequently believed, consists of many preparatory activities, many ancillary enterprises, many years of seed-sowing, many decades of shepherding, educating, and developing a few congregations, and many attempts to help churches apply Christianity to all of life. As the whole intricate operation is carried forward, church growth will take place, it is held, in whatever degree is pleasing to God and according to his timetable.

During recent years a growing body of pastors and missionaries, and perhaps a majority of those who direct old-line missions, would say: "Carrying on the whole program of God in the world is the mission of the church. While winning women and men to Christian faith is undoubtedly part of the program, it is by no means the chief part. In places church-planting evangelism must be muted, so that other instruments in the orchestra may be heard. Christian unity, racial harmony, economic justice, service of the poor and ignorant, education of the existing churches, and many other emphases—all are parts of mission." Leaders with these convictions assume that church growth may or may not take place as the vast general program is quietly carried forward; but since mission is being carried on, church growth really does not matter.

In line with this assumption, pastors, lay leaders, and even some missionaries do their assigned work whether churches grow or not. Sometimes duties are assigned by the mission, sometimes by the church. This pastor concentrates on exegetical preaching, that one on shepherding the flock. This missionary teaches in a theological training school, that one runs a hospital, and the third does student work or evangelistic touring. All carry out their assignments on the unformulated assumption that as each does the work people will be reconciled to God in Jesus Christ, to the extent that they can be.

Theological rationalization of this position is very common. Some lean heavily on verses like Mark 16:15, which commands us to preach the gospel to every creature and believe that the task is done when the gospel is proclaimed by literature, radio, voice, or kind act—whether any believe or not, whether any churches are established or not. Others argue, with less biblical justification, that the era of planting churches is over; and still others, that planting churches is not the chief purpose of missions in any case.

Fear of ecclesiastical aggrandizement, failure of nerve in postwar Europe, shock of loss of empire, jealousy for the position of Christ rather than the church, defensive thinking induced by lack of church planting, and other factors all tempt church leaders to play down plans for the actual communication of the gospel, that is, the establishment of cells of believing, baptized Christians open to the irradiation of the Holy Spirit and alive to the clamant needs of men and societies.

THIS ASSUMPTION A SERIOUS ERROR

As we seek to understand church growth we should recognize that this common assumption is a serious mistake. Church growth seldom comes without bold plans for it. Only those who disregard the evidence can believe that church growth is a by-product of multifaceted Christian activity. The assumption is contrary to the New Testament practice. We do not see the apostles carrying out a genial program of *koinonia, diakonia,* and *kerygma* and the churches happily rising here and there like dandelions in a well-watered lawn. There we see Paul and Barnabas throwing their lives into a tremendous program of church planting, racing against time to reach as many as possible with the message of salvation before the Lord returned. There we have the picture of Paul in Corinth arguing in the synagogue every sabbath and persuading Jews and Greeks. The record is careful to point out that Paul was occupied with preaching, testifying to the Jews (with abundant proofs from the Law, Psalms, and Prophets) that the Messiah was Jesus. When the Jews opposed and reviled him, he shook out his garments and said to them, "Your blood be upon your own heads. I am clean. From now on I will go to the Gentiles" (Acts 18:4-11).

But he did not go empty-handed. He took Crispus, the ruler of the synagogue, and all his household, a God-fearer who had been attending the synagogue, Titius Justus, and all his household, and many others into the new church that he established.

Before Paul arrived at Corinth, he had been practicing his bold plan for planting churches, and after he left he continued using the same effective plan. He would have been amazed at any idea that the church grows as an unplanned by-product of the full Christian life or that the true end is a just society to which the church is strictly instrumental.

The only way the good news of Jesus Christ can possibly reach the myriads of earth is for fantastic church planting to take place. . . . The only way Christian values, economic justice, racial brotherhood, social betterment, or democracy can spread is for multitudinous cells of baptized believers to be formed in which the word is preached and the sacraments are observed. It is inconceivable that the Spirit of God will so operate on human beings in these tumultuous and revolutionary times that some new religion that knows nothing of Jesus Christ and the Bible will arise and sweep all men into itself. It would be the height of foolishness to opt for such a religion before it has even appeared.

One can well believe that, under the guidance of the Holy Spirit and the Bible, devoted Christians from the churches of the world will develop new forms of the church that are loyal to Jesus Christ as God and Savior and believe in the Bible as their sole rule of faith and practice. But if such forms do arise, they will not happen by themselves. They will come as the result of careful planning on the part of consecrated Christians.

EVERY GREAT FORWARD MOVEMENT HAS PLANNED FOR CHURCH GROWTH

As we consider the place of planning in church growth, we recall the great growth of the Methodist Church around the world. Wesley's class meetings did not arise by chance as he led a devout Christian life. He created

them. He standardized them. He required new believers to form themselves into them. He monitored them. As long as he hoped that through
them the Anglican Church might be renewed, he called them class meetings. When that hope faded, or in countries where the Anglican Church
was merely one of many denominations, class meetings became
Methodist churches and continued to be planted according to plan. Revival meetings on a grand scale were held in order to save people, whose
salvation was not complete till they were firm members of Methodist
churches. Wesley, Asbury, Coke, and others would have laughed at any
idea that church growth took place by itself without any planning.

Time would fail me were I to recount the bold plans that undergirded
the great extension of churches in all six continents. Even the spread of
Pentecostal congregations in Brazil from none in 1916 to thousands in
1990—as unstructured a spread as can be found on earth—was certainly
not an unintentional by-product of full-orbed mission touching all of life.
Some famous leaders of the Assemblies of God in Brazil have baptized
ten, twenty, and thirty thousand people. These baptisms did not happen
by accident. They were planned. The great growth of the Assemblies of
God in Brazil came as a result of bold plans for church growth carried out
by the common people. An essential element of these plans was the conviction that wherever believers went, it was their duty and privilege to win
their fellows to similar belief in the Lord and to bind them together in a
regularly worshiping, praying, praising, and evangelizing congregation.

The sentimental supposition of some that "Christian presence,"
"working for secularization," "witnessing to Christ by kind deeds," "industrial evangelism that seeks to improve laboring conditions," "discerning God in the revolution and lining up with him" will through some mysterious process result in as much communication of the gospel as they
should, hangs in mid-air without a shred of biblical or rational evidence
to support it. World evangelization is concerned with the more than three
billion who are yet completely unchurched, completely under the domination of sub-Christian or anti-Christian ideologies, value systems, and
religions. Churching these billions will never happen of itself as an unplanned by-product of kind Christian activity.

It must immediately be added, however, that planting churches is only
the first half of the Great Commission. The second half is to "teach them
all things whatsoever I have commanded you." All must applaud the
church pressing ahead to perfect those who have become disciples of
Christ and these in turn applying Christ's principles to the social,
economic, and political structures of their neighborhoods and nations. The

program of perfecting those of the billions who become disciples of Christ is entirely praiseworthy. Leading them on to more and more appropriation of the mind of Christ, more and more infilling of the Holy Spirit, and more and more ethical and aesthetic advance, is unqualifiedly good. On this point most Christians will agree.

Nevertheless, if we are to understand the place of the church in the real world confronting us, we must see that before the great ethical goals can be achieved, first there must be many churches. Only churches that exist can be perfected. Only babies who have been born can be educated. Only where practicing Christians form sizable minorities of their societies can they expect their presence seriously to influence the social, economic, and political structures. The church must, indeed, "teach them all things," but first it must have at least some Christians and some churches. What it must totally reject is the naive idea that God will act in and through those who reject his Son and his revelation so much better than he will through those who accept his Son and his revelation, that it should cease at once from planned church planting and try to create a vague community of justice and goodwill among all.

WHAT DO WE MEAN BY BOLD PLANS
FOR CHURCH PLANTING?

Vague general work and shifting emphasis from discipling to some form of perfecting is not what we mean by bold plans. Neither emphasis will liberate people from bondage to evil nor "diffuse the fragrance of his knowledge" (2 Cor. 2:14). Bold plans mean something far more positive. In understanding church growth it is not enough to see the faulty assumptions that prevent maximum multiplication of sound churches. We must go on to devise and operate intelligent and adequate plans for establishing church after church throughout whole populations.

Reading a book or two on the dynamics of mission and the growth of Christ's churches is merely a glance in the right direction. Stating a church growth concept of mission is not enough. Espousing a purpose to plant churches is only a beginning. Copying a plan by which the Lord has multiplied churches somewhere else is merely a part of the preliminary exploration. Knowing enough about a piece of the mosaic to hazard a guess as to what might win its people to Christ and his church is one of the bricks in the foundation—no more. God's obedient servants should not deceive themselves that any of these introductory activities is their goal.

Their goal is to devise an intelligent plan for planting churches—one that fits their population, is similar to plans that have multiplied churches in other populations of this sort, and can be carried out with the resources God has put into their hands. The plan should be adequate. If their piece of the mosaic contains fifty thousand people, their plan should be large enough to disciple the whole piece. No one expects that all fifty thousand will become and remain devout Christians—but because the compassionate Lord holds the door open for every one and faithful ambassadors beseech each to be reconciled to God, an adequate plan should make becoming a disciple of Christ a real option to every one of the fifty thousand. No plan is adequate that aims at creating a tiny enclave of two hundred and so elevating its members by lift and redemption that they are unable to communicate Christ to their kinfolk. Church leaders should beware of petty plans. Plans for establishing power centers of liberated and liberating persons (churches) should, then, be both intelligent and adequate.

Putting such plans into operation is the true goal. A good plan on paper does nothing. Only as it becomes incarnate in flesh and blood does it achieve anything. It may be born in imagination or given to the Christian in dreams, but until it is drenched in sweat and sprinkled with blood it remains the talent laid away in a napkin. It is better to put an imperfect plan into operation than to carry on splendid church and mission work while waiting for the perfect plan to appear.

It is a sound principle that each national church evangelizes its neighborhood, and missionaries residing there help the church do so; but in case some national church sits calmly by, neglecting a homogeneous unit prepared to accept the gospel, God will not hold the mission guiltless that also sits calmly by, sharing the neglect. If the mission cannot inspire the church to action, it should draw a circle around each moribund congregation and in the vast territory outside the circles put into operation an intelligent and adequate plan for multiplying churches. The work is urgent, the day is far spent, and God wants his lost children found. No church has the right to cordon off populations hungry for the word, neither feeding them nor permitting other churches to do so. "Dog in the manger" comity is displeasing to God. The sovereignty of each church should not be inflated to mean that its indifference to the salvation of the peoples of its land binds the hands of God's people elsewhere. When the Holy Spirit sends Paul to Rome, if he finds the church already there made up of Judaizers who resist his message, he should not argue that missionaries must subordinate themselves and their convictions to "the great national church in Italy."

The Christian and Missionary Alliance, a church of 192,000 members in North America in 1977, has shown the way to other denominations. It resolved to double this membership, reaching 384,000 by 1987. It then added in its members overseas and found it had 952,000. It resolved to double this also, reaching the high total of 1,904,000 by 1987. Then Louis L. King, the president of the whole church, penned these significant words:

> To reach these goals we are calling the church to a renewed emphasis on evangelism, to maximum participation, to planning at every level, to teaching and training for outreach, to accurate reporting, to sacrificial giving, and to much intercessory prayer.

The whole story is told in the *Church Growth Bulletin* for September 1979. I know of no better example of hard, bold plans, and of no more dramatic examples of positive results. In 1987, the centennial year of the C&MA, the worldwide goals were reached.

Operating intelligent, adequate plans for seeding a countryside with new churches necessarily involves adjusting these plans in view of the outcomes. Certain aspects of the plan do not work, others produce far better than anticipated, still others give promise of improved performance if modified and regulated. Adjustment, modification, and regulation are not New Testament words, but they describe a New Testament reality. In Luke's account of the first thirty years of church planting he indicates again and again modification of the plan to fit changed circumstances. When the *ecclesiae* began to include not only born Jews but also uncircumcised God-fearers, new departures in the *kerygma* were made by the apostle Paul. When the synagogue was no longer available as a place to argue, testify, and prove that according to the Law, the Psalms, and the Prophets the Messiah was Jesus of Nazareth, new evangelistic and worship centers had to be found. When the poor of the Hellenistic Christians were neglected, deacons had to be appointed to wait on tables. When the initial thrust of spontaneous expansion through the Jerusalem refugees slowed down, a new form of propagation through church representatives sent out by a church was instituted.

SUITED TO THE STAGE OF MISSION

World evangelization may be regarded as the process through which God makes known to all peoples his plan of salvation and calls them from death to life and responsible membership in his church.

Looked at from the viewpoint of the agents of reproduction, one may say that in most regions of earth, world evangelization passes through four stages—exploration, pioneer labors, scattered successes, and substantial Christianization. Plans must fit each stage. Looked at from the viewpoint of the reproduction achieved, one may say that the church passes through four stages. *Exploration* becomes "resolve of missionaries to evangelize a new population." *Pioneer labors* become "well-supported outposts of the church." *Scattered successes* become "strong clusters of congregations organized into beginning presbyteries, conventions, conferences, and dioceses rooted in a few of the populations." *Substantial Christianization* becomes "the church organized into permanent unions, conferences, conventions, presbyteries, dioceses and synods, well-rooted in most pieces of the marvelous mosaic that makes up the national population."

Adequate plans for the propagation of the gospel must recognize these stages and fit each. For example, in North America as a whole evangelization is in stage four. The plans suited to this stage are quite different from those employed by the North American church as it carries on mission in Palestine or Kalimantan.

To be realistic one must at once add that North America is far from a homogeneous whole. The situation in Canada is different from that in Florida. A well-rooted church comprising a fifth of the total population in British Columbia, for example, will at one and the same time carry on stage one evangelization among the new immigrants to Canada from Hong Kong and Uganda and stage four evangelization among those who have been in Canada for several generations. Similarly in Java, as the church impelled by the Holy Spirit carries on its work of proper expansion, it will at one and the same time do stage four evangelization in some sections of the population, stage three in others, and stage two or one in others. In Andhra State in South India, the Convention of Telugu Baptist Churches among unbelieving Malas and Madigas will be carrying on stage four evangelization, but among the Brahmin and Kshatriya castes will be carrying on stage one.

THE FOUR STAGES

Having placed the four stages of world evangelization in proper perspective, let us consider each.

First comes that of *exploration*. The church (or more commonly, some churchly sodality or modality) has resolved to evangelize an un-reached people group. Quite properly it sets about discovering everything possible about this homogeneous unit, which may be composed of hard-core rationalists of the universities, French Canadians in upper New York, the sixty thousand Korean miners at work in Germany, the Nishis in north-east India, or a tribe in south central Zaire. It will not only learn about this segment of society, but will also explore how to evangelize it and how the evangelizers will continue evangelizing until churches start multiplying in it.

For missionaries overseas, this will mean finding a place to live, learning the language, being misunderstood, persecuted, banished, or killed, establishing beachheads of one sort or another, commending them-selves by good works and holy lives, winning the first converts, and found-ing the first few congregations.

Because the first congregations are started by outsiders, they will in-evitably have a foreign flavor. Despite the best effort of the advocates, the population being evangelized will think that to become Christian is to leave our community. If the expansion is into a new language area, the first translations of the Gospels or other portions of Scripture tend to be awkward. First congregations everywhere tend to be made up of those who before their conversion were already at outs with their own people. Nevertheless, these first congregations are a great triumph. Hundreds of that culture or subculture are now living as Christians. Christ has his way in their lives. They believe in him and have become new creations in him. They feed on his word and are being transformed into his likeness. They are having a beneficial effect on their societies.

The second era of world evangelization is that of *well-supported out-posts*. In a scattered but systematic way the whole population has been exposed to the gospel and outposts established throughout it. If the popu-lation is—let us say—Mexican Americans in Texas and the evangelizers the Southern Baptists—then Baptist strategists, having found out where the Mexican Americans are numerous and how receptive different sec-tions of that community are, have planted a network of Baptist churches in every county of the state. Churches are most numerous where there are concentrations of Hispanic-name Americans. Special attention is paid to recent arrivals, because these are usually responsive to the gospel.

During the second era of missions, the congregations still have a somewhat foreign flavor. To become Christian, to join these new congre-gations is still regarded by the great majority of the population as "leav-ing our people." So becoming a Christian tends to be more a social than a religious step. When, for example, a son in a strong Lutheran family becomes a Roman Catholic, his parents feel he has betrayed them. When Muslims move to Christian faith, all the members of their family feel they have left them. So a sweeping movement is not likely. Second stage congregations (well-supported outposts) grow slowly. Nevertheless, if the founding church or mission continues to support and buttress these outposts, they increase steadily. Because they are there, stage three becomes possible.

In stage three, *strong clusters* of congregations arise in various places. The third stage begins as here and there in the target population responsive segments, moved by cultural compulsion or other action of the Holy Spirit, begin to turn to Christ in a multi-individual way. Enough of them become followers of Jesus Christ so that Christians become numerous. Converts feel, "We are not leaving our people. We are charting a way that all the rest sooner or later will follow." Congregations begin to think of themselves as advance guards of their people. During this era the church grows strong. Denominations come to number fifty thousand, a hundred thousand, or half a million communicants. Schools and seminaries prepare leaders. Hymnbooks, prayer books, and good translations of the Bible are printed. Regular worship in well-built churches becomes common. Christian ways of burying the dead, marrying, and celebrating festivals are developed and become precious to Christians. Pastors, elders, deacons, teachers, district superintendents, evangelists, and seminary professors are trained to function in an indigenous way. The institutional church, while faithful to God and the Bible, takes on a thoroughly national hue.

The good lives of Christians, the good deeds they do, their labors for justice and the public good, and the transformations of life that faith in Christ brings are noted by neighbors. The persecution and ostracism that plagued the early stages of the church die down. The church prospers and appears likely to survive. It becomes strong in more and more communities throughout the nation.

During stage three, transition to national leaders is very largely completed. Outside leaders, noticeable in stages one and two, have turned over to local leaders. In stage three, missionaries should not go home but turn over authority and go on to yet unconverted populations. Contrary to much popular opinion, missionaries are sent not to help younger churches, but to multiply churches in new segments of the population.

In stage four of the expansion of the church, substantial Christianization of the population has taken place. A third, a half, two-thirds, or nine-tenths of the population has become Christian.

It must be remembered that a church may be at stage four in regard to one homogeneous unit, and at stage one in regard to another. Thus the church in Jerusalem in the year A.D. 45 was at stage four in regard to the Jewish masses, and at stage one in regard to the Italian army of occupation. Thus the Reformed Church in America is at stage four in regard to the well-to-do whites in scores of suburban areas of the United States, but has yet to enter stage one in regard to the Puerto Rican multitudes in New York, Buffalo, Cleveland, Detroit, and Chicago.

What does this mean in regard to hard, bold plans for church growth? This, that an essential duty of each congregation and denomination is to ponder the stage of evangelization in which it finds itself and to devise adequate plans that fit that stage. In addition, it will no doubt feel called to play its proper part in the ongoing task of world evangelization. This may mean additional plans for stage one, two, or three evangelization in adjoining populations.

THE TWO TRACKS

Especially during stage four, the church ought to surge out in ceaseless ardent evangelism that proceeds on two tracks, bringing back two kinds of fruit. Along track one it will conduct evangelism irrespective of homogeneous units or different kinds of people. If a Syro-Phoenician child needs healing, it will heal her. It will invite all sinners to repent and become members of a congregation in which all Christians are accepted as equally people of God, having equal access to the throne. Congregations will arise in which "There is no such thing as Jew and Greek, slave and freeman, male and female" (Gal. 3:28 NEB).

Along the second track, evangelism will seek to bring those who believe into congregations made up of their own kith and kin, their own kind of people. This may sound impossible to Christians who have been reared in conglomerate congregations where all growth has taken place from a dribble of converts from many different backgrounds. To some who are fighting the battle for brotherhood, the very idea of track two evangelism, which brings in congregations composed of one kind of people, smacks of segregation. Its theological validity is questioned. Church leaders have doubts whether this second track is really Christian. However, when it is remembered that the rapid spread of congregations through one homogeneous unit, through one segment of society is a mode of growth that God has abundantly blessed, doubts will be resolved.

Through the ages, as men and women have left non-Christian faiths for Christ, most of them have come along track two. God blesses track one. He also blesses track two. Rather than attack either of these ways of coming to Christ, the task is to understand them and use both.

WILL ALL BELIEVE?

But now a question arises. Does not the Bible say that many are called but few are chosen? Is there any biblical authority for supposing that all people will hear the gospel, believe, and be saved? Should we labor to disciple every segment of humanity, every piece of the marvelous mosaic? The questions are fair and must be answered.

The Bible teaches and Christians consequently believe that Christ will be Lord in every segment of humanity. (See Matthew 28:19; Luke 24:47; John 1:29; 3:16; Romans 16:26; 2 Corinthians 4:15; Philippians 2:9-11; Revelation 5:9; 7:9; and many other passages.) In every piece of the complex mosaic, Jesus Christ will be acknowledged as Lord to the glory of God the Father. Every tribe and tongue and kindred and nation, every class and economic level, every community rural and urban, will come to its true fulfillment in him.

However, the Scriptures do not support the notion that all this will happen before the Lord returns. Before his second coming, on the contrary, much rejection of the good news and much rebellion against God may be expected. The exact proportion of each piece of the mosaic that will believe can safely be left in the hands of a just judge. In the meantime, the duty of every Christian is to press forward fervently proclaiming Jesus Christ as God and only Savior, and persuading men and women to become his disciples and responsible members of his church. We should be confident that in God's good time every knee will bow and every tongue will confess.

As we rejoice in the transient triumphs of technology, science, space travel, public health, and brotherhood, we rejoice in the eternal triumphs of the gospel. We are unashamed triumphalists. Error, we are sure, will give place to truth. Cruelty will give way to kindness. False and inadequate ideas of God and man will give way to the revelation that it has pleased God to give to all human beings through the Bible and his Son, our savior.

In all six continents, world evangelization is well begun. The church does not stand in the sunset of the Christian mission to the world. Rather, the missionary movement stands at sunrise. The era of greatest advance lies ahead. A mighty stream of witnesses and lay evangelists will stream out, across the bridges of God, to the hundreds of millions living in darkness. Some of these are our neighbors and relatives. Many are unreached peoples in our own and other lands. God intends for them all to hear.

The apostle Paul in the closing verses of the Epistle to the Romans declares that the gospel was revealed by command of the eternal God himself precisely to bring these myriad peoples (ethnic units) to the obedience of the faith. Christ commands his followers to go into all the world and disciple *panta ta ethne*—all the classes, castes, and other segments of mankind—in all six continents.

Hard, bold plans to carry out this unswerving purpose of God are demanded. The Holy Spirit impels the church to this central task and reveals what plans, allocations of resources, and petitions to God he wishes Christians to make. Understanding church growth begins in obedient enlistment in this cause of Christ, continues through intellectual discernment of the many factors that affect growth, and ends in great joy as Christians come bearing many sheaves and hear their Lord say, "Well done, good and faithful servant."

REFERENCES CITED AND CHURCH
GROWTH READING LIST

ANNAN, Nelson
  1987 *More People! Is Church Growth Worth It?* Wheaton, IL: Harold Shaw. A fine easy-
         to-understand exposition of church growth principles written from the Christian
         (Plymouth) Brethren perspective. Each chapter has discussion questions.
APPLEBY, Jerry L.
  1986 *Missions Have Come Home to America.* Kansas City, MO: Beacon Hill Press. An
         up-to-date challenge for reaching out to America's ethnic groups.
ARN, Charles, Donald McGavran, and Win Arn
  1980 *Growth: A New Vision for the Sunday School.* Pasadena, CA: Church Growth Press.
         The first book to make explicit application of church growth principles to the
         growth of Sunday school.
ARN, Win
  1987 *The Church Growth Ratio Book.* Pasadena, CA: Church Growth Press. A practi-
         cal checklist expressing 27 church growth principles in numerical ratio format.
ARN, Win, ed.
  1979 *The Pastor's Church Growth Handbook.* Pasadena, CA: Church Growth Press. A
         very interesting compilation of articles that have appeared in *Church Growth:
         America* magazine over the last few years.
  1982 *The Pastor's Church Growth Handbook, Vol II.* Pasadena, CA: Church Growth
         Press. More of the above. An excellent and practical source.
ARN, Win and Charles Arn
  1982 *The Master's Plan for Making Disciples.* Pasadena, CA: Church Growth Press.
         One of the key concepts of church growth theory is to identify people movements
         that travel along natural webs of relationships. The Arns call this "oikos" evange-
         lism and develop the principle in detail in this book.

ARN, Win, Carrol Nyquist, and Charles Arn
  1986 *Who Cares About Love?* Pasadena, CA: Church Growth Press. Research on mea-
       suring the "love care quotient" of churches and denominations shows a corollary
       between love and numerical growth.
BARRETT, David B.
  1982 *World Christian Encyclopedia.* Oxford, England: Oxford Press. A classic, exhaus-
       tive data source on the status of Christianity in every country of the world with
       growth projections to 2000. A standard reference.
BARTEL, Floyd G.
  1979 *A New Look at Church Growth.* Scottdale, PA: Mennonite Publishing House. A
       contextualized application of church growth principles for Mennonites avoiding
       to the extent possible overidentification with the Fuller Seminary brand of church
       growth and yet including the principles.
BEASLEY-MURRAY, Paul and Alan Wilkinson
  1981 *Turning the Tide: An Assessment of Baptist Church Growth in England.* Swindon,
       England: British Bible Society. This is a landmark volume because it contains the
       first published scientific study of the applicability of Wagner's "seven vital signs"
       to an empirical situation. Five were affirmed; two were questionable.
BOALS, Barbara M.
  1961 *The Church in the Kond Hills: An Encounter with Animism.* Nagpur: National
       Christian Council of India.
BOLTON, Robert J.
  1976 *Treasure Island: Church Growth Among Taiwan's Urban Minnan Chinese.*
       Pasadena, CA: Wm. Carey Library. This goes beyond the Minnan Chinese them-
       selves and analyzes the rise of Christianity in Taiwan.
BONTRAGER, G. Edwin and Nathan D. Showalter
  1986 *It Can Happen Today! Principles of Church Growth from the Book of Acts.* Scott-
       dale, PA: Herald Press. An excellent, biblically based exposition of church growth
       principles written to teach laypeople and motivate them for growth. A teacher's
       manual is available also.
BROCK, Charles
  1981 *The Principles and Practices of Indigenous Church Planting.* Nashville, TN:
       Broadman. One of the best current books on how to plant churches cross-cultur-
       ally.
CHO, Paul Yonggi
  1981 *Successful Home Cell Groups.* Plainfield, NJ: Logos. This book, by the pastor of
       the world's largest church, is not just about home cell groups, but church growth
       in general. It is very practical and highly recommended.
  1984 *More Than Numbers.* Waco, TX: Word Books. Cho explains his theories of church
       growth in one of the top books in the field.
CLOUGH, John E.
  1915 *Social Christianity in the Orient: The Story of a Man, a Mission, and a Movement.*
       Philadelphia, PA: American Baptist Publication Society.
CONN, Harvie M., ed.
  1976 *Theological Perspectives on Church Growth.* Nutley, NJ: Presbyterian and Re-
       formed Publishing Company. Several authors examine the strengths and weak-
       nesses of the Church Growth Movement from the perspective of Reformed the-
       ology. The criticisms are generally well informed.

COXILL, H. Wakelin and Kenneth Grubb, eds.
 1962 *World Christian Handbook*. London, England: Lutterworth.
 1968 *World Christian Handbook*. London, England: Lutterworth.
DASENT, G. W., trans.
 1960 *The Story of Burnt Nyal*. London: Dent & Sons. New York: E. P. Dutton. First published 1861.
DAVENPORT, D. Dewayne
 1978 *The Bible Says Grow: Church Growth Guidelines for Church of Christ*. Church Growth/Evangelism Seminar, Box 314, Williamstown, WV 26187. Donald McGavran writes the introduction to this fine summary of church growth principles contextualized for the Restoration Movement churches.
DAVIS, John Merle
 1943 *How the Church Grows in Brazil*. New York, London: Department of Social and Economic Research and Counsel, International Missionary Council.
DAYTON, Edward R.
 1983 *That Everyone May Hear: Reaching the Unreached*. Monrovia, CA: MARC. A brief, easy to comprehend, summary of the contents of the next book on the list.
DAYTON, Edward R. and David A. Frazer
 1980 *Planning Strategies for World Evangelization*. Grand Rapids, MI: Eerdmans. This is one of the finest books on missiology written. It is for the serious Christian interested in strategizing the missionary task.
DE SILVA, Ranjit
 1980 *Discipling the Cities in Sri Lanka: A Challenge to the Church Today*. Peradeniya, Sri Lanka: Church Growth Research Centre. A comprehensive analysis of urban church growth with many maps, charts, and graphs.
DOUGLAS, J. D., ed.
 1975 *Let the Earth Hear His Voice*. Minneapolis, MN: World Wide Publications.
DUDLEY, Roger L. and Des Cummings, Jr.
 1983 *Adventures in Church Growth*. Washington, D.C.: Review and Herald Publishing Assn. A well-written, well-organized, well-researched book written from the perspective of Seventh Day Adventist church growth. This introduces valuable research data useful for all denominations and is strong on community survey instruments.
ELLIOTT, Ralph H.
 1982 *Church Growth that Counts*. Valley Forge, PA: Judson Press. A sharp criticism of the Church Growth Movement from a theological perspective somewhat more liberal than its Fuller advocates. Some strengths of church growth are admitted and an alternate way of looking at growth suggested.
ELLIS, Joe S.
 1986 *The Church on Target: Achieving Your Congregation's Highest Potential*. Cincinnati, OH: Standard Publishing. A practical, motivating introduction to applying church growth principles to the local church. While addressed to Restoration Movement adherents, it is broad enough to help all Christians interested in effective outreach.
ENNS, Arno W.
 1971 *Man, Milieu and Mission in Argentina: A Close Look at Church Growth*. Grand Rapids, MI: Eerdmans. A historical view of how Protestant churches have grown in the Argentine cultures.

ENYART, Paul C.
1970 *Friends in Central America.* Pasadena, CA: Wm. Carey Library. The origin and growth of Quaker churches in Guatemala, Honduras, and El Salvador.

EXMAN, Gary W.
1987 *Get Ready . . . Get Set . . . Grow! Church Growth for Town and Country Congregations.* Lima, OH: CSS Publishing Company. This takes its place as a top book on small churches, geared to encourage them to grow. It is full of practical insights and tools for small church growth. While written from a Methodist perspective, its scope is transdenominational.

FALWELL, Jerry and Elmer Towns
1984 *Stepping Out on Faith.* Wheaton, IL: Tyndale Press. This is a book on faith and church growth. Ten brief case studies of new Liberty Baptist Fellowship churches provide the data for excellent theorizing on church planting.

FREND, W. H. C.
1952 *The Donatist Church.* Oxford, England: Oxford University.

GAMALIEL, James Canjanam
1967 "The Church in Kerala: A People Movement Study." A Master of Arts Thesis in the School of World Mission and Institute of Church Growth, Fuller Theological Seminary, Pasadena, CA. Unpublished.

GATES, Alan Frederick
1979 *Christianity and Animism in Taiwan.* San Francisco, CA: Chinese Materials Center. A thorough study of how animism and traditional religion have penetrated Taiwanese life through the ages, and suggestions as to how Christianity can meet the challenge.

GERBER, Vergil
1973 *God's Way to Keep a Church Going and Growing.* Glendale, CA: Regal Books. The classic "Gerber Manual" which has been translated into over forty languages of the world.

GIBBS, Eddie
1979 *Body Building Exercises for the Local Church.* London: Falcon. A creative application and adaptation of Wagner's church pathology to churches in England. This book models how church growth principles can be contextualized.
1982 *I Believe in Church Growth.* Grand Rapids, MI: Eerdmans. This is the most complete introductory textbook on church growth available. Gibbs, who is an evangelism professor at Fuller, writes with a combination of sound scholarship and a style that offers delightful reading.
1987 *Followed or Pushed? Understanding and Leading Your Church.* London: MARC Europe. A thorough, practical, readable look at the kind of church leadership that will be a positive growth factor.

GIBBS, Eddie, ed.
1984 *Ten Growing Churches.* London: MARC Europe. Some churches are growing in England, and in this book ten pastors of growing churches have described and analyzed their growth experiences.

GLASSER, Arthur F.
1976 "An Introduction to the Church Growth Perspective of Donald Anderson McGavran," in *Theological Perspectives on Church Growth,* ed. H. M. Conn. Nutley, NJ: Presbyterian and Reformed Publishing Company.

GLASSER, Arthur F. and Donald A. McGavran
1983 *Contemporary Theologies of Mission.* Grand Rapids, MI: Baker Book House. This

book shows how advanced aspects of the theology of church growth stand in relationship to WCC and Roman Catholic theology.

GOFORTH, Jonathan
1943 *When the Spirit's Fire Swept Korea.* Grand Rapids, MI: Zondervan.

GREENWAY, Roger
1971 *Urban Strategy for Latin America.* Grand Rapids, MI: Eerdmans.
1978 *Apostles to the City.* Grand Rapids, MI: Baker Book House.

GRIMLEY, John B. and Gordon E. Robinson
1966 *Church Growth in Central and Southern Nigeria.* Grand Rapids, MI: Eerdmans. One of the earlier books written under McGavran's supervision. Excellent background material for West Africa.

GRISWOLD, Roland E.
1986 *The Winning Church.* Wheaton, IL: Victor Books. A fine popular introduction to basic church growth principles. Griswold makes church growth very practical.

HAMILTON, Keith
1963 *Church Growth in the High Andes.* Lucknow, India: Lucknow Publishing House.

HAMILTON, Michael
1981 *God's Plan for the Church—Growth.* Gospel Publishing. This is the first church growth book written from the Pentecostal perspective.

HEDLUND, Roger E.
1970 *The Protestant Movement in Italy: Its Progress, Problems and Prospects.* Pasadena, CA: Wm. Carey Library. An important book for understanding the challenges for church growth in Europe and among Catholics.

HINTON, Keith
1985 *Growing Churches Singapore Style.* Singapore: Overseas Missionary Fellowship Ltd. Using contemporary Singapore as a model, Keith Hinton draws out many church growth principles that can be universally applied.

HOEKSTRA, Harvey
1979 *The World Council of Churches and the Demise of Evangelism.* Wheaton: Tyndale House.

HOGE, Dean R. and David A. Roozen, eds.
1979 *Understanding Church Growth and Decline 1950-1978.* Philadelphia, PA: The Pilgrim Press. The most exhaustive study of patterns of growth in mainline U.S. churches yet undertaken. This came from a two-year consortium of researchers that met at Hartford Seminary. A chapter on the Church Growth Movement was contributed by C. Peter Wagner.

HOLLAND, Clifton L.
1974 *The Religious Dimension in Hispanic Los Angeles: A Protestant Case Study.* Pasadena, CA: Wm. Carey Library. An encyclopedic compilation of facts with valuable insights as to how Hispanic churches grow in the U.S.A.

HUNTER, George G. III
1979 *The Contagious Congregation.* Nashville, TN: Abingdon. Hunter, a respected United Methodist leader, writes a valuable book containing fresh insights into local congregational growth.
1987 *To Spread the Power: Church Growth in the Wesleyan Spirit.* Nashville, TN: Abingdon. One of the outstanding leaders in the field identifies and describes six church growth "mega-strategies," traces them to Donald McGavran and John Wesley, and applies them effectively to churches today.

HUNTER, Kent R.
   1983a *Foundations for Church Growth*. New Haven, MO: Leader. One of the best intro-
          ductions to church growth principles. This is written from a Lutheran point of view
          but the ideas are practical for all.
   1983b *Your Church Has Doors: How to Open the Front and Close the Back*. Church
          Growth Analysis and Learning Center. Church growth expert Kent Hunter ex-
          pounds on eight "keys" to open doors to growth in your church: faith, aftercare,
          incorporation, integrity, assimilation, accountability, pruning, and amputation.
   1985   *Your Church Has Personality*. Nashville, TN: Abingdon. A ground-breaking book
          that lays out the meaning of philosophy of ministry. Kent Hunter, a leading church
          growth consultant, draws on wide experience to produce this practical guidebook
          which will help any pastor who uses it. He includes biblical and theological foun-
          dations, role models, and how-to sections for writing your church's philosophy of
          ministry.
IGLEHART, Charles
   1957   *Cross and Crisis in Japan*. New York: Friendship.
JACQUET, Constant H., ed.
   1967   *Yearbook of American Churches*. New York: National Council of the Churches of
          Christ.
JENSON, Ron and Jim Stevens
   1981   *Dynamics of Church Growth*. Grand Rapids, MI: Baker Book House. This adds to
          church growth literature by bringing to bear the Campus Crusade insights, by lay-
          ing a strong biblical base, by incorporating management principles, and by offer-
          ing practical suggestions for action at the end of each chapter.
JOHN PAUL II
   1978   *Redemptor Hominis*. Rome: Libreria Editrice Vaticana.
JOHNSTONE, Patrick J.
   1986   *Operation World: A Handbook for World Intercession*. Pasadena, CA: STL Books
          and Wm. Carey Library. Country-by-country, Johnstone outlines valuable secular
          and religious data, then lists areas where earnest prayer is needed.
KELLEY, Dean M.
  (1977) *Why Conservative Churches Are Growing*. Macon, GA: Mercer University Press.
   1986   This was probably the most discussed religious book in the decade of the seven-
          ties. It deals with the function that churches have in society and shows how liberal
          churches usually turn out to be socially weak institutions. It is a must for students
          of church growth.
KESSLER, J. B. A.
   1967   *A Study of the Older Protestant Missions and Churches in Peru and Chile, with
          Special Reference to the Problems of Division, Nationalism and Native Ministry*.
          Goes, Netherlands: Oosterbaan & Le Cointre, N.V.
KEYES, Lawrence E.
   1983   *The Last Age of Missions*. Pasadena, CA: Wm. Carey Library. The most up-to-date
          summary we have of the research on Third World missions.
KRAFT, Charles H.
   1979   *Christianity in Culture*. Maryknoll, NY: Orbis Books. This book is a modern clas-
          sic. It wrestles with the problems involved in transforming Christianity from one
          culture to another.
KRAMER, Bert
   1982   *Growing Together*. Everyday Publications Inc., 421 Nugget Avenue, Unit 2, Scar-

borough, ON, Canada M1S 4L8. A small, concise introduction to church growth by and for Plymouth Brethren.

KRASS, A. C.
 1967 "A Case Study in Effective Evangelism in West Africa," *Church Growth Bulletin,* Vol. IV, No. 1, Pasadena, CA.

KWAST, Lloyd Emerson
 1971 *The Discipling of West Cameroon: A Study of Baptist Growth.* Grand Rapids, MI: Eerdmans. From this case study, Kwast extrapolates many universally valid principles of church growth.

LATOURETTE, Kenneth S.
 1936 *Missions Tomorrow.* New York: Harper.
 1938 *The Thousand Years of Uncertainty.* New York: Harper.

LAWSON, E. LeRoy and Tetsunao Yamamori
 1975 *Church Growth: Everybody's Business.* Cincinnati, OH: Standard. A solid, but now rather dated, introduction to church growth principles by two disciples of McGavran.

LEVAI, Blaise, ed.
 1957 *Revolution in Missions.* Vellore, South India: The Popular Press.

LIAO, David C. E.
 (1972) *The Unresponsive: Resistant or Neglected?* Pasadena, CA: Wm. Carey Library. A
 1979 study of the homogeneous unit principle as illustrated by the Hakka Chinese in Taiwan. The lack of growth there may be due to poor methods rather than inherent resistance.

McCURRY, Don M.
 1978 "Is Muslim Evangelism Possible?" *Church Growth Bulletin.* September 1978, p. 220.

McGAVRAN, Donald A.
 (1955) *The Bridges of God: A Study in the Strategy of 1981 Missions.* New York: Friendship Press. This is the foundation document of the Church Growth Movement. A classic that should be read by all students of church growth.
 1956 "A Study of the Life and Growth of the Disciples of Christ in Puerto Rico." Unpublished manuscript.
 1958 *Multiplying Churches in the Philippines.* Manila: United Church of Christ in the Philippines.
 (1959) *How Churches Grow: The New Frontiers of Mission.* New York: Friendship Press.
 1966 This contains much of McGavran's thought that cannot be found in other writings.
 1962 *Church Growth in Jamaica.* Lucknow, India: Lucknow Publishing House.
 (1970) *Understanding Church Growth.* Grand Rapids, MI: Eerdmans. The classic text-
 (1980) book by the father of the 1990 Church Growth Movement, this is the essential starting point for any serious student of the field. The 1990 edition is revised by C. Peter Wagner.
 1973 "Events of Special Significance," *Church Growth Bulletin,* Vol. X, No. 2 (November 1973), pp. 366-77.
 1974 *The Clash Between Christianity and Cultures.* Grand Rapids, MI: Baker Book House.
 1979 *Ethnic Realities and the Church: Lessons from India.* Pasadena, CA: Wm. Carey Library. A penetrating analysis of the homogeneous unit principle showing how it has affected church growth in India. The insights apply to peoples all over the world.

1984 *Momentous Decisions in Missions Today.* Grand Rapids, MI: Baker Book House. This book highlights the theological and methodological issues in missiology with a strong appeal for the ongoing need for cross-cultural missionaries and church planting among the unreached.

1988 *Effective Evangelism: A Theological Mandate.* Phillipsburg, NJ: Presbyterian and Reformed Publishing Company. McGavran's views on theological education, church growth theology, homogeneous units, and other issues plus some personal memories on the Church Growth Movement.

McGAVRAN, Donald A., ed.

1964   *Church Growth Bulletin.* Three volumes as follows:

to 1979   1. Donald A. McGavran, ed., *Church Growth Bulletin, Volumes I-V,* September 1964 through July 1969. South Pasadena, CA: Wm. Carey Library, 1969.

2. Donald A. McGavran, ed., *Church Growth Bulletin Second Consolidated Volume, Volumes VI-XI,* September 1969 through July 1975. South Pasadena, CA: Wm. Carey Library, 1977.

3. Donald A. McGavran, James H. Montgomery, and C. Peter Wagner, eds., *Church Growth Bulletin Third Consolidated Volume, Volumes XII-XVI,* September 1975 through November 1979. Santa Clara, CA: Global Church Growth, 1982.

(1965) *Church Growth and Christian Mission.* New York: Harper & Row. Pasadena, CA:
1976   Wm. Carey Library.

1972   *Crucial Issues in Missions Tomorrow.* Chicago, IL: Moody.

1977   *The Conciliar-Evangelical Debate: The Crucial Documents 1964-1976.* South Pasadena, CA: Wm. Carey Library. This is an expanded version of *Eye of the Storm: The Great Debate in Missions,* first published in 1972.

McGAVRAN, Donald A. and Win Arn

1973   *How to Grow a Church.* Ventura, CA: Regal Books. Using a question-and-answer format, McGavran sets forth his thoughts on American church growth.

1977   *Ten Steps for Church Growth.* San Francisco, CA: Harper & Row. A substantial sequel to *How to Grow a Church* with many new insights from the authors.

1981   *Back to the Basics in Church Growth.* Wheaton, IL: Tyndale. A biblical perspective on church growth, so related to the spiritual dimension that it could be read as a devotional exercise.

McGAVRAN, Donald A., John Huegel, and Jack Taylor

1963   *Church Growth in Mexico.* Grand Rapids, MI: Eerdmans. A very insightful case study of why churches have or have not grown.

McGAVRAN, Donald A. and George G. Hunter III

1980   *Church Growth: Strategies That Work.* Nashville, TN: Abingdon. One of the best primers on the Church Growth Movement, this book also provides practical tips on motivating people of growth, training laity, helping small churches grow, and planting new churches.

McGAVRAN, Donald A. and Norman Riddle

1979   *Zaire: Midday in Missions.* Valley Forge, PA: Judson Press. A very important analysis of the dynamics of growth of one of the fastest-growing churches in Africa.

McNEE, Peter

1976   *Crucial Issues in Bangladesh: Making Missions More Effective in the Mosaic of Peoples.* Pasadena, CA: Wm. Carey Library. A model of thorough, extensive, and sensitive church growth research. This won the McGavran Church Growth Award.

MALDONADO, Oscar
1966 "Camillo Torres," *CIF Reports,* Vol. V, No. 6. Cuernavaca, Mexico: Center of Intercultural Formations.

MASIH, Samuel M.
1964 "Civil Rights and the World Mission of the Church." *Social Action Letter,* February 1964, Indianapolis, IN: United Christian Missionary Society.

MILES, Delos
1981 *Church Growth: A Mighty River.* Nashville, TN: Broadman. This is a broad up-to-date summary of the entire field of church growth. While it does not go deeply, it does touch virtually all the bases.

MILLER, Herb
1983 *Fishing on the Asphalt: Effective Evangelism in Mainline Denominations.* St. Louis, MO: Bethany Press. This is the best church growth book I have seen written from the mainline perspective. It avoids any mention of the Church Growth Movement and its leaders, but incorporates church growth research findings.

MIZUKI, John
1978 *The Growth of Japanese Churches in Brazil.* Pasadena, CA: Wm. Carey Library. This book digs deeply into the history of the church in Brazil and looks optimistically into the future.

MONTGOMERY, Jim
(1971) *Fire in the Philippines.* Carol Stream, IL: Creation House. The remarkable saga of
1975 the growth of the Foursquare Church in the Philippines. This church grew with very little help from foreign missionaries or foreign funds.

MONTGOMERY, James H. and Donald A. McGavran
1980 *The Discipling of a Nation. Global Church Growth Bulletin.* This is one of the most important church growth books of recent years. It documents and analyzes the growth of several denominations in the Philippines using the research categories found in *The Church Growth Survey Handbook* (Waymire and Wagner).

MYLANDER, Charles
1979 *Secrets for Growing Churches.* New York: Harper & Row. This book draws many practical applications for American churches from general church growth principles. Written by a pastor who is seeing it happen in his church.

NELSON, Amirtharaj
1975 *A New Day in Madras: A Study of Protestant Churches in Madras.* Pasadena, CA: Wm. Carey Library. While Madras is considered the most Christian city in India, Nelson shows that much more growth can take place if the proper strategy is followed. An excellent contribution to urban literature.

NELSON, Marlin L.
1976 *The How and Why of Third World Missions: An Asian Case Study.* Pasadena, CA: Wm. Carey Library. One of the finest studies on how sending agencies are developing in the newer churches.

NEWBIGIN, LESSLIE
1979 "Context and Conversion," *International Review of Mission,* Vol. LXVIII, No. 271 (July 1979), pp. 301-12.

NORDYKE, Quentin
1972 *Animistic Aymaras and Church Growth.* Newberg, OR: Barclay. The huge Aymara tribe living in the high Andes in Bolivia and Peru is very receptive to the gospel. Here is a challenging story of how God is working there with universal growth insights.

NOREN, Loren E.
c. 1963 *Urban Church Growth in Hong Kong 1958-1962:* Third Hong Kong Study, 3 Lancashire Rd., Kowloon, Hong Kong. Privately produced.

NOVAK, Michael
1971 *The Rise of the Unmeltable Ethnics.* New York: Macmillan.

ORJALA, Paul R.
1978 *Get Ready to Grow.* Kansas City, MO: Beacon Hill. Written as a denomination-wide study book by a professor in the Nazarene Theological Seminary, this book sold over 50,000 copies in the first three months and has circulated all through the Church of the Nazarene.

ORR, J. Edwin
1964 *The Second Evangelical Awakening: An Account of the Second Worldwide Evangelical Revival Beginning in the Mid-Nineteenth Century.* Fort Washington: Christian Literature Crusade.
1965 *The Light of the Nations: Evangelical Renewal and Advance in the Nineteenth Century.* Grand Rapids, MI: Eerdmans.

PARSHALL, Phil
1980 *New Paths in Muslim Evangelism: Evangelical Approaches to Contextualization.* Grand Rapids, MI: Baker Book House. A ground-breaking book that is opening many doors to more effective strategy planning for reaching Muslims. How to be a Christian in a Muslim way.

PENTECOST, Edward C.
1974 *Reaching the Unreached: An Introductory Study on Developing an Overall Strategy for World Evangelization.* Pasadena, CA: Wm. Carey Library. This is especially good on predicting resistance or receptivity of people groups.

PICKETT, J. Waskom
1933 *Christian Mass Movements in India.* Lucknow, India: Lucknow Publishing House.
1956 *Church Growth and Group Conversion.* Lucknow, India: Lucknow Publishing House.
1960 *Christ's Way to India's Heart.* Lucknow, India: Lucknow Publishing House, third edition.

POINTER, Roy
1984 *How Do Churches Grow? A Guide to the Growth of Your Church.* Hauts: Marshall, Morgan and Scott. This book is as good a summary of the state of the art of the Church Growth Movement as is available. Roy Pointer writes primarily for the British audience, but in a style and with a freedom that is very appealing to American readers.

RANDALL, Max Ward
1970 *Profile for Victory: New Proposals for Missions in Zambia.* Pasadena, CA: Wm. Carey Library. An excellent example of how to analyze a mission field, diagnose the situation, and plan for future evangelization.

READ, William R.
1965 *New Patterns of Church Growth in Brazil.* Grand Rapids, MI: Eerdmans. One of the original, ground-breaking studies of church growth written under McGavran's supervision.

READ, William R., Victor M. Monterroso, and Harmon A. Johnson
1969 *Latin American Church Growth.* Grand Rapids, MI: Eerdmans. To date the only continent-wide church growth study ever made. This is a treasure house of information about churches in Latin America.

REEVES, R. Daniel and Ron Jensen
  1984 *Always Advancing*. San Bernardino, CA: Here's Life Publishers, Inc. An up-to-date book introducing church growth principles with new information on church typology and philosophy of ministry.

ROBINSON, Gordon E. and John B. Grimley
  1966 *Church Growth in Central and Southern Nigeria*. Grand Rapids, MI: Eerdmans. One of the earlier books written under McGavran's supervision. Excellent background material for West Africa.

SARGUNAM, Shree M. Ezra
  1974 *Multiplying Churches in Modern India: An Experiment in Madras*. Federation of Evangelical Churches in India. A skillfully planned and executed strategy for multiplying urban churches that actually is working.

SCATES, David R.
  1981 *Why Navajo Churches are Growing: The Cultural Dynamics of Navajo Religious Change*. Navajo Christian Churches (595 Colanwood, Grand Junction, CO 81501). The rise and current growth of Catholic, Mormon, and Protestant churches. A combination of historical and anthropological insights.

SEAMANDS, J. T.
  1968 "Growth of the Methodist Church in South India." Unpublished dissertation, Asbury Theological Seminary, Wilmore, KY.

SHEARER, Roy E.
  1966 *Wildfire: Church Growth in Korea*. Grand Rapids, MI: Eerdmans. One of the pioneer country-wide studies done under McGavran. Essential for understanding dynamics of growth in Korea.

SHENK, Wilbert R., ed.
  1973 *The Challenge of Church Growth: A Symposium*. Elkhart, IN: Institute of Mennonite Studies. A directed and well-informed criticism of the Church Growth Movement by scholars writing from the Anabaptist perspective. An especially perceptive essay by John Howard Yoder is included.

  1983 *Exploring Church Growth*. Grand Rapids, MI: Eerdmans. A critical evaluation of the Church Growth Movement. Seven of the twenty-two chapters specifically point out perceived weaknesses in church growth theory. Some chapters ignore church growth research.

SHEWMAKER, Stan
  1970 *Tonga Christianity*. Pasadena, CA: Wm. Carey Library. A realistic analysis of how the gospel has spread in this tribe in Zambia with practical suggestions for future growth.

SKIVINGTON, S. Robert
  1977 *Mission to Mindanao: A Study in the Principles of Church Planting Strategy for the Philippines*. Quezon City, Philippines: Conservative Baptist Publications. A skillfully designed strategy for the spread of the gospel in one of the key areas of the world.

SMITH, Ebbie C.
  1970 *God's Miracles: Indonesian Church Growth*. Pasadena, CA: Wm. Carey Library. A complete view of Indonesia and how churches have grown in the distinct regions of this huge nation.

  1976 *A Manual for Church Growth Surveys*. Pasadena, CA: Wm. Carey Library.

  1984 *Balanced Church Growth*. Nashville, TN: Broadman. As fine a brief, understandable introduction to church growth as we have. Smith has included discussion of the major areas of church growth, focusing on worldwide application.

SMITH, James C.
1976 "Without Crossing Barriers: The Homogeneous Unit Principle in the Writings of Donald McGavran." Unpublished doctoral dissertation at The School of World Mission, Fuller Theological Seminary, Pasadena, CA.

SMITH, W. Douglas, Jr.
1978 *Toward Continuous Mission: Strategizing for the Evangelization of Bolivia.* Pasadena, CA: Wm. Carey Library. Much more than a focus on Bolivia, this book draws out principles of ethnohistory, ethnotheology, and ethnostrategy for missiology in general.

STOCK, Frederick and Margaret Stock
1975 *People Movements in the Punjab: With Special Reference to the United Presbyterian Church.* Pasadena, CA: Wm. Carey Library. A complete history of Presbyterian missions in Pakistan with comparisons to many other denominations as well.

SUBBAMMA, B. V.
1970 *New Patterns for Discipling Hindus: The Next Step in Andhra Pradesh, India.* Pasadena, CA: Wm. Carey Library. A focus on Lutheran church growth with practical suggestions for reaching the middle to upper castes.

SUNDA, James
1963 *Church Growth in West New Guinea.* Lucknow, India: Lucknow Publishing House.

SWANSON, Allen J.
1970 *Taiwan: Mainline Versus Independent Church Growth: A Study in Contrasts.* Pasadena, CA: Wm. Carey Library. The growth dynamics of such groups as the True Jesus Church and the Assembly Hall Church as compared to more traditional churches.

SWANSON, Allen J., ed.
1977 *I Will Build My Church: Ten Case Studies of Church Growth in Taiwan.* Pasadena, CA: Wm. Carey Library. Important lessons for church growth can be learned from each of these churches in Taiwan.

TAIWAN PRESBYTERIAN SYNODICAL OFFICE
c. 1966 *Announcing the Second Century—Basic Facts and Discussion Materials.* (Title translated from the Chinese). Taipei: Taiwan Presbyterian Synodical Office.

TAYLOR, Jack E.
1962 *God's Messengers to Mexico's Masses: A Study in the Religious Significance of the Braceros.* Privately published, Eugene, OR.

TEGENFELDT, Herman G.
1974 *A Century of Growth: The Kachin Baptist Church of Burma.* Pasadena, CA: Wm. Carey Library. A solid study of the evangelization of a people group.

THOMAS, Winburn
1959 *Protestant Beginnings in Japan.* Rutland, VT: Tuttle and Company.

TIPPETT, Alan R.
1965 "Numbering: Right or Wrong," *Church Growth Bulletin,* Vol. I, No. 3.
1967 *Solomon Islands Christianity: A Study in Growth and Obstruction.* New York: Friendship Press. One of the most thorough studies in print of how churches have grown in a particular country.
1970 *Church Growth and the Word of God.* Grand Rapids, MI: Eerdmans. An excellent study of how the Bible undergirds church growth theory.
1971 *People Movements in Southern Polynesia: A Study in Church Growth.* Chicago: Moody. An analysis of the spread of the gospel among Tahitians, Maoris, and Tongans with valuable theoretical conclusions.

1987   *Introduction to Missiology.* Pasadena, CA: Wm. Carey Library. A collection of forty of the best writings of a pioneer of anthropologically oriented missiology, compiled by Charles and Marguerite Kraft.

TIPPETT, Alan R., ed.

1975   *God, Man and Church Growth.* Grand Rapids, MI: Eerdmans. This was a festschrift written by twenty-six of Donald McGavran's colleagues and students in honor of his seventy-fifth birthday. A church growth collector's item.

TOWNS, Elmer L.

1987   *Winning the Winnable.* P.O. Box 4404, Lynchburg, VA 24502, Church Growth Institute. A skilled integration of church growth principles with evangelism. Excellent application of resistance-receptivity theory and other practical ideas.

TOWNS, Elmer L., John N. Vaughan, and David J. Seifert

1981   *The Complete Book of Church Growth.* Wheaton, IL: Tyndale. An amazingly thorough textbook on various case studies of growth analyzing a number of approaches to ministry in American churches and including a substantial chapter on "The Fuller Factor."

TOYNBEE, Arnold

1956   *An Historian's Approach to Religion.* London, New York: Oxford University.

TUGGY, A. Leonard

1968   *Philippine Society and Church Growth in Historical Perspective.* A Master of Arts Thesis in the School of World Mission and Institute of Church Growth, Fuller Theological Seminary, Pasadena, CA. Unpublished.

1971   *The Philippine Church: Growth in a Changing Society.* Grand Rapids, MI: Eerdmans. A notable and carefully documented account of the spread of the faith in one of the world's most explosive growth areas.

TUGGY, A. Leonard and Ralph Tolliver

1971   *Seeing the Church in the Philippines.* Manila, Philippines: O.M.F. Publishing Company.

VAUGHAN, John N.

1984   *The World's Twenty Largest Churches.* Grand Rapids, MI: Baker Book House. Case studies of the superchurches of the world (including U.S.A.) with analyses of the growth factors.

1985   *The Large Church: A Twentieth Century Expression of the First Century Church.* Grand Rapids, MI: Baker Book House. This book provides a wealth of historical and contemporary information on large churches in the U.S.A. and other parts of the world. Vaughan gives special attention to the satellite group structure that many superchurches have developed.

VICEDOM, G. F.

1962   *Church and People in New Guinea.* London: Lutterworth; World Christian Books, No. 38.

WAGNER, C. Peter

1970a   *Latin American Theology.* Grand Rapids, MI: Eerdmans. A look at early liberation theology from a church growth perspective.

1970b   *The Protestant Movement in Bolivia.* Pasadena, CA: Wm. Carey Library. A complete history of all the Protestant groups in Bolivia from the beginning to 1968. Includes a section on Evangelism in Depth.

1971   *Frontiers of Missionary Strategy.* Chicago, IL: Moody.

(1976)   *Your Church Can Grow: Seven Vital Signs of a Healthy Church.* Ventura, CA:
1984   Regal Books. Wagner's first book on American church growth has now become a

basic document in the field. It is in its thirteenth printing. Over 120,000 copies are in print.

1979a *Your Church Can Be Healthy.* Nashville, TN: Abingdon. A description and analysis of the causes and symptoms of eight major growth-inhibiting diseases of American churches.

1979b *Your Spiritual Gifts Can Help Your Church Grow.* Ventura, CA: Regal Books. Written from both a biblical and a practical point of view, this book shows how activating twenty-seven spiritual gifts can have a beneficial effect on church growth.

1979c *Our Kind of People: The Ethical Dimensions of Church Growth in America.* Atlanta, GA: John Knox Press. The only book-length treatment of the homogeneous unit principle of church growth and its application to American churches.

1981 *Church Growth and the Whole Gospel: A Biblical Mandate.* New York: Harper & Row. Taking the critics of church growth seriously, this book probes the relationship of church growth to social ethics in depth. It is a scholarly theological statement that brings new light to the issues.

1983 *On the Crest of the Wave.* Ventura, CA: Regal Books. A popular book on missions telling what is going on in the world and the means God is using to make it happen.

1984 *Leading Your Church to Growth: A Guidebook for Clergy and Laity.* Ventura, CA: Regal Books. This is the first book dealing exclusively with how both clergy and lay leadership can influence church growth for good or for bad, depending on how they perform. A substantial chapter on lay followership is also a first. The book advocates strong pastoral leadership to equip the laity for ministry and shows how this can be developed into a positive growth factor.

1986 *Spiritual Power and Church Growth.* Almonte Springs, FL: Strang Communications. The exciting story of the phenomenal growth of Latin American Pentecostalism is interwoven with church growth principles so that other churches can learn from that growth and hopefully experience the same thing.

1987 *Strategies for Church Growth.* Ventura, CA: Regal Books. An up-to-date guidebook for ways and means of planning evangelistic strategy that will lead to church growth.

1988a *How to Have a Healing Ministry without Making Your Church Sick.* Ventura, CA: Regal Books. A framework for understanding supernatural signs and wonders from a non-Pentecostal point of view and suggestions for implementation in the local church.

1988b *The Third Wave of the Holy Spirit.* Ann Arbor, MI: Servant Books. A briefer "fast food" version of the above *How to Have a Healing Ministry.*

1988c "Church Growth," *Dictionary of Pentecostal and Charismatic Movements,* Stanley M. Burgess and Gary B. McGee, eds. Grand Rapids, MI: Zondervan. A 10,000-word summary of explosive Pentecostal and charismatic church growth worldwide.

WAGNER, C. Peter, ed.

1972 *Church/Mission Tensions Today.* Chicago, IL: Moody.

1986 *Church Growth: State of the Art.* Wheaton, IL: Tyndale. Sixteen church growth experts contribute to this major work, sharing up-to-date research and thinking on aspects of the American Church Growth Movement. It includes historical material, an annotated reading list, and a glossary of church terms. Completely indexed.

WAGNER, C. Peter and Edward R. Dayton, eds.

1979 *Unreached Peoples '79.* Elgin, IL: David C. Cook.

1980 *Unreached Peoples '80.* Elgin, IL: David C. Cook.

1981 *Unreached Peoples '81.* Elgin, IL: David C. Cook.

WAGNER, William L.

1978 *Growth Patterns of German-Speaking Baptists in Europe.* Pasadena, CA: Wm. Carey Library. A thorough, documented study that incorporates many church growth principles and shows how they operate in Europe.

WALKER, F. Deaville

1942 *A Hundred Years in Nigeria.* London: Cargate Press.

WALTNER, Orlando A.

1962 "The General Conference Mennonite Church in India." An unpublished manuscript resulting from research done at the Institute of Church Growth, Eugene, OR.

WASSON, Alfred W.

1934 *Church Growth in Korea.* New York: International Missionary Council.

WAYMIRE, Bob and C. Peter Wagner

1984 *The Church Growth Survey Handbook.* Milpitas, CA: Global Church Growth Bulletin. This 8 1/2 × 11 workbook is a step-by-step methodology for doing church growth research. It is the authors' hope that it will serve to standardize the recording and reporting of church growth worldwide.

WELD, Wayne C.

1968 *An Ecuadorian Impasse.* Chicago, IL: Evangelical Covenant Church. One of the early church growth studies of a nation, focusing on Christian and Missionary Alliance, Evangelical Covenant, and Foursquare.

WILLCUTS, J. L.

1979 *Friends in the Soaring Seventies.* Newberg, OR: Oregon Yearly Meeting of Friends.

WILLIAMSON, Wayne B.

1979 *Growth and Decline in the Episcopal Church.* Pasadena, CA: Wm. Carey Library. The author is an Episcopal priest who applies church growth principles learned at Fuller to his own church.

WINTER, Ralph D.

1966 "Gimmickitis," *Church Growth Bulletin,* January 1966.

1974 "The Highest Priority: Cross Cultural Evangelism," in *Let the Earth Hear His Voice,* J. D. Douglas, ed. International Congress on World Evangelization. Minneapolis, MN: World Wide Publications.

1977a "Who Are the Three Billion?" *Church Growth Bulletin,* Vol. XIII, No. 5 (May 1977), pp. 123-26.

1977b "Who Are the Three Billion? Part II," *Church Growth Bulletin,* Vol. XIII, No. 6 (July 1977), pp. 139-44.

WOLD, Joseph Conrad

1968 *God's Impatience in Liberia.* Grand Rapids, MI: Eerdmans. A fresh look at missions in Africa with well-researched case studies from Liberia.

WONG, James

1973 *Singapore: The Church in the Midst of Social Change.* Singapore: Church Growth Study Centre. An excellent study of urban church growth by a practitioner who has applied church growth theory effectively.

WONG, James, Peter Larson, and Edward Pentecost

1973 *Missions from the Third World.* Singapore: Church Growth Study Centre. The pioneer research on Third World missions, this book is a classic.

YEAKLEY, Flavil R., Jr.

1977 *Why Churches Grow.* Nashville, TN: Anderson's. A social scientist summarizes his Ph.D. dissertation on the reasons for growth among the Churches of Christ. Although he mentions the Church Growth Movement, he does not write from that perspective.

ZUNKEL, C. Wayne

1986   *Strategies for Growing Your Church.* Elgin, IL: David C. Cook. One of the few church growth books written for the average layperson. Zunkel has explained all the major church growth principles in plain English with copious examples and professional artwork for overhead transparencies.

1987   *Church Growth Under Fire.* Scottdale, PA: Herald Press. A straightforward apologetic for church growth covering the field in broad brush strokes. An excellent starting point for the theologically informed beginner.

INDEX

311

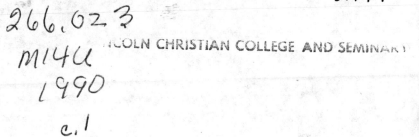